ROGER CORMAN

FEED ME!

ROGER CORMAN

*Blood-Sucking Vampires, Flesh-Eating
Cockroaches, and Driller Killers*

Beverly Gray

Enjoy!
Beverly
Gray

THUNDER'S MOUTH PRESS
NEW YORK

Roger Corman: Blood-Sucking Vampires, Flesh-Eating Cockroaches, and Driller Killers

© 2000, 2004 by Beverley Gray

Originally titled *Roger Corman: An Unauthorized Biography of the Godfather of Indie Filmmaking*

Published by
Thunder's Mouth Press
An Imprint of Avalon Publishing Group Incorporated
245 West 17th St., 11th Floor
New York, NY 10011-5300

Library of Congress Cataloging-in-Publication Data is available.

ISBN: 1-56025-555-2

9 8 7 6 5 4 3 2 1

Printed in the United States of America
Distributed by Publishers Group West

To Bernie, for round-the-clock computer help.
To Hilary, for cogent critiques in multicolored ink.
To Jeffrey, for well-timed hugs.

And to all my fellow Roger Corman alumni who've gone on
to make a difference in the film industry.

ACKNOWLEDGMENTS

For BEHIND-THE-SCENES assistance, I'm grateful to Paul Almond, Steve Barnett, Flo Bloch, Rachel Bloch, Joseph Bosco, Frances Doel, Robert Dorian, Paul Hoffman, Louis Morneau, Adam Simon, Frank Weimann, and Ashley Wrobel, as well as my eggstraordinary agent, Stuart Bernstein. Special thanks to the tireless Mary Menzel and to the remarkably patient Jim Parish. I'm also indebted to Dan O'Connor and the gang at Thunder's Mouth Press.

The following institutions facilitated my research: Beverly Hills Historical Society, Beverly Hills Public Library, Beverly Hills Unified School District, Burton Historical Collection at Detroit Public Library, Margaret Herrick Library of the Academy of Motion Picture Arts and Sciences, Santa Monica Public Library, Science Fiction Writers of America, UCLA Arts Library, and USC Cinema-Television Library. Archivist Margaret Kimball at Stanford University's Green Library was especially helpful.

My sincere appreciation to everyone I interviewed for this book. I also thank the members of my extended family for favors large and small.

CONTENTS

INTRODUCTION

I FIRST LAID eyes on veteran Hollywood filmmaker Roger Corman in the summer of 1973, when he interviewed me for a job as his assistant. Our chat took place on Los Angeles' famed Sunset Strip, in the rather shabby penthouse that served as the headquarters for Corman's company, New World Pictures. The forty-seven-year-old moviemaker had gotten my name through the Phi Beta Kappa chapter of the University of California at Los Angeles (UCLA), where I was completing a doctorate in English. It was typical of Roger to seek out someone with lofty academic credentials: he loved to shore up his credibility by hiring underlings with fancy academic degrees and titles.

On that first morning, I was impressed (as everyone always was) by Corman's handsome face, deep voice, and good-humored manner. We had a serious talk about motion-picture aesthetics, and he told me that one condition of my employment would be a promise to read and discuss with him Siegfried Kracauer's *Theory of Film* (1960). Of course I complied, wondering how this ponderous tome would shed light on the making of Corman's cinematic staples: low-budget monster movies and biker flicks. I'm still wondering. He never mentioned Kracauer again.

After sixteen lively months as Corman's all-purpose assistant, I left New World in 1975 to return to academia. Several jobs and two babies later, I was persuaded by Roger to become the story editor at Concorde–New Horizons, the new company he had founded in 1983. Signing on in 1986, I once again plunged headfirst into the madcap world of economy filmmaking. My duties included overseeing writers, consulting with young directors, and earning the occasional script credit on horror films and thrillers—including *Immortal Sins* (1991) and *Beyond the Call of Duty* (1992)—that needed emergency fixes. Life was not dull. I never knew what challenge the next business day would bring. One April afternoon in 1994, Corman called me into his office. There, dwarfed by huge paintings that had been done on the cheap by a grad student imitating Ellsworth Kelly, we had what turned out to be another pivotal conversation.

Roger told me his fears for his company's financial health. (This was nothing new, as he had these concerns every week or so.) Then he brought up the plight of a close friend of mine. She had been an early Corman employee, beginning in the 1960s when he was just starting out, and she had taught me a great deal when I first came on board at New World. Later, she'd moved into more lucrative positions with more prestigious film companies. But she'd hit on hard times, and was now desperate for work. It was a nice gesture on Corman's part to make a place for her on his staff. It was not so nice, however, to give her my job.

The upshot was that after eight years of loyal service, I was rewarded with two weeks' notice. All the while, Roger insisted that I had been an exemplary employee. He told me to write myself a glowing recommendation. ("Don't be modest," he said.) He promised to sign it. I later discovered that, in typically shrewd Corman fashion, he'd hired my old friend on a cut-rate basis, which meant that while lending a hand to someone in need, he was actually saving the difference between her salary and my own. So his altruism, though undoubtedly genuine, was also to his material benefit. But such is Roger Corman: Truly the buck stops with him, in more ways than one.

• • •

Now that six years have passed and my career has taken me in unexpected new directions, I can step back and mull over my relationship with Roger

Corman. At times he treated me graciously, at other times coldly. Some days he was solicitous of my needs, while on others he issued outrageous demands. He could make me feel like a valued part of his organization, or like a minor functionary to be casually swept aside. In other words, I'm no different from the hundreds of other employees who have worked for Corman over the years. Most of us will admit to both gratitude and frustration. We recognize that we've been given the unparalleled opportunity to learn the fascinating business of making movies from an expert. Yet emotionally we've been put through the wringer, all in the service of a man who seems bent on squeezing every last dollar out of every last screen project. Director Deborah Brock spent four years at the head of the Concorde–New Horizons post-production team. When we spoke in Santa Monica, California, on October 14, 1998, she summed up the experience of many Corman employees. "It was like you were constantly having the worst day of your life. But in between having the worst day of your life you could have a lot of fun. So it was continually elating and horrible."

Roger Corman (b. 1926) is, of course, a show-business legend. No one in Hollywood before or since has had a film career quite like his, in terms of both longevity and scope. Since 1954 he's directed fifty low-budget features, and produced nearly ten times that many. This is a staggering number, especially given that all but a handful have made money. (On May 14, 1998, Corman told the *Hollywood Reporter*'s Kirk Honeycutt that of his more than four hundred feature films to date, perhaps fifteen had failed to turn a profit.)

But Corman's fiscal track record is hardly the sole basis for his celebrity. As a movie director in the 1960s, he captured the rebellious spirit of the youth revolution, while also crafting Edgar Allan Poe (1809–49) adaptations that spoke deeply to a new generation of moviegoers. As a company head, he found ways to blend action, sex, humor, and message into hip entertainments. In one ten-year period, beginning in 1973, his New World Pictures was North America's premier distributor of foreign-language films. While introducing such greats as Ingmar Bergman, Federico Fellini, Akira Kurosawa, and François Truffaut to new audiences across North America, New World also inspired younger companies like Miramax (founded in 1979) to carve out a lucrative niche as importers of art-house cinema. Moreover, Corman's own brand of guerrilla filmmaking, which exploits every possible source of low-cost production values, still has an impact on today's independent film scene.

Above all, Roger Corman prides himself on starting scores of filmmakers on their way professionally. His role as mentor to such big-league directors of today as Francis Ford Coppola, Martin Scorsese, Jonathan Demme, John Sayles, and James Cameron has been well-publicized. And it's no secret that some of Hollywood's brightest stars—including Jack Nicholson, Peter Fonda, and Sylvester Stallone—learned their craft on his projects. Equally important, Corman alumni can be found in every arena of the film industry. Roger's offices have spawned many of today's producers, writers, agents, casting directors, sales executives, and marketing mavens. Respected editors, cinematographers, designers, makeup artists, and effects specialists all have cut their teeth on Corman productions. Most of these people are not household names. Still, Hollywood would never be the same without them. During our conversation on February 3, 1999, veteran actor David Carradine put it best: "It's almost as though you can't have a career in this business without having passed through Roger's hands for at least a moment."

When I found myself cut adrift from Concorde–New Horizons in 1994, I put in calls to a long list of people who had formerly been on the Corman payroll. Some were now directors; others line producers; still others held executive positions at major Hollywood studios and film companies. Many were strangers to me, but I quickly realized that we all belonged to the same secret society. Once they knew that I, too, had experienced life at a Corman company, they were wonderfully generous in giving advice and sending job leads my way. The clear assumption was that anyone who had worked for Roger over an extended period of time had the goods to make it in show business. During my Concorde stint, some of us had ordered bomber jackets that identified us, only half facetiously, as members of the Roger Corman School of Film. What I discovered after leaving Concorde is the existence of an informal Roger Corman Alumni Association, whose legions of members are dedicated to ensuring one another's career survival. We figure that, having survived Roger, we can accomplish just about anything.

This book owes much to the Roger Corman graduates who so kindly shared their memories with me. I have spoken to nearly eighty former Cormanites, from every phase of his long filmmaking career. Some conversations were brief, but more typically they ran well over an hour. Alumni have welcomed me into their homes and offices; they have phoned me from distant cities, and even traveled to meet me. I was treated so well partly because many remembered me as a colleague and friend. There's also the fact, however, that Roger Corman inspires discussion.

Those who have worked for Roger all hope to unravel the Corman enigma. It's easy to trade stories about his cheapness, his chutzpah, and his sometimes tawdry tastes. There is, however, an air of mystery about him that everyone wants to penetrate. Director Joe Dante (*Gremlins, Matinee*) believes Corman has depths that few will ever plumb. As Dante told me in the course of a long chat on November 5, 1998: "It's not an accident that none of the books [about Corman] have really captured him as a person, because he's very guarded. And I don't know how many people can say they really, truly, know Roger. Because he does have a persona that he puts on in order to deal with people. And he's had it for years."

• • •

To meet Corman for the first time is to be surprised. Many who know his reputation as a longtime maker of B movies expect to find a tough old codger, pounding the table and smoking big cigars. Actress Pam Grier, interviewed on camera for the 1998 KCET-TV documentary *Roger Corman: Shoot to Thrill*, admits that before landing her first Corman screen role in the early 1970s she anticipated a "three-hundred-pound Neanderthal raving maniac, with a silk shirt and gold chains and loafers but no socks." Instead, Roger is tall, slender, and casually conservative in his dress. Though now in his seventies, he can still look almost boyish. Veteran distribution executive Pamm Vlastas, who talked with me on October 7, 1998, remembers that when she met Roger in 1975, he seemed an "elegant, dashing, very polite, rather shy person." That hint of shyness has stayed with him. So has his gift for making a newcomer feel welcome and important. No wonder journalists love him.

One of Corman's most memorable traits is his photogenic smile. Another is his deep, resonant speaking voice. Beach Dickerson, a jack-of-all-trades who was an early member of the Corman filmmaking circle, mentioned on October 2, 1998, "I love the voice above all. He can seduce you into anything." Which explains, perhaps, why generations of Corman people have found themselves agreeing to tackle jobs that are plainly impossible. Post-production chief Deborah Brock, too, recalls Roger's distinctive voice and diction. She told me, "If you've ever noticed how he speaks, it's the royal 'we'." When working for Corman early on, she whispered to a fellow employee, "Who does he mean by 'we'?" The answer came back, "Him and God, okay?"

Images of royalty also surface in screenwriter Daryl Haney's recollections. When we talked in late 1998, Haney stressed that "there was a certain majesty in the way [Corman] carried himself. Something also in the seeming serenity of the way he would talk to you: it was almost Buddha-like." But Haney also compares his old boss to a hyperactive child: "If he knows too much about something, he begins to lose interest. I think there's a certain amount of seeking novelty on Roger's part. And he has to move on. If he lingers too long, he becomes restless."

Though known for his public graciousness, Corman can retreat into himself. Haney, who recalls that Corman "would seem to listen to everything that you were saying," also admits that "there was a slight sense of detachment about him at the same time." On September 15, 1998, photographer Ellen Mark recounted for me her favorite Corman memory. During the filming of *Death Race 2000* (1975), she chanced to find herself standing near Corman: "I just remember the man was so totally consumed with something. . . . [He was] so totally self-absorbed that the world could have blown up and he wouldn't have noticed."

The list of contradictions surrounding Corman seems endless. He is an intensely private man who thrives on public attention. Many of his pictures have outlaws as heroes, but his own lifestyle is fundamentally conservative. He made his reputation as a trendsetter, but he endlessly recycles the ideas of others. Corman is both gutsy and timid, both open-minded and stubborn, both notoriously cheap and surprisingly generous. While serving as a father figure to generations of young filmmakers, he has stayed in many ways a child at heart. Perhaps most fundamentally, he maintains an uneasy balance between art and commerce that makes him, in the words of one former employee, "the most conflicted person I know."

The late writer-director Howard R. Cohen first met Corman in 1972. In September 1998, seven months before his fatal heart attack, he shared with me many stories of Corman's helpful and generous acts. During our long conversation, however, Cohen also spoke feelingly of a broken promise that in 1990 ended their working relationship. Cohen insisted to me that "there are two of him. There's the one you talk to and the one you do business with. The one you talk to I still like a lot."

· · ·

Is Roger Corman aware of his own complexities? Says one Corman veteran, "I don't think he will ever understand himself." In the late 1960s, at the time he shot *The Wild Angels* and *The Trip,* Corman spent several years in psychoanalysis. Employees from that period remember him delving into Freudian psychology with characteristic gusto. At the same time, he could not grasp why his analyst kept charging him for missed sessions. According to a former Corman staffer, the analyst finally decreed that "unless Roger really wanted to change, there was no point in continuing on."

Although Corman may not be given to self-scrutiny, his alumni delight in trying to sum him up. During my research for this book, their comments to me took on a *Rashomon*-like quality. As director Rodman Flender *(Idle Hands)* quipped, "Maybe we all see what we want to see in Roger." Screenwriter Robert King called Corman "a Machiavellian businessman, using people to the utmost, knowing they are thriving on the glamour of Hollywood." Writer-director Howard R. Cohen characterized him as a master teacher, remarkably willing to share his tricks of the cinema trade. Randy Frakes, who did special effects on several Corman projects, hailed him as "the last of the filmmaking moguls who has some intimate knowledge of filmmaking."

As I delved further, producer John Broderick underscored for me the dangers of Corman's exploitative business tendencies, labeling him "a Fagin" (in reference to the character in Charles Dickens's *Oliver Twist*) and "a very sick guy." Veteran screenwriter Charles B. Griffith, who has clashed with Corman over the years, wrote to me in mid-November 1998 that Roger "uses half his genius to degrade his own work, and the rest to degrade the artists who work for him." Most alumni, though, focused on Corman's positive side. Director-producer Deborah Brock noted that "just when you think he's the shit of the world, he turns around and does something of extraordinary niceness."

If any aspect of Roger Corman's career has been romanticized, it is his role in launching new talent. This is the basis on which producer Brad Krevoy (*Dumb & Dumber, Kingpin*) hopes to persuade the Academy of Motion Picture Arts and Sciences to grant Corman an honorary Oscar for lifetime achievement. But the fact that the Academy's president, Robert Rehme, is himself a former New World sales executive hardly makes Corman a shoo-in for such an accolade. Rehme clarified for me, on December 3, 1998, that no one has ever received an Oscar chiefly for giving others a start in the industry. Still, Cormanites are used to doing the impossible, and Krevoy (who once handled Concorde business affairs) seemed convinced that his campaign will eventually achieve its goal. Not all alumni feel Roger deserves such lofty recognition: they mention his wasted potential, his failure to achieve personal artistic greatness. The vast majority, however, would be delighted to see this near-mythic figure recognized by the film industry that has long reaped benefits from the Corman farm league.

• • •

Since I've left Corman's employ, Roger and I have talked cordially on several occasions. In September 1994, a few months after my stay at Concorde ended, he phoned me at home with news that a start-up company had a job opening. I appreciated the tip, although I was slightly bemused by the authoritative way he directed me to check it out immediately. Years later, when I was on a short deadline for a *Hollywood Reporter* assignment, Roger kindly made time for a late-night phone interview. But Corman has played no part in my research for this book. In writing about a famous Hollywood independent, I have wanted to maintain my own independence, freely drawing conclusions even while striving to stay true to the facts at hand. When I worked for Roger, he often finished a conversation with the phrase, "Use your own best judgment."

And so I have.

Part One

THE EARLY YEARS

(1926–47)

A BOY'S LIFE

There was no way I couldn't be interested in movies,
growing up where I did.

ROGER CORMAN, 1996

IT'S TEMPTING TO imagine Roger Corman starting life in a
gothic castle, with flags flying above and dark secrets in the dungeon below.
Such, however, was not the case. Nor did he lead a solitary childhood in a tum-
bledown mountain cabin, with only a sled named *Rosebud* for company.

In point of fact, Roger William Corman was born in Detroit, Michigan,
on April 5, 1926, and spent his early years in the middle of the middle class.
Roger's father, William Corman, had grown up in St. Louis, Missouri, where
he studied engineering at Washington University, graduating at the top of
his class. William served as a naval engineer in the First World War, then
moved to Detroit, where he met his wife-to-be, a legal secretary named Anne
Hugh, on a tennis court. During Roger's boyhood, William Corman worked
for Detroit's McCray Steel Company, designing bridges, roads, and dams.
One of his projects was a dam for Greenfield Village, an ambitious re-creation
of nineteenth-century American life begun in Dearborn, Michigan, in 1929
by automobile magnate Henry Ford.

William Corman was to be a dominant influence throughout his son's
life. In his 1990 autobiography, *How I Made a Hundred Movies in Hollywood
and Never Lost a Dime,* Roger Corman speaks of his dad as being extremely

intelligent and logical. "To him, intellect was probably more important than emotion. If he didn't express as much feeling as some fathers, there was never any question that he loved us." To those who know the adult Roger Corman, the emotional reticence he attributes to his father seems one key to the character of the son as well.

Though both William and Anne Corman were the children of immigrants, they apparently maintained few ties to their Old World heritage. Roger grew up without taking much interest in his family tree. Veteran employee Frances Doel once told me that when she asked where his ancestors had come from, Corman had shrugged that in all likelihood they were just Huns wandering across the face of Europe. He did inherit his mother's Catholicism, but this meant primarily that he and younger brother Gene (born Eugene Harold on September 24, 1927) were baptized. Characteristically, Corman was quick to acknowledge his religious roots when they might prove useful to him. In the 1960s, when he considered filming a World War II drama, *The Spy in the Vatican,* he instructed an assistant to get the Pope on the phone and arrange for a few weeks of shooting in Vatican City. Over her protests that the pontiff and his staff might not go along with this plan, Roger calmly advised her to "tell them I'm a registered Catholic." He also pooh-poohed her fears that the Vatican might be displeased with the existing script's slant on the role of the Church in World War II, saying, "In that case, we will make up a script to send them."

Religion may not have played a large role in the Corman household, but respect for education was seen as a paramount value. The family was then living in the Six Mile Road section of Detroit, six miles north of downtown, in a neighborhood of small brick houses, green lawns, and tall shade trees. The local junior high school, Post Intermediate, had been built in 1930. It housed over two thousand adolescents from a pleasant mix of ethnic groups, with Jews, blacks, and Italian-Americans comfortably coexisting with the white Anglo-Saxon Protestant majority. Corman did well enough there to skip a grade, which meant that for years he was fated to be the youngest and smallest in his class.

When not involved with his studies, Corman liked reading adventure stories and attending Sunday movie matinees; *Mutiny on the Bounty* (1935) was a favorite. He also played basketball, tackle football, and ice hockey with the neighborhood boys, though not often enough to suit the family patri-arch. (In a *People* magazine profile dated November 17, 1980, Roger recalled that his father "told me to go out and play more instead of reading.") Another of young Corman's chief enthusiasms was gas-powered model airplanes, which he crafted out of rice paper and balsa wood in the bedroom he and Gene shared. His skill at maneuvering radio-controlled aircraft with three- or four-foot wingspans stood him in good stead when, years later, he recruited boys with model planes to help shoot the aerial-combat footage for his World War I drama, *Von Richtofen and Brown* (1971).

At least one Hollywood producer connects the boy who loved to fly toy airplanes with the Roger Corman of today. Thom Mount, whose credits include *Bull Durham* and *Tequila Sunrise* (both 1988)—as well as Corman's own return to directing, *Frankenstein Unbound* (1990)—spoke to me at length on November 13, 1998. Mount insisted that "in another lifetime, Roger Corman could easily have been [automobile industrialist] Henry Ford. He could easily have been [airplane pioneer] Wilbur Wright. He tin-kers, he invents things, he loves invention, he loves improvisation, he loves opportunistic, mechanistic experiment. . . . If you can regard him from a little distance, what you see is a tremendous native American lyricism that's not very far removed from the great eccentric American entrepreneurs."

Young Corman had time to pursue hobbies because he was never expected to hold a part-time or summer job. In his 1990 memoir he notes that his dad dissuaded him from getting a paper route, saying, "You'll have your whole life to work." These words have proved prophetic: today, as a filmmaker in his seventies, Roger shows few signs of slowing down. But in light of William Corman's reputation as a shrewd businessman wholly devoted to the work ethic, it's instructive that he allowed young Roger a childhood free of the obligation to pay his own way.

Not that money worries were unknown to the Cormans. This was, after all, the era of the Great Depression. Though William Corman held on to his job, his salary was reduced, and many around him were scrambling to find any work at all. It was a time when economic uncertainties made wastefulness the enemy, and elevated thriftiness into a cardinal rule. For the Corman family, the household frugalities that made perfect sense in the 1930s became part of a lifelong pattern. Anne Corman, who, thanks to years of smart investments, enjoyed a tidy fortune in her old age, was remembered by her son's employees as buying day-old vegetables and reusing postage stamps. And Roger Corman himself is notorious among his staffers for writing memos on tiny scraps of paper with the stub of a pencil. To the often extravagant motion-picture industry he brings a sense of strict fiscal self-control that occasionally borders on fanaticism.

Despite William Corman's money anxieties during the 1930s, he managed to retire from engineering in 1940 at age forty-three. Health concerns were part of the reason he chose to move his family to Beverly Hills, California. Until his death in 1978, William devoted himself to managing his investment portfolio and overseeing his two sons' business affairs. From the early days, Roger Corman's staffers remember him poring over the company books and questioning expenditures. The very first Corman assistant, Kinta Haller, described William Corman for me on January 5, 1999, as having been cool, analytical, and direct, with an independent streak tempered by a strong sense of family solidarity. In sum, he bore a striking resemblance to the man his son would grow up to be.

•   •   •

When Roger Corman arrived in Beverly Hills in 1940, he found a city much different from Detroit. Beverly Hills was incorporated in 1914 by a developer who named it after his hometown, Beverly Farms, Massachusetts. From the first, the city featured wide avenues with easy, sweeping curves; its streets were carefully planted with palms and acacia. The image of Beverly Hills as home to Hollywood's finest was bolstered in 1919 when silent-movie superstars Mary Pickford and Douglas Fairbanks, married in private life, built their sumptuous estate, Pickfair. A migration of other film stars to the city followed, and elegant mansions soon appeared; but celebrities were not the only residents, and more modest houses could be had circa 1940 for under $10,000.

The new Corman abode, on Almont Drive between Olympic and Wilshire Boulevards, was located in that less fancy part of the city known as "the flats." Still, the neighborhood proved to be attractive and well tended. Today, South Almont preserves a sense of calm and order. Its one-story Spanish-style stucco homes, interspersed with the occasional vaguely Tudor cottage, show signs of recent remodeling. One thing Corman would not recognize from 1940 is the welter of parking restrictions spelled out on signs that line the curb.

Present-day Beverly Hills is a place of lively commercial activity: Businesses on both Wilshire and Olympic attract traffic that tends to spill over onto residential streets. Not so in the early 1940s, when Beverly Hills was a small, sleepy village of 30,000 citizens who took pride in low taxes and tended to vote Republican.

At age fourteen, Roger Corman entered Beverly Hills High School, long respected for its academic excellence. The school, built in 1927, boasts an elegantly sprawling campus, complete with archways, colonnades, and a clock tower. The well-landscaped school grounds feature tennis courts and a gymnasium complete with swimming pool. Corman has noted, in his memoir and elsewhere, that among the school's 1,600 students he rubbed shoulders for the first time with people who had wealth and social position. And it is true that some of his classmates were the scions of famous Hollywood families: Lita Warner, Carlotta Laemmle, and young Adolph Zukor all graduated with him in the summer of 1943. But another graduate of that vintage, Malcolm Florence, made clear when we spoke in early 1999 that celebrity kids did not dominate the social scene at Beverly High. Florence, who in 1943 held the post of Boys' League president, remembers a middle-class environment enlivened by the occasional touch of glamour. His own father worked as a maître d' at the exclusive Beverly Hills Hotel, and families of many other Beverly High students had equally tangential entertainment-industry connections.

Florence fondly thinks back to his teenage years, when a shopping excursion to downtown Los Angeles meant taking the bus to Fairfax Avenue in what is now known as the Park La Brea area, then catching a double-decker for the rest of the ride. As a treat, he'd sometimes stop in at the Orpheum Theatre, where the father of classmate Rube Wolf was a well-known bandleader. (Wolf's job was to accompany the stage show that preceded the featured movie attraction.) Florence also recalls more local pleasures: hanging out at Simon's Drive-In restaurant in the heart of the Beverly Hills business district, taking a date to hear Cab Calloway at the Casa Mañana in Culver City. Teen vices then were mild. Florence informed me that "bad boys at Beverly High smoked cigarettes in the parking lot."

But these were also the years when America found itself pushed into World War II. By the time Roger Corman became a high-school senior, in

September 1942, the local newspapers were full of stories of young men marching off to battle. Given the fervent patriotism of the time, several of the high school's teachers enlisted, and the campus was busy with scrap drives, war bond sales, and the formation of a Boys' Emergency Corps. The summer 1943 edition of *Watchtower,* the school yearbook, is solemnly dedicated to those alumni "who so courageously have given their lives for their country."

In this era of innocent fun and grave social concern, Corman managed to pursue his own interests. He studied science and math, but also discovered the short stories of Edgar Allan Poe, little knowing that one day he would bring eight of them to the screen. Having grown to be a six-footer, Roger tried basketball, but was never an important part of the team. Though he joined the High-Y, a kind of fraternity, he couldn't get up the courage to ask a girl for a date until his senior prom. At school he focused on activities involving journalism and writing, eventually sharing the post of front-page editor of *Highlights,* the weekly student newspaper. He also enrolled in the popular Radio Speech course through which students presented original short plays on Los Angeles radio station KMPC.

Mal Florence, today a veteran sportswriter for the *Los Angeles Times,* remembers Corman from both the *Highlights* staff and the Radio Speech class. He told me Corman was "a nice guy, good sense of humor." He hasn't forgotten Roger's deep, rich, speaking voice and precise diction; he always assumed Roger's father had movie connections, and that Roger himself was an aspiring actor. The gregarious Florence stresses he didn't know Corman well. He acknowledges, as so many others have, that Corman (who in later years could make assistants tremble with an angry glance) was at base probably quite shy.

In the Summer 1943 edition of *Watchtower,* Roger's senior photo reveals a handsome and serious young man, his hair neatly parted, gazing directly into the camera. There's not a hint of the dazzling smile that has disarmed journalists and members of the film community through the decades. Anyone flipping through that yearbook will find few other Corman appearances, though he is pictured among the members of Quill and Scroll, the school's journalism honor society. Elsewhere in *Watchtower,* Roger's brother Gene can be spotted among the junior class: he stands out as one of very few students wearing glasses.

Although the adult Roger Corman has always been known for his keen intellect, he was by no means a star pupil at Beverly High. At graduation, he received no service awards for his extracurricular activities, nor was he honored by the school's Lektos Society for outstanding achievement in any one specific academic discipline. Even more surprising, he was not among those students who received gold seals on their diplomas for maintaining top grades throughout high school. Members of Beverly High's scholastic honor society, those who had earned the requisite number of A's on their report cards at semester's end, were known as Palladians. Corman was not among their ranks in either half of his senior year. But when he graduated along with some 260 other seniors in June 1943, he was part of a group of eighteen honored with the Fideles Award. The *Beverly Hills Citizen* for June 11, 1943, explains this accolade as a prize for good attendance.

•   •   •

Corman's lackluster high-school record is noteworthy because of his insistence in later years on using degrees and honors as a way of screening potential employees. In 1974 I photocopied a page from something called *Monicker* magazine, in which Roger obliquely referred to me in describing the academic achievements of his staff at New World Pictures. In language that may seem quaint by current standards of political correctness, he noted that "the two girls going out today just to test titles, one is a Ph.D. and a Phi Beta Kappa in English, from UCLA, the other is a Phi Beta Kappa from UCLA. My story editor is a First in English from Oxford which is the equivalent of a Phi Beta Kappa, and there's hardly anybody in the office who does not have an A-minus average."

As part of this stress on scholastic achievement, Corman has long had a tendency to inflate credentials. Though his longtime story editor, Frances Doel, is indeed a graduate of England's Oxford University, and though she is hugely admired by all who know her for her intelligence and good sense, she makes no claim to have received a First. Corman himself admitted in 1975 to *New York Times Magazine*'s Bill Davidson that his earliest press releases had falsely portrayed him as a Rhodes scholar, recipient of one of the highest honors bestowed upon graduates of American universities. And some high-level employees who worked with Corman for years still believe that he graduated from college Phi Beta Kappa.

To an extent, such grandiose misstatements can be blamed on the instinct for hype that is part and parcel of the film industry. Corman's publicity team has, for decades, specialized in planting in the trade press bogus items designed to enhance the Corman image. (One example of this is the March 18, 1987, issue of the *Hollywood Reporter* which announced that Corman was considering selling his film library to a forty-year-old financial whiz for the extraordinary sum of $500 million.) If questioned directly, however, Corman can sometimes be engagingly forthright. When the interviewer from *Monicker* asked about his college years, Roger acknowledged that although he was a graduate of Stanford University, "I was not Phi Beta Kappa and I find it very nice that I've got all these Phi Bet [sic] girls working here."

In 1943 Stanford was a well-respected school, but students seeking entrance did not face the horrendous odds that today's candidates must endure. The application process was straightforward: In the spring of your senior year in high school, you submitted (along with your $5 nonrefundable registration fee), a letter from your high-school principal verifying your scholastic promise, an indication of suitable standardized-test scores, and a transcript indicating not less than a B average in academic coursework. Stanford's student population at the time, however, was far smaller than the 13,000 of today, and only about 450 men (along with 250 women) were allotted spots in the entering class of 1943–44. The 7,054 students in residence that year included a mere 2,412 regular undergrads, plus 916 graduate students. The largest percentage of the student body consisted of the nearly 3,500 young men enrolled in the Army Specialized Training Program (or ASTP), then housed on the bucolic 8,000-acre campus in Palo Alto, on the peninsula forty miles south of San Francisco.

So the number of male civilians at Stanford was relatively small, and not many of Corman's Beverly High classmates joined him up north at the school affectionately known as "The Farm." For one thing, many young men of that era were forced to defer college until their military service was over. And even for residents of Beverly Hills, a choice of schools rested heavily on what the student's family could afford. The cost of a Stanford education in the 1940s seems extraordinarily low by today's standards: male students could expect to spend a mere $350 per quarter (including university fees, room, board, and incidentals). Still, with the Depression barely over, this sum was enough to give pause to many. Roger's classmate Mal Florence, who entered the military soon after high school, later relied on the G.I. Bill to pay his way through the University of Southern California (USC). But Corman, who was only seventeen when he graduated from Beverly Hills High, was still young enough to be safe from the military draft. Fortunately for him, his parents were willing, and able, to shoulder the financial burden of a Stanford education.

A GENTLEMAN
AND A SCHOLAR

*I've never met a successful director, writer, or producer
who wasn't intelligent.*

ROGER CORMAN, 1992

It HAD LONG been preordained that Roger Corman would
study engineering in college. His determination to follow in his father's
footsteps hints again at the powerful presence of William Corman in his
older son's life. Roger entered Stanford planning to become an aeronautical
engineer, then switched to electrical engineering, and, in 1947, was awarded
an industrial engineering degree. Though Corman gradually concluded
that engineering would not be his life's work, the field's emphasis on effi-
ciency and management clearly appealed to one side of his nature.

Few filmmakers are engineers by training. But those who have known
Corman as a director and producer often comment on his distinctive engineering approach to the making of motion-pictures. In our conversation of
September 25, 1998, film producer Brad Krevoy speculated that Corman's
engineering studies, coupled with his family's deeply ingrained frugality, led
him to revolt against the wastefulness endemic in Hollywood. Krevoy
pointed out that Roger's movies stress economy above all: they are short and
precise, taking pains to make much out of little. Paul Rapp, who served as
production manager and assistant director on many of Corman's early pictures, told me in fall 1998 that "Roger had a theory about how many takes,

how many feet of film. This was all very calculated. . . . We were dictated by how many feet of film we had, and how many takes we could take. And how many setups we had to achieve in a given time."

Corman's earliest assistant, Kinta Haller (originally Kinta Zebal) spoke to me of the delight her boss took in getting maximum use out of time and materials: "He's always written movies in three days, shot them in three days, used the same sets to shoot two or three movies. He loves that because that's the efficient engineer in him. He loves that sense of being practical. You've had the expense of building the set, making the monster, now let's get as much as we possibly can out of it. . . . That really makes him happy." Another employee theorized that at the center of Corman's personality is the engineer's zest for problem-solving: "I think one of his great joys in life is to come into total chaos and to straighten it out. And I think this has something to do with his engineering background. I sometimes think Roger actually, on some levels, creates problems so that he can solve them."

This same employee went on to explore the complex dichotomy between Corman the engineer and Corman the creative artist. "On the one hand, as a result of his upbringing, and as a result of his undergraduate work, he does have this very formal, black-and-white, engineering approach to life. He is definitely a man who sees no shade of gray. And yet he's in a business that's nothing but shades of gray, nothing but compromise, nothing but groups of people working together. He would like to engineer a picture. He would like it to be just straight ahead—you envision it a certain way, that's the way it works. Of course, that's not filmmaking. And of course he knows that, in the other half of his brain." The employee could not resist seeing Corman as schizophrenic, in the older sense of that term. "There are two of him. There's the very strict, black-and-white, scientifically oriented, brook-no-nonsense, 'this is the way it should be, this is the way it is' . . . that's one side of him. And yet, there is this other side that's creative, loves that whole process, can spot, or at least was able to spot, talent. I think he's a man constantly at war with himself as a result of that."

This view of Corman as a divided soul is shared by screenwriter Charles B. Griffith (*The Little Shop of Horrors*) who, in the course of our long e-mail correspondence, described his old filmmaking colleague in terms of "the engineer's brain torturing the artist's impulses." In fact, those who know

Roger make something of a game of pointing out the dramatic contradictions within his personality. It's irresistible to connect this vision of him as a man wracked by warring urges with the stories of Edgar Allan Poe, which played so prominent a role in Corman's teenage years. In Poe's "William Wilson," for instance, the protagonist battles a mysterious other who turns out to be himself. (Something of the same climactic self-confrontation would later turn up in Corman's version of Poe's "The Masque of the Red Death," filmed in 1964.) Another Poe motif (best exemplified in the story that in 1960 became Corman's *House of Usher*) is that of the tainted family inheritance. The tantalizing link here is to William Corman and his profound influence on his son's life choices. The longtime employee who spoke of Roger Corman's warring impulses also described the family patriarch for me: "He struck me as a very demanding, authoritarian, strict disciplinarian-type father. He was the engineer without the other side." So the young man who first chose and then recoiled from engineering was in a sense engaged in a battle with that part of himself that was the keeper of his father's legacy.

•   •   •

Though Corman later had the opportunity to probe his tangled inner life through psychoanalysis, this was doubtless not a top priority in the 1940s, during his college years at Stanford University. As an entering student, he plunged into the extracurricular whirl, quickly becoming co–sports editor of the *Stanford Daily*. (In one of his "Sideline Slants" columns, dated November 15, 1943, Roger touts the expertise of the *Daily*'s sports staff as "pigskin prognosticators," noting that he himself leads the pack by having correctly predicted the outcome of eighty-six out of ninety-eight of the season's collegiate football games.) At a time when the potential of radio was just starting to be recognized on university campuses, he auditioned for Stanford's first radio drama workshop, and played a minor role in an audio production of Arch Oboler's *The Special Days* that was broadcast on a station in San Francisco. As the issue of the *Daily* for May 19, 1944, notes, Corman and his partner, a fellow student named Frances Smith, took second place in a "mixed golf tournament" held to support a school charity project.

But by the end of his freshman year, Roger could no longer put off thinking about his military service. It was spring 1944, and the war overseas continued to dominate life in Palo Alto. Because so much of the dorm space on campus had been allotted to the ASTP student soldiers, Stanford's fraternities had been formally shut down. Rooms in the frat houses, renamed in honor of presidents of the United States, were allotted to male civilians, so that Corman's Lincoln Hall residence was actually the former Phi Kappa Psi house. Stanford's varsity athletic teams had been terminated for the duration of the war. Thus, as a sports writer, Corman was reduced to covering intramural matches between campus groups. (The hallowed athletic rivalry between Stanford and the University of California at Berkeley played itself out that year as a competitive war-bond drive. As the school that raised the most money, Stanford gained possession of the coveted ax trophy.) In his column for April 21, 1944, Corman formally said farewell to his co–sports editor, Jim Weinberg, who was leaving for the Army.

On June 6, 1944, a banner headline in the *Daily* screamed, "INVASION OF EUROPE ON." Ten days later, near the close of the spring quarter, Corman wrote his last column as sports editor. He did not mention that he was about to enter a U.S. Navy officer training program known as the V-12, thus ensuring himself of a chance to complete his engineering studies while having some control over his future military assignment.

The V-12 program, open to those who passed a rigorous academic test, sent him to the University of Colorado at Boulder as an apprentice seaman. At the end of two and a half years of study, which included regular engineering classes as well as specialized coursework in naval science, he was slated to be commissioned as an ensign. The need to wear a uniform, learn to march, and use naval terminology was doubtless a constant irritant to the very independent minded Corman, whose career has shown disdain for regimentation in any form. Fortunately for him, the war ended before his hitch was complete. His autobiography recounts how he left the Navy in spring of 1946. At the time of his discharge, he made it a point of honor to refuse the higher rank offered him by a friendly clerk in place of his lowly "apprentice seaman" designation.

Also in his book, Corman gives a harrowing account of his return to civilian life. On his first night back in northern California, all his belongings disappeared out of an unsecured footlocker. On his second night, he hitched a ride to a fraternity party in Berkeley and ended up being robbed at knifepoint. These two events turned out to be a formative introduction to the real

world. From this point on, Corman would take much better care to hold on
to what was his.

But first there was an academic degree to complete. After returning to
Stanford in the summer of 1946, Roger seemed to be in a great hurry. He
joined one of the reinstated fraternities, Sigma Alpha Epsilon, but no longer
dabbled in journalistic pursuits. Although radio courses were now an established part of the campus Speech and Drama curriculum, he apparently
did not take advantage of these. One younger student who did was Monte
Jay Himmelbaum, who, at Corman's graduation, was awarded the
NBC–Stanford Radio Institute Scholarship. Later, under the name of Monte
Hellman, he made several films for Roger, and has achieved cult status
among cinéastes worldwide for such atmospheric screen works as *The
Shooting* (1967) and *Two-Lane Blacktop* (1971).

From Corman's own perspective, his college graduation ceremony on
June 15, 1947, was a rather low-key affair. He had actually been granted his
B.S. from the university's esteemed School of Engineering in January of that
year, at the end of fall quarter. Given his interrupted stay at Stanford, as well
as the absence of emotional commitment to his official field of study, it is
surely not surprising he won no particular academic recognition. This lack
didn't keep him, in later years, from hinting (as he did to *Show* magazine's
Digby Diehl in 1970) that he finished college "with all the honors."

The 1947 edition of the *Quad*, the Stanford yearbook, opens with a
dedication to "those Stanford men who gave their lives that we might live in
peace." Though Corman was by now listed on school records as a World War
II veteran, he had been spared the horrors that many of his generation had
seen. His graduation photo in the *Quad* reveals a handsome, serious young
man. He faces forward, but his eyes are evasive, even secretive. He looks
thoughtful, like someone at a crossroads in his life.

•   •   •

By the time Corman returned to Los Angeles in spring 1947, he had decided
to enter the film business. To some extent, the attraction was money and
glamour. Mark Thomas McGee, in his book *Faster and Furiouser: The Revised
and Fattened Fable of American International Pictures* (1996), claims that
Roger had promised himself he'd be a millionaire by the time he reached age
thirty. Corman's 1990 autobiography puts the matter in a rather different

light: "I knew even then that if you wanted to make a lot of money in southern California you went into real estate. My interest in films was for the creative satisfaction and the excitement."

It seems quite clear that at this point of his life, twenty-one-year-old Corman was in love with movies. In an era when formal film study was almost nonexistent (certainly, there were no film courses or cinema societies at Stanford at that time), he discovered, and was bowled over by, the works of such directors as John Ford, Alfred Hitchcock, and Howard Hawks. (On June 12, 1991, when Roger's star was unveiled in front of 7013 Hollywood Boulevard, I was among the guests who heard him express great satisfaction that it was located—per his request—next to Hitchcock's.) Corman's affection for classic screen westerns later inspired some of his own more ambitious films: *Battle Beyond the Stars* (1980) was a futuristic rendering of *The Magnificent Seven* (1960), and *Space Raiders* (1983) began as an outer-space variant on *The Wild Bunch* (1969). In conversation Roger refers often to *Red River* (1948) and *Shane* (1953), and he still hopes to do his own remake of a British film he remembers fondly, Carol Reed's screen adaptation (1951) of the Joseph Conrad novel *An Outcast of the Islands* (1896).

The fact that Roger is partial to Hollywood-style action movies (as well as hard-boiled film noir) should not imply that he scorns the art film. He has long admired Akira Kurosawa's samurai epics, and his *The Masque of the Red Death* (1964) pays homage to the black-cloaked Death figure in Ingmar Bergman's *The Seventh Seal* (1957). In the early 1970s, when someone gave Corman a dog, he named it Po, after the film he has often called his very favorite, Sergei Eisenstein's *Battleship Potemkin* (1925). His genuine respect for international cinema helped pave the way for the exhilarating period, during the heyday of New World Pictures, when he reigned as North America's leading distributor of foreign-language features.

The young man who left Stanford filled with dreams of making movies could not realize that, after forty years in Hollywood, his enthusiasm for the motion-picture form would be destined to fade. Producer-director Deborah Brock recently summed up what many others have noticed: "I think he definitely started out loving movies. I don't think he particularly cares about them now." The Roger Corman of today watches films not for pleasure, but rather out of a sense of obligation. A staff member who has worked closely with him in recent years has heard him say more than once, "I never want to see another movie. But it's the only thing I know how to do." It's a surprising sentiment for someone who so deliberately chose the life of a filmmaker. But a man in his seventies is entitled to feel a bit weary.

Back in 1947, as a brand-new college graduate, Corman was not in the least weary. In fact, he was impatient to get started on his new career. But the Hollywood film community was hardly standing by with arms outstretched to welcome the young man into the fold.

Part Two

AMERICAN INTERNATIONAL PICTURES

(1948–70)

Chapter 3

ONE FOR THE MONEY

What turned me on was film, not only as an art form but as an exciting way to make money.

ROGER CORMAN, 1978

HOWARD R. COHEN, who wrote some forty Corman films, recounted to me one version of how Corman got his start in the movie business. Roger once told Cohen that when he became a messenger at Twentieth Century–Fox, "they promised me that when a job opened up in some other department, they would let me move into it. And two jobs opened up on the same day, amazingly. And they gave me a choice. One was in the writing department, and one was in the accounting department." According to Cohen, Corman then smiled and said, "You know, today I could have been a really great accountant."

The anecdote is charming, but not quite accurate. Corman's movement into the story department was not nearly as simple and inevitable as this tale would make it seem. And Roger would probably never have made a great accountant. For all his financial savvy, his talents have never lain in the area of computation and record keeping. He acknowledges this in his memoir, discussing a college aptitude test that "proved" he could succeed in virtually any field, other than bookkeeping and accounting. Honesty has never been the issue: if you work for Corman, you can expect to get paid. (In an industry built on empty promises, television writer Bill Rabkin gave Corman the ultimate accolade in assuring me that "he paid on time, and his checks always cleared.") But when it comes to keeping track of financial intricacies, not to mention copyright matters and long-term rights to acquisitions, Roger has always shown a decided lack of interest. His own predilection is for being where the action is: making the deal, making the picture.

In the late 1940s, though major changes were just around the corner, the action was still almost entirely confined to the big Hollywood studios. Those who wanted to make movies had to find their way into a closed system. So the question remains: How did a young man armed with nothing but great expectations manage to get his big break?

Initially, it seemed hopeless. At age twenty-one, Corman spent long months trying to find a toehold in the industry. At one point, his memoir relates, he settled for an engineering job at a local firm, U.S. Electrical Motors. By his third day, he realized he could not accept engineering as his life's direction. He quit on Thursday morning, unwilling even to finish the first week.

Finally, in 1948, a friend's father pulled some strings, and Roger was hired as a messenger on the Twentieth Century–Fox lot in West Los Angeles, where Darryl F. Zanuck held sway and Betty Grable, Victor Mature, Anne Baxter, and Tyrone Power were among the contract stars. The job paid $32.50 a week, but Corman hardly considered this low. For months he hustled, even working without pay on weekends, to prove himself worthy of a loftier post. Then, in 1949, an opening came up, and he was duly named a Fox story analyst at the then princely salary of $65 a week. His excitement faded after much time spent writing coverage of lackluster novels and "spec" scripts that would doubtless never be made into films. (I have among my keepsakes a typed synopsis, dated June 16, 1949, of a fantasy novel called *Slaves of Sleep* by the founder of Scientology, L. Ron Hubbard. It was sent my way in the 1970s by a Fox story editor as a friendly gesture, because Roger Corman was the analyst who had summarized the book, in serviceable though hardly elegant prose.)

While working for Fox, Corman got his first taste of the way big studios operate. His autobiography describes how, on his own initiative, he retrieved a reject from the slush pile, suggested changes, and sent it off to a Fox executive as a vehicle for contract star Gregory Peck, who was looking for a classy, offbeat western. The script, retitled *The Gunfighter* (1950), became a major critical and popular hit, and the executive earned a big bonus. Roger's complaint is that his own contribution was wholly overlooked. Disillusioned, he quit his job, and parlayed his G.I. Bill benefits into what he called a "semester" at England's Oxford University, forty miles north of London.

Corman's term at one of Oxford's oldest and most prestigious institutions, Balliol College, involved studying modern English literature (mostly E. M. Forster, D. H. Lawrence, and T. S. Eliot) and playing a bit of tennis. After six months, he headed for Paris, where, in the company of a young crowd of expatriate Americans, he frequented jazz clubs and discussed existentialism. He also dabbled in screenwriting, but his professional aspirations seemed to be largely on hold. The European adventure ended about a year after it had begun, when Corman, his money running out, returned home, and faced his need to reenter the real world.

The Oxford experience, brief though it was, contributed to Corman's respect for great literature. It also added another highbrow touch to his résumé. Well over a decade later, when his reputation as a director of independent films was solidifying, he was honored by the Oxford University Film Society. This event, on September 3, 1966, helped give rise to exaggerated notions about Corman's youthful Oxford stay. In the next few years, several articles (including Lawrence Dietz's 1967 piece in the *New York World Journal Tribune*) would call attention to Corman's master's degree from Oxford. On July 31, 1969, Variety announced that Corman was establishing a $1,000 annual scholarship at Oxford, "where he received his Master of Arts degree in English." Needless to say, he had earned no master's degree, and it was wholly unlike him to commit to a long-range program of charitable giving. So the reader can be forgiven for suspecting once again the fine hand of Roger's publicist at work.

• • •

All this was well in the future in 1951, when the twenty-five-year-old Corman, newly back from Europe, discovered there were no openings at Twentieth Century-Fox. His former story editor helpfully recommended him for a slot at the Jules Goldstone Literary Agency. He spent the early 1950s in a series of industry-related jobs, toiling as a grip at KLAC-TV and reading scripts for literary agencies around town. In 1953, while at the Dick Irving

Hyland (Literary) Agency, Corman finally achieved a breakthrough. Allied Artists (formerly Monogram Pictures), a small but ambitious film company, offered $3,500 for a script he had co-written, based on his original story, "The House in the Sea." Corman immediately quit his agency job to work, gratis, on the low-budget production, which was directed by Nathan Juran and featured Richard Conte as an outlaw caught up in a chase across the desert. By the time the black-and-white thriller was released, it had been retitled *Highway Dragnet* to exploit the popularity of *Dragnet* (1952–55), the hit TV series, and Corman was credited as both writer and associate producer. His disappointment with the film's shoddy production values faded in time, as he discovered that his career had not been irreparably damaged. But his first hands-on filmmaking experience had convinced him that efficiency was the key to artistic success. On his second feature, he intended to hold the reins himself.

That second movie was inspired by an item in the *Los Angeles Times,* about how a local company called Aerojet General was testing an electric-powered one-man submarine. Corman talked Aerojet into giving him free use of this vaguely futuristic craft, then set about raising the $12,000 he'd need to shoot the six-day film that eventually became *The Monster from the Ocean Floor* (1954). His autobiography relates how, seeking financial backing, he first appealed to his parents, who pointed out that they had already put him through Stanford University. Corman, however, was not to be denied. Paul Almond, an attorney-turned-producer who once handled business affairs at Corman's New World Pictures, described his former boss to me as someone who can be as unstoppable as an avalanche. "Roger is the kind of person that you would want to go up against any impossible situation, because if there was a way—either by being charming, talkative, compelling—this is the man that would figure out a way to do it, at little or no cost." In this case, Corman artfully persuaded his college fraternity brothers and their families to become investors. And he found a young actor, Wyott ("Barney") Ordung, who would gladly try his hand at directing for a piece of the action. Corman the movie producer was off and running.

The success of this black-and-white venture was owed partly to Gene Corman, who had followed his elder brother to Stanford but actually was the first of the two to land a job in the entertainment field. Gene started college with prelaw aspirations, then briefly considered premed, but graduated in 1948 with a bachelor's degree in the social sciences. Returning to Los Angeles, he parlayed a passion for tennis and an engaging social manner into a budding career as an agent. Former Corman assistant Kinta Haller told me, during the course of our chat, that she viewed Gene as more willing than his brother or his father to be a company man. He was to spend seven years at the Music Corporation of America (MCA) talent agency, representing such stars as Joan Crawford, Fred MacMurray, Harry Belafonte, and Ray Milland. In 1954 it was Gene who helped Roger set up a distribution deal with Robert Lippert of the Lippert Releasing Company. The $60,000 advance from Lippert (against a sale price of about $110,000) allowed Roger to pay off his debts on *The Monster from the Ocean Floor* and begin planning his next production.

Given the Corman tradition of family solidarity, Gene's involvement in his brother's first big movie project was not surprising. Still, their kinship hardly guaranteed constant goodwill between the two. On November 17, 1998, veteran screenwriter Chuck Griffith e-mailed me an account of the persistent gossip surrounding the Cormans—"that the father was a hovering presence, a casual achiever, superior to both sons combined, who had sent them into competition with each other and with himself."

Griffith never witnessed the rumored one-upmanship between the brothers, but many former Corman employees—particularly those from the early New World Pictures years when Gene's own small production company occupied a corner of Roger's office suite—describe tensions and tempers flaring. Director Paul Bartel (*Eating Raoul*) recalls the relationship of the two Cormans in the 1970s as "cool but not cold. I certainly never saw any signs of brotherly love. . . . I had the impression that the main family value in the Corman family was money, and that it really was about who could amass the most money and the most valuable goods." But Kinta Haller, who came on the scene in the late 1950s, disputes the notion of a fierce rivalry between the siblings: "They're two brothers, very ambitious. I think the ties that bound them together and kept them working together were far more intense than any rivalry."

Gene Corman collaborated with Roger on several early pictures, and was also to try producing films on his own, first for American International

Pictures and then for major studios. The World War II epics *Tobruk* (1967) and *The Big Red One* (1980) are among his most important feature credits. Unlike his maverick brother, Gene seems comfortable working in the mainstream. He was a television executive for Twentieth Century–Fox in the mid-1980s, and achieved his greatest professional success as the Emmy-winning producer of *A Woman Called Golda,* a 1982 Paramount TV mini-series that starred Ingrid Bergman as Israeli prime minister Golda Meir. (Bergman garnered both an Emmy and a Golden Globe for this, her final role before her death.) The brothers' differences even extend to the voting booth: Gene has called himself a dyed-in-the-wool Republican, while Roger once informed his young children (in the presence of then assistant Anna Roth) that Democrats are naturally superior in terms of both "IQ and compassion."

What's most interesting about Gene is the way he diverges from the family code of personal austerity. Everyone who's known the two Cormans remarks on the contrast in their lifestyles. Roger's tastes run to contemporary minimalism, and his homes have always reflected this; Gene has lived for years in a venerable Beverly Hills Tudor-style house replete with antiques. Roger prides himself on wearing the same nondescript clothing for decades; Gene owns an array of handsome pullover sweaters. Gene was the family's first art collector, bucking William Corman's fears that paintings and sculpture were an extravagance and much too risky to be considered a worthwhile investment.

Frank Moreno, longtime New World head of sales, explained to me in late 1998 the essential distinction between the brothers: "Gene is going to enjoy every minute of life, and Gene'll spend whatever it takes to do it." Paul Almond, a later New World business executive, puts it this way: "Gene was a total sport. Gene would pick up a tab. Roger never picks up tabs." There may well be, as some have suggested, a significant link between Gene's personal warmth and his liberal attitude toward money, which stand a world apart from Roger's emotional reticence and tightfisted approach. One former employee sees money as the fundamental indicator of Roger Corman's rigidly controlled personality: "It would be very tough for me to imagine him making any disclosures about himself as a human being the way most people I know do. And I think money, in a weird psychological way, is a part of him. So when he has to pay out, when he gives up money, it's truly an emotional sacrifice he's making. It's far beyond being cheap and frugal. . . . For him to give up money is literally to give up a piece of himself."

•   •   •

Despite its shoestring budget, *The Monster from the Ocean Floor* won some respectful reviews. *Variety* said, "Here's an oddity—a well-done quickie. . . . Roger Corman's production supervision has packed the footage with commercial values without going overboard." Buoyed by his success, twenty-eight-year-old Corman immediately planned a second feature. This black-and-white film, the aptly titled *The Fast and the Furious* (1954), was a 73-minute race-car drama shot in nine days on a $50,000 budget. Far more ambitious than its predecessor, it featured name actors Dorothy Malone and John Ireland, with Corman signing Ireland for well under his usual price by letting him co-direct the film, along with Edward Sampson. But *The Fast and the Furious* also marked Corman's first opportunity to step behind the camera himself, when, for one climactic sequence, he served as a second-unit director. Roger also filled in as a stunt driver, and has confided to journalist Ed Naha (in *The Films of Roger Corman: Brilliance on a Budget,* 1982) that he ruined one take by failing to let the hero pass him in a key racing sequence: "I got so excited about driving a real race car that I drove to win the race."

Corman's passion for racing did not abate. In later years, fast sports cars—including, briefly, a Lotus—proved to be one of his few self-indulgences. Low-budget director Jim Wynorski, whose career was kick-started when he became New World's head of advertising in 1980, shared with me an incident that reveals Corman's car mania. Corman was driving a Los Angeles freeway with Wynorski when somebody cut them off. "I remember going down the 10 Freeway, with him hitting eighty, ninety [miles per hour], trying to beat this guy to the exit who had cut him off. He was living *Eat My Dust!* [1976] for real. And I thought, 'There's a reason he made all those car movies. He likes cars. He likes fast cars. . . .' I figured I was safe. For some reason, I felt the Roger Corman angels were hovering over that car."

Jim Wynorski may be right about the Roger Corman angels. And divine intervention may have been part of the mix in 1954, when everything seemed to be going Corman's way. In his first year out, he had produced two features for his own tiny company, Palo Alto Productions. He had a modest production office above a quasi English pub called the Cock 'n' Bull on Los Angeles' sometimes tawdry but always trendy Sunset Strip. He was starting to assemble the stock company of actors and crew who would stand by him on many of his early screen ventures. And *The Fast and the Furious* brought him a three-picture distribution deal with American Releasing Corporation.

This new company, headed by film exhibitor James Nicholson (1916–1972) and entertainment attorney Samuel Z. Arkoff (b. 1918) was formed in 1954 to take full advantage of the so-called Consent Decree, a Supreme Court anti-trust ruling that stripped the major studios of their power over motion-picture theater chains. American Releasing Corporation's mission was to supply product to the drive-ins and smaller theaters, at a time when the majors were phasing out the lower-budget "B movies" they had used in the past to fill double bills.

(Corman's personal resistance to the use of the term "B movie" to describe his own projects stems from the fact they aren't intended to be paired with star-driven "A movies," as in the old days of the studio system. He first labeled his own features "exploitation films," using a common exhibitors' term for low-cost pictures that rely on showmanship to appeal to a broad popular audience. Such movies, "exploiting" hot topics of the day, had been on the rise since the mid-1940s, as an article in *Variety* for January 4, 1946, makes clear. *Variety* gave as an example of an exploitation film RKO's *Back to Bataan,* released in 1945 very close to the time of the actual incident it portrayed. But, of course, the exploitation label quickly came to imply a cheaply made picture with strong sexual content. Later, as the rise of such blockbusters as *Jaws* [1975] and *Star Wars* [1977] gave the horror and science-fiction genres increased respectability, Corman began applying to his own product line the more dignified term "genre films." Still, he does smile graciously when he is called "the King of the B's.")

American Releasing soon changed its name to American International Pictures, or AIP. Over the course of two decades it would grow to be the largest and most influential independent film company in Hollywood. In the beginning, Corman was AIP's only supplier of film product. Once he proved he could deliver the goods, he was soon making multiple AIP features a year. Mel Welles, who acted in his first Corman movie, *Attack of the Crab Monsters,* in

1957, recently described for me Corman's basic AIP deal: Upon delivering a completed film, he would receive $50,000 as a negative pickup fee, plus a $15,000 advance on the projected foreign sale. Though he was also guaranteed a percentage of the movie's eventual profits, Corman never counted on this potential income. His strategy was to come in under $65,000 per film, so as to have working capital for his next project. The fact that he would plan every third or fourth feature to be ultralow-budget (below the $30,000 range) would help ensure a healthy profit in the long run.

The story of Corman averaging between ten and twelve AIP films a year in his heyday is an exaggeration. Corman himself mentions in his memoir having turned out over a dozen movies during one frantic two-year period, 1956–57, though only half of these were for AIP. In a typical year he might make three or four AIP features, along with others released through such companies as Allied Artists. In any case, his output in this era was remarkable. His ability to work fast and cheap rested heavily on his organizational skills and his seeming imperviousness to outside pressure. Welles, to whom I spoke in early 1999, sees this as a case of a man having found his niche. He told me he particularly admired Corman's "ability to make decisions when they had to be made, like tear pages out of the script, [and say,] 'Wrap it up, we're not going to shoot this.' No matter how tough the decision was in terms of what it might do to the picture, he was able to make it."

•   •   •

One decision Corman made early on, immediately after completing *The Fast and the Furious,* was to wear the director's hat himself. An obvious advantage was that, by personally directing the film, he would no longer have to pay someone else to do the key job. Nor would he have to work within the confines of someone else's artistic vision. His very next feature, *Five Guns West* (1955), saw Corman in command, though not in total control of his nerves. In 1980 Roger described to Ed Naha what happened en route to the set on his first day of shooting. When he discovered it was starting to rain, "I drove to the side of the road and, as casually as possible, threw up. I then proceeded to the set."

R. Wright Campbell was present for Corman's directorial debut on *Five Guns West,* which costarred John Lund and Dorothy Malone. Campbell had been given $200 to write the script, and like most Corman writers then and now, he considered himself grossly underpaid. (In 1956 he would double his money on Corman's tropic adventure film, *Naked Paradise*, and in 1958 would receive an Oscar nomination for scripting the Lon Chaney biopic, *Man of a Thousand Faces*.) Campbell recalled for me via e-mail that "when I mentioned to Roger that every actor and craftsman on *Five Guns West* would make more than I did for creating it, he asked me if I wanted to act. So I played one of the leads."

During the filming of a campfire scene, Campbell noticed that Corman sat with his nose buried in the script instead of watching the actors. Roger explained he was making sure they got their lines right. The legend, according to former assistant Frances Doel, is that this was his pattern in the earliest films: If the actors said all their dialogue correctly, he'd yell, "Cut!" and if they got the dialogue wrong, he'd go for another take. At some point, veteran cinematographer Floyd Crosby quietly took him aside and suggested he needed to look through the lens occasionally. Doel likes that story, whether or not it's true. For her it indicates that "the idea that he teaches all of us, about movies being a visual medium, is something he had to learn, which is maybe why he's so insistent on it."

In any case, Corman's technical prowess quickly increased, and he no longer made economic gaffes like asking for multiple retakes of the same stunt when the stuntman expected to be compensated for each one. As time passed and Roger's filmography grew, the consensus is that he was happiest planning mechanical effects and action sequences, and least happy giving direction to actors. This despite the fact that he conscientiously attended classes with well-known Hollywood acting coach Jeff Corey in order to gain insight into the actor's world.

In truth, most of Roger Corman's early actors were not much more experienced than he was. Many (including Jack Nicholson) began as would-be writers who had been pressed into on-camera service on the spot. Veteran character actor Dick Miller, whom I interviewed on September 11, 1998, first planned to be a writer, too, but ended up playing both an Indian and a cowboy in *Apache Woman* (1955), Corman's second film as a director. For this he was paid about $300. Miller was to make six Corman films in 1957 alone, and ultimately his pay improved. Mel Welles told me of his own entry into the so-called Corman Repertory Company, "which for actors was a good deal because you could always count on him whenever you needed a week's work. And he was always good to work with. He was very affable in the early days, and he was very quick in the shooting. . . . You knew you were going to work long hours and get $500 and that's it. And you were going to work a week, because that's all it took to shoot the picture. I really enjoyed my relationship with Roger."

"To be honest," claims Dick Miller, "[Corman] never really directed much. He set up the shots . . . he seemed to know where the next shot was going to be, because he'd be yelling, 'Cut!' while he was walking, and everybody would grab a reflector or something and just follow him to the next setup." This was good training in the long run: Miller is still known in the film industry as a one-take actor.

Miller emphasized to me that Corman's willingness to leave his actors alone in front of the camera was one secret of his success. "Why worry about your actors if you can get good people, the best available on the money you have? Because then you don't have to direct them. I don't recall him ever telling me how a line should be read, or telling the actors I was working with what our motivation was. He did the technical end. He set up the shots, which were very basic, and let the people—who were good people— go, let them wail. That concept was right."

Like most serious critics, Gary Morris finds the acting in Corman's pictures uneven. But Morris, whose book *Roger Corman* (1985) hails the moviemaker as an auteur master, is unwilling to dismiss the sometimes inspired, sometimes inept performances as anything other than part of a grand design. To him, the Corman oeuvre is replete with self-portraits of the artist trapped in a universe beyond his control. In the sort of solemn pronouncement that often makes Corman alumni howl with laughter, Morris states that the "bad acting" (the quotation marks are his) represents both Corman's "fear of accepting *in toto* the god-like role of the director and his use of actors as blanks or ciphers inhabiting a world of total pointlessness." Even Morris, however, acknowledges that Corman may also have felt intimidated by the enforced contact with his screen players.

To veteran actress Beverly Garland, who starred in five early Corman releases, Roger's hands-off attitude toward actors indeed stems from his fundamental bashfulness, which he strove mightily to overcome. As she explains, Corman won over his cast by taking their work seriously, and by willingly sharing in the hardships of low-budget filmmaking, as when they all camped out in an abandoned hotel in the middle of the Louisiana bayous to make *Swamp Women* (1955). Still, Corman could be maniacal about getting the job done. On *Gunslinger* (1956), Garland remembers thinking, "If the cameraman drops dead, Roger will just pick up the camera and we'll continue on." To her, Corman could do anything: "The only thing he couldn't do was put on a red wig and really look too much like Allison Hayes. But he might've, if he had to!"

The wig might well have become necessary, because it was on *Gunslinger* that costar Hayes fell off a horse and broke her arm. She finished the western regardless. So did Garland, who badly sprained her ankle during a shot in which she had to run down a flight of stairs. The following day, with the movie's climactic catfight scheduled, she couldn't even hobble, until Roger summoned a doctor who injected her with a painkiller—"and in a few minutes I could walk, I could jump, I could do everything. And I worked all day." Ultimately she paid the price: "I didn't work for three or four months after that, because I couldn't walk very well. But that's Roger; the show goes on."

Corman applied this throw-caution-to-the-winds approach to himself as well. Actor and jack-of-all-trades Beach Dickerson remembers a 1961 Puerto Rico trip "when we were shooting *The Creature from the Haunted Sea* and it was literally hurricaning, and the trees were bent [over], and he was defying the gods. . . . He was determined to get that last damn shot." Dickerson notes that Corman has always "pushed himself to the limit. Now it hasn't satisfied him. Except financially. But you can only spend so much money. How many candy bars can you eat?"

Dickerson's rhetoric brings up the valid question of what Roger was trying to accomplish. Certainly, he wanted to make money. But something additional seemed to be at stake. Actor Dick Miller honed in on this for me: "He was turning out a product that made him money. But at the same time, I used to get an inkling from some of his discussions that he was very sincere and very serious about his work. It's hard to say [he was] artistic on a picture made for $17,000, but I think he was sincerely trying to make a good movie. There were guys around in those days who said, 'Let's make a movie. You get your cheap script and cheap actors, and we'll make this cheap movie.' And Roger, I think, was thinking, 'Let's get the best we can.'"

So from the very start, Corman was balancing aesthetics and economics. On November 5, 1998, I spoke jointly to some successful filmmakers who in the 1970s had gone from being Corman buffs to Corman protégés. Reviewing Roger's early career, director Joe Dante insisted, "I don't know if he was ever an artist, but he was serious about making movies." To which his old friend and colleague, producer Jon Davison (*Airplane, Robocop*), chimed in, "And he made better cheap movies than anybody else did."

• • •

Corman's movies stood out from the other low-budget Hollywood films of the era because they always gave the viewer something extra: a clever idea, a distinctive performance, a modicum of style. This is borne out by generally favorable reviews in industry publications. Of *It Conquered the World* (1956), the *Hollywood Reporter* said, "Roger Corman's production is well integrated with science fact and fantasy for enough believability to maintain interest and excitement." Even a weaker effort like *Swamp Women* (1955) earned some praise, partly for the filmmaker's decision to experiment with color cinematography. In *Variety*'s words, "Roger Corman's direction, somewhat over-melodramatic, fully utilizes the bayou area to pictorial advantage, with Fred West's Eastman Color camera-work also aiding here."

To attract top personnel to these projects, Corman was willing to overlook personal failings. Dick Miller remembers this approach backfiring in the case of Paul Birch, a veteran character actor with a reputed serious drinking problem. Birch disappeared midway through the filming of *Not of This Earth* (1956), forcing Corman to hire a not-very-similar stand-in to complete this inventive sci-fi thriller. Somehow, it worked.

When it came to gathering a crew, Corman looked for adaptability and experience. Despite his well-deserved reputation for cheapness, he initially paid top dollar, offering his key personnel union-minimum salaries and guaranteed overtime, even though he was shooting with nonunion crews in a far more informal working atmosphere than that found at major studios. Kinta Haller explains, "When Roger started directing himself, he knew that he needed people to help him. He knew he needed the best to get that movie made, and he was not going to hire people who were inadequate.

Later on, when he knew more and could do more himself, that may have changed. But when I knew him, he had some excellent crew people, and he treated them very well."

Corman's crews generally included Chuck Hannawalt, a key grip who (says Haller) "could run Roger around by the nose, because Roger had so much respect for Chuck's ability to get a film made." Another regular was head cameraman Floyd Crosby, "a tough old guy" with the bearing of a general who had won an Oscar in 1932 for his work on *Tabu* as well as a Golden Globe in 1953 for *High Noon*. Such veterans were augmented by rising talents like art director Daniel Haller. (Roger's high-school pal Jack Bohrer served as his assistant director on many productions.)

Actors, writers, and craftspeople all loved working for Corman because he gave them the freedom to be creative. He was also loyal to them personally, but only up to a point. Those expecting to find a lifelong home in the Corman Stock Company were doomed to disappointment, because Roger was far too pragmatic to make decisions based on sentiment alone. Chuck Griffith, who wrote some of Corman's most memorably outrageous films, conveyed this to me poignantly in a November 20, 1998, e-mail from his home in Australia. "I thought we'd move up as a group. But when he moved to the [Edgar Allan] Poe pictures, he dumped all his old writers, who were clearly small-town types without actual futures."

Film critic Gary Morris expresses the common wisdom: "Part of Corman's fascination lies in his ability to convince artists like [Floyd] Crosby, [Chuck] Griffith, and [Daniel] Haller to work with him when major studio options would have been open to them." But the fact is that most people stuck with Corman because they were not being offered more prestigious gigs. The majority of Cormanites, then as now, viewed their stint in his B movie factory as a means to a professional end. Kinta Haller's assertion that "I don't think that anybody that I know of was so loyal to Roger that they'd turn down a better opportunity" is borne out by the career of her husband Dan, whom she met and married while in Corman's employ. After designing sets for some of Corman's best-known films, Dan Haller moved into a solid career as a TV director and never looked back.

Longtime character actor Mel Welles agrees that those who worked for Corman did so largely because the doors of the major studios were closed to them. "Roger was a way to get to do what you wanted to do, in a business that screens you out rather than welcomes you in. It was a way to sharpen your beak and move on." So if Corman was using others to advance his own career, they were using him as well.

The principle of mutual exploitation also applied to Corman's social life. Unlike brother Gene, who had married an attractive blonde fashion model in 1955, Roger was still unattached at age thirty. In this period he was dating a number of his leading ladies. One of these was the effervescent Beverly Garland, who told me she was flattered by the attention: "Roger cannot be around people that are not bright. It drives him crazy. I always felt very good about myself, because I always thought, 'I must be bright, or he wouldn't talk to me.'" Garland remembers Corman on a date as charming in his shyness. But while she regarded him as mesmerizing, she could never have fallen in love. "What I found fascinating was the way he did business; the way his mind worked. . . . I loved to see Roger on the set, directing. That was part of his fascination for me."

No one has ever suggested that Corman chose actresses for major screen roles in order to curry favor with them romantically. He was far too serious about his movies to use the casting process as a way to advance his love life. Yet Howard R. Cohen, who once broached Gayle Hunnicutt's name to Corman for a part in an upcoming movie, had the distinct impression that after a relationship with an actress had cooled, Corman was no longer willing to have her on his set. Beverly Garland concedes that Cohen had a point. "That could be right. Roger dated me and I went my own way." Though she had starred in such early Corman classics as *Not of This Earth* (1956), and though she would go on to a successful career in TV series like *My Three Sons* (1969–72) and *Scarecrow and Mrs. King* (1983–87), she was not hired by Corman again until 1995. That was the year she traveled to Russia on short notice to play opposite Ben Cross in a gothic horror piece called *Hellfire*, directed by a young Corman hopeful, David Tausik. *Hellfire* was an arduous shoot, complicated by cultural misunderstandings, and Garland told me she found herself thinking, "Why doesn't Roger come over here and help us out?" In her mind, "I knew that if Roger stepped off that plane, came to the studio in Moscow, everything would be solved."

• • •

By the start of 1957, the thirty-one-year-old Corman had made fifteen features, averaging five a year. In 1958 he would move from his bachelor apartment into a small (1,700 square feet) but sleek new canyon home on Lindacrest Drive in Beverly Hills. His parents dropped by frequently to make sure the young man was well stocked with spare lightbulbs and other domestic necessities. Home ownership, though, did nothing to enlarge Corman's social life. He was not a party-giver, and when the Corman Stock Company was not hard at work, there was little fraternizing between the boss and his hirelings.

Roger's air of self-containment was due partly to his shyness, and partly to his sense of having a private mission. Once again, former assistant Kinta Haller provides insight: "I think he always was very much his own man. While he had many relationships and many friends, I think they were fairly detached relationships. . . . When there was a mutuality of interests he worked with lots of different people; when that mutuality of interests changed, he kept going in his own direction. I don't know that he ever has felt any loss because of that. I feel he's always done what he needed to do for himself, with his own vision of where he wanted to go and the way he wanted to get there."

Though such an attitude was hard on the old cronies who came to feel they had been left in the dust, it made sense for a man on the move. And Roger Corman was definitely out to make his mark on the motion-picture industry.

MAKER OF MONSTERS

Don't show the monster too much at the beginning.

ROGER CORMAN, 1997

ROGER CORMAN'S APPROACH to shooting horror films in the 1950s and thereafter is best captured in a segment of *Directors on Directors,* an interview program made for Italian television in 1997. Speaking on-camera to Concorde–New Horizons alumnus Adam Simon, Corman explains his long-held theory that good horror movies at first reveal the monster only through hints and glimpses, so that "each member of the audience creates their individual monster." Corman, of course, knows a thing or two about monster flicks. He's especially savvy about low-rent monsters—when the special effects leave something to be desired, it's wise to hide the creature as long as possible.

Corman's wholehearted embrace of the horror genre is one reason he quickly became AIP's top moneymaker, far outpacing such other early AIP regulars as Edward L. Cahn (*The She Creature,* 1956) and Bert I. Gordon (*Attack of the Puppet People,* 1958). From the start, Roger instinctively grasped horror's appeal to the vast youth audience that in the late 1950s was just coming into its own. The first wave of baby-boomers saw Corman films in theaters; a later generation watched them when they aired in the 1970s on the popular syndicated TV show *Creature Features.* Director Joe

Dante recently clarified for me one aspect of these films' appeal: "The whole thrust of these cheap movies was that they were movies your parents wouldn't want you to see."

Portly character actor Mel Welles, who has made the rounds of nostalgia conventions geared to horror fans, reveals that today's fifty-year-olds consider *Attack of the Crab Monsters* (1957) a special favorite, because "it was the first film that ever frightened them." The matinee audiences for Roger Corman's early monster flicks contained boys (it's an overwhelmingly male genre) who would one day be among Hollywood's leading filmmakers. Writer-director Howard R. Cohen pointed out to me that "you can see the [Corman] influences in Steven Spielberg and in all the guys who are doing stuff now, in that age group. They grew up with that fast-paced action—sudden shock—horror. It's all there."

Another hint that Corman had his finger on his film-going audience's pulse was his ability to respond instantly to the big events of the day. For instance, on October 4, 1957, the Soviet Union launched *Sputnik,* the first man-made satellite to orbit the earth. Three weeks later, Roger and company wrapped the 66-minute *The War of the Satellites,* a black-and-white science-fiction drama designed to cash in on young people's new fascination with outer space. Within three months, it was on screens across the nation.

Corman's enthusiasm for movies that are, as he likes to put it, "ripped from the headlines" has continued. When a devastating earthquake rocked San Francisco in 1989, and when Los Angeles exploded in civil unrest in 1992, Corman immediately planned quickie films to capitalize on the excitement. He sent camera crews to photograph devastated cityscapes, and put writers to work on timely scripts. But by then, distracted by bureaucratic headaches within his own company, Roger lacked the flexibility he'd had in the 1950s to rush an up-to-the-minute motion picture into production. In any case, by the 1990s there were no longer drive-in theaters eager to snap up Corman's latest offerings. So the timely movies he envisioned never happened. In 1957, however, Roger Corman seemed like a visionary . . . and a magician.

•   •   •

In 1959 Roger Corman and his brother Gene launched Filmgroup to distribute their own self-financed product, thus bypassing the need to have outsiders oversee their bookings. Reporter Ian Spear's 1956 column for *Boxoffice* had lauded Corman as "a refreshing new type of producer-director, the young man, [is] gifted with imagination, daring and entirely unhandicapped by the do's and taboos over which many more experienced film fabricators are currently stubbing their financial toes." One example of Roger's audacity was his decision to make two movies at the same time for his new company. The films were shot in the dead of winter in the Black Hills of South Dakota, using essentially the same cast and crew. Roger produced and directed *Ski Troop Attack* (1960), an ambitious World War II epic; Gene was concurrently producing *Beast from Haunted Cave* (1960).

Both features were written by Chuck Griffith, who still remembers Roger's instructions for the latter: "Give me *Naked Paradise* [a 1957 Roger Corman–directed feature] at a gold mine . . . with a blizzard instead of a hurricane. Oh, and add a monster." (Later, for 1961's *The Creature from the Haunted Sea*, Griffith would move the monster underwater and try a comedic tone.) *Beast from Haunted Cave* marked the directorial debut of a young UCLA film school graduate known as Monte Hellman. Corman had lost $500 investing in Hellman's local stage production of Samuel Beckett's *Waiting for Godot*. The Canadian film journal *Take One* quotes Hellman as saying that "I thought I'd better pay him the money back by doing some films for him." Presumably, this was Monte's little joke. He also noted to *Take One* that Roger was the only man in Hollywood who was entrusting directing gigs to recent graduates of film schools.

Though Gene Corman was credited as producer on *Beast from Haunted Cave*, those involved agree that, as always, Roger took charge of the whole enterprise. His aim was to keep the budgets at $50,000 or below, and Hellman has recalled for me how Corman's cost-consciousness affected the morale of those involved. "He told everyone in town that we were UCLA film students doing a student film, so we got hotel rooms for, I think, a dollar a night, but we had two people in a room so it was fifty cents a night per person, and we were shooting in ten below zero and he served salami sandwiches on plain white bread for lunch. I think if we'd had just a cup of soup. . . . Those kind of economies don't pay off in the long run. You get a lot of bad will that's generated."

Paul Rapp worked on both pictures, receiving what he calls "one very uncomfortable salary" for his services as assistant director, prop man, and head of wardrobe. He also played a major screen role, and (since he was the only one present who knew how to ski) acted as stunt coordinator. An additional duty was chauffeuring Corman and a load of props from Los Angeles to the South Dakota location. In the fall of 1998, he described the trip: "Of course, stopping was not considered possible. It was out of the question. Fortunately the car broke down as we coasted into Denver, and we were forced to take a motel room." Rapp says he gained key insight into Roger's character while watching him brush his teeth: "It was obsessive. It was like a machine. It was like a robot. It was all calculated."

Filmgroup handled about ten features over a three-year period. It relied heavily on Gene's connections with theater-chain owners, until Gene—weary of being saddled with the business side of running a distribution company—left to produce films at Twentieth Century–Fox. Filmgroup's remaining pictures subsequently found distribution through AIP. Roger told Todd McCarthy and Charles Flynn, for their 1975 book *Kings of the Bs*, that Filmgroup was far too tiny to make serious money: the company's profits were in the range of $3,000 one year, $1,500 the next. Nonetheless, Corman's yen to be his own distributor was to resurface on a far grander scale with the founding of New World Pictures in 1970.

• • •

By the end of the 1950s, working primarily through American International Pictures, Corman was cranking out monster movies, action adventures, science fiction, and tough gangster films like *Machine Gun Kelly* (1958), which gave Charles Bronson a memorable role and won the filmmaker serious respect in Europe. No matter what the genre, he was making money. In 1957, when asked by *Variety* for the secret of his success with youthful moviegoers, Corman attributed it to a "nearly complete reliance" on a representative poll of students from twenty-five American high schools. In truth, his methods were not nearly so scientific. Instead of twenty-five carefully chosen high schools, Corman based his sample on a school or two in close proximity to Hollywood. Every generation of Corman assistants has faced the ritual of trekking to a nearby public high school at lunchtime, armed with a clipboard. (I well remember my 1974 stint at my Los Angeles alma mater, Hamilton High, where I nervously dodged administrators to ask students to choose among lurid titles, concepts, and snippets of poster art.)

Corman alumni debate whether Roger paid much attention to the results of these casual surveys. He did have a penchant for taking polls, which writer Chuck Griffith ascribes to his underlying lack of faith in his own judgment. But Kinta Haller, who found the polling reflective of Corman's scientific orientation, assured me, "I don't think he is ever influenced by it. I think he still uses his own counsel to go and do what he wants to do." Nonetheless, for all of his vaunted decisiveness, Roger likes to fall back on popular opinion. In recent years assistants have been sent to shopping malls instead of high-school campuses, but their ad hoc surveys have played a key role in the retitling of *Paranoia* (which became *Brain Dead*, 1990), in the choosing of video-box art for *Stripped to Kill* (1987), and in the hiring of comic actor Harvey Korman for a major role in *Munchies* (also 1987).

Veteran screenwriter Howard R. Cohen agreed with Haller that such attempts at research rarely supplanted Roger's own decision-making. Cohen felt, however, that for Corman staffers, these excursions had a value of their own, in forcing them to "deal with the people, deal with the audience, go out and meet human beings." Ironically, said Cohen, this was something the boss himself didn't do. "Part of Roger paying such low salaries is that we really believed that he had not been in a grocery store in thirty years. Which may be true. He didn't know what things cost. It was not so much cheapness as innocence" about life's daily realities.

Whatever value the poll-taking might have had as an educational opportunity was clearly lost on Joe Dante and Allan Arkush, who, in the early 1970s, were young Corman editors and all-purpose acolytes. When we spoke in November 1998, they gleefully detailed how they had outsmarted the Corman "system." Dante explained to me, "The problem with the title-testing was that after a while, the people who went out there to do this got wise to the fact that they didn't have to do it. So instead of going to actually ask high-school kids what the titles were, they would go get a hamburger. They would just write the responses themselves and bring back the information that they wanted." For Arkush (who has gone on to a successful career as a TV director), the point was that the results of the surveys were usually very predictable: "Are you going to go see *Tidal Wave* or *The Submersion of Japan*? It's not a contest."

. . .

In a syndicated-TV featurette aired on *PM Magazine* in 1987, Corman expounded on the handling of suspense in movies: "You break the tension one way, and it's horror. You break the tension another way, they laugh." Corman's first attempts at horror comedies blending fear and laughter were to win him a new category of fans.

The horror comedies, notably *A Bucket of Blood* (1959) and *The Little Shop of Horrors* (1960), marked something of a departure from Corman's early pictures because of their accent on dark humor. Though Corman can show a sly wit in conversation, most who know him agree he is a fundamentally serious person who prefers making serious movies. Randy Frakes, a visual-effects specialist on several New World projects in the early 1980s, maintains that Corman "did not like much humor in his films. To his credit, he likes people to take things seriously. If you look at his [Edgar Allan] Poe films, they're dead serious. They're precisely trying to do what Poe did—scare the hell out of you." Those acquainted with the early films agree that *The Little Shop of Horrors, A Bucket of Blood,* and a third horror comedy, *The Creature from the Haunted Sea* (1961), were aberrations; Joe Dante cites the legend that Corman needed to have the scripts' humor explained to him. The consensus is that the guiding spirit behind these films was writer Charles B. Griffith, whose talent for outrageously mordant comedy came to full flower in this period—and that flower was something of a Venus flytrap.

Chuck Griffith recalls that when he first broached the idea of trying a comedy, Corman turned him down flat, saying, "We don't do comedy or drama, because you have to be *good*. We don't have the time or money to be good, so we stick to action." When Griffith handed in a story outline for *A Bucket of Blood,* about a nebbish who finds recognition in hip art circles after exhibiting his plaster-covered murder victims as sculpture, Corman was put off at first by its comedic overtones. Ultimately he was convinced by Griffith's logic that "since you're going to make it in five days for $35,000, you can't lose." According to Griffith, Corman needed to ask, "How do you direct comedy?" Griffith, who came from a family with roots in vaudeville, advised him that the key to directing comedy was to make sure the actors played the nonsense straight, which, of course, made it work.

Corman's own accounts of the filming of A *Bucket of Blood* have down-played Griffith's role in instigating the project, focusing instead on the challenge of a five-day shoot. The AIP film, though a favorite of many Corman buffs for its biting satirical edge, certainly betrays its quick-and-dirty schedule and ultralow budget. In an era when others were embracing color and wide-screen technology, the 66-minute feature was shot in glorious black-and-white. Dick Miller, who landed one of his best roles as the would-be artist Walter Paisley, told me, "If they'd had more money to put into the production so we didn't have to use mannequins for the statues, if we didn't have to shoot the last scene with me hanging with just some gray makeup on because they didn't have time to put the plaster on me, this could have been a very classic little film. The story was good, the acting was good, the humor in it was good, the timing was right, everything about it was right—but they didn't have any money for production values, and it suffered."

Although A *Bucket of Blood* was not a big box-office winner, Corman decided to repeat the experiment for Filmgroup. The genesis of *The Little Shop of Horrors* has often been told: Corman discovered that he could get two days' use of the sets left standing on the lot at Chaplin Studio (now a recording studio) in Hollywood, where he was renting office space. Incorporating the dark tone of the previous movie, but removing much of its satiric edge, Chuck Griffith cranked out the story of a dim-witted flower-shop assistant who breeds a plant that thrives on human blood. Dick Miller, determined not to repeat himself, turned down the leading role of Seymour Krelboined but appeared as the petal-munching Burson Fouch. The young Jack Nicholson contributed an unforgettable cameo as a masochist in a dental chair ("No novocain—it dulls the senses"). Corman stalwart Jonathan Haze became the hapless Seymour, and Mel Welles was shop owner Gravis Mushnik, playing a variation on a character type he had been using at showbiz parties for years. Chuck Griffith himself supplied the plant's distinctive voice. The budget totaled about $27,500, and the film's threadbare look became part of the fun.

Welles insists that, after the mediocre showing of A *Bucket of Blood, Little Shop* only got made because he and Chuck Griffith persuaded Corman to give it a try. As Welles told me in early 1999, "You see, the reason that *The Little Shop of Horrors* worked is because it was a love project. It was *our* love project. We had to beg [Corman] to do the picture, because he didn't like horror comedies."

To Welles, *A Bucket of Blood* had only limited success with moviegoers because Dick Miller played his role so convincingly that it was hard for most viewers to be amused by his plight. But *Little Shop*'s goofy humor was almost lost to audiences. Exhibitors of the day, pointing to the greedy Mushnik character along with the clearly Jewish Mrs. Shiva (whose relatives keep dying), suspected the film of being anti-Semitic, and therefore chose not to book it. Mel Welles, himself Jewish, admits that he gave the film's Mushnik a Turkish Jewish accent and mannerisms, but he sees the humor of the film as playful; certainly, there was no intent to defame any ethnic group. Still, it was only because AIP desperately needed a film to pair with a horror import from Italy, Mario Bava's *Black Sunday,* that *Little Shop* found itself in general release in May 1960.

Little Shop may have started as a second feature, but its uniqueness was quickly recognized. Horror-movie fans flocked to see it, and among the young and the hip, the words "FEEEEED MEEE!" were soon in common use. Though the *New York Times* did not deign to review the entry, *Variety* was at least semipositive, calling it "a sort of rowdy vegetable that hits the funny bone in about the same way that seeing a man slip on a banana peel does." *Variety*'s critic concluded with the thought that "horticulturists and vegetarians will love it, particularly on Arbor Day."

By the time he made *Little Shop of Horrors,* Dick Miller had played feature roles in nearly a dozen Corman films. But over the years, his once comfortable relationship with Corman had begun to show some strain. Miller still treasures the fact that after *A Bucket of Blood,* Corman called him "the best actor in Hollywood," though he wryly noted to me that "[Corman] probably took it back afterwards!" Miller attributes the cooling of their relationship partly to a volume that came out of France around this time, entitled *Corman avec Miller* (which translates as *"Corman with Miller"*). The feisty actor maintains that this book "burned [Roger's] ass. Because he resented that the French . . . I was like Jerry Lewis over there; I could do no wrong. He didn't like the idea of sharing credit. They thought there was some kind of union there, some kind of co-joining of talents, that this was the basic plan. Roger would direct them, and I would be in them."

Mel Welles confirms that this obscure French volume, *Corman avec Miller,* did exist. But he will not agree with Miller that Corman resents sharing credit. A case in point: "He's never resented me and Chuck [Griffith] taking credit for the exteriors of *The Little Shop of Horrors.*" It seems the two days of interiors shot by Corman had to be augmented by two nights of outdoor location shooting on Skid Row in downtown Los Angeles. This work was done entirely by Welles and Griffith, using their ingenuity to keep expenditures to almost nil. They paid winos ten cents apiece to be extras, and for two bottles of scotch got the use of the nearby Southern Pacific Railway yard for an entire evening. Having persuaded the crew to back a locomotive away from actor Bobbie Coogan, who was lying on the track, they would later print the shot in reverse to simulate Coogan (playing a drunken tramp) being run over by the train. (The next day, says Welles, Twentieth Century–Fox paid the railway company $15,000 to perform the same service.) In all, for $1,100, Welles and Griffith contributed fifteen minutes' worth of exteriors to a picture that ran seventy minutes total. Welles has made sure I know that whenever Corman appears on a forum to discuss *Little Shop,* the director graciously recognizes the role of Welles and Griffith in making it all happen.

• • •

In his historical survey *The Horror People* (1976), writer John Brosnan quotes AIP's co-founder Samuel Z. Arkoff, speaking in 1970 about the long-range prospects for his movies: "When you come down to it, I don't think there are any of us in the film industry making anything today that will be of more than passing historical interest fifty years from now." Something of the same logic seems to have informed Roger's own carelessness about copyrighting the motion pictures he owned outright. Up until 1978, copyrighting a film required some simple bureaucratic procedures, chiefly the posting of a "notice of copyright" in the film's credits and the shipping of a print to the Library of Congress, which struck Corman as a needless expense. His failure to protect such pictures as *Little Shop* at the time of their first release has driven to distraction many a later Corman attorney. According to Dick Miller, "His thinking was, 'We're going to make this movie, it's going to play in a couple of theaters for a month or two, and then it's garbage.' He never saw into the future, is what I'm saying. So when *Little*

Shop of Horrors [the theatrical musical] came down, he was up the creek. He had to establish on all kinds of phony, problematic bases that this was his property. He didn't own it. He didn't have any right to it. It was public domain from the minute he made it."

When Howard Ashman and Alan Menken's musical version of *The Little Shop of Horrors* became an off-Broadway hit in 1982, Corman discovered that his earlier laxness was now costing him money. Television stations were frequently airing his 1960 film, and people were even circulating pirated home-video versions. In order to sell his own authorized videos, Roger needed to locate the master print. But given the usual chaotic state of record-keeping at his company, no one had any idea where it was. It fell to a young staff editor named Steve Barnett to track down the elusive print.

Roger, as usual, had never bothered to make what's called an "interpositive" as a backup in case of damage. Barnett has detailed for me how he located the original *Little Shop* negative at a film lab's storage facility. The optical soundtrack was also there, but not the "three-stripe," the magnetic tape of the dialogue, music, and effects soundtracks. An optical soundtrack is celluloid, and can be extremely fragile when it's old. Barnett remembers that "I was deathly afraid to put the soundtrack into the printer, for fear it would crumble and we would lose it forever." Fortunately, Gene Corman suggested that the magnetic tape of the film might be somewhere in the vault at a local sound lab, possibly stored under another name. So Barnett's sleuthing continued. "Down there in the basement of Ryder Sound in Hollywood, dusting off all these old boxes, we found this one stack that said, 'Passionate People Eater'—barely visible. The ink was on masking tape and it was evaporating. So we almost didn't know what it was." It was, in fact, what Barnett had been seeking, labeled with the film's working title.

After Barnett made his discovery, he quickly went to work making copies of *Little Shop*'s various elements. "I wanted as much protection for it as I could get, as much for Roger's own good as for what I felt was this amazing piece of film history. I was just thrilled to be able to protect something that I'd watched as a kid on television. And so if you buy the authorized video now, it's this pristine, beautiful copy. I don't think Roger knew I went as far as a fine-grain interpositive and an internegative—but he knows now, so there you go."

Barnett's determination to preserve the Corman legacy was to be matched by many other staffers at both New World (1970–83) and Concorde (1983–present); young men and women who grew up with Corman motion-pictures have fought hard to keep their boss from recycling negatives, erasing magnetic-tape stock, and consigning old press materials to the trash heap. They've lodged protests when he insists on recutting an original negative to make a television version, or shipping it overseas for use by foreign distributors. The Corman mania for reusing and discarding is intended to save money as well as space, but the staff still labors to teach the boss that this is a false economy; several have told me about the creative ways in which they've dodged official edicts, trying to save Roger from himself.

• • •

There's no question that *The Little Shop of Horrors* has taken on a life of its own. To the vast amusement of those who made it, the film has been subjected to much serious intellectual scrutiny over the years. Howard R. Cohen learned from Chuck Griffith that while *Little Shop* was being edited, "there was a point where two scenes would not cut together. It was just a visual jolt, and it didn't work. And they needed something to bridge that moment. They found in the editing room a nice shot of the moon, and they cut it in, and it worked. You come out of one scene, there's the moon, you go to the next scene. Worked like a charm. . . . Twenty years go by. I'm at the studio one day. Chuck comes running up to me, says, 'You've got to see this!' It was a magazine article—eight pages on the symbolism of the moon in *Little Shop of Horrors*." Mel Welles, who holds a Ph.D. in psychology, possesses a twenty-four-page treatise authored by a Beverly Hills psychotherapist which delves into such arcane matters as the use of color imagery in this black-and-white film (today, there also exists a computer-colorized version).

But it was, of course, the 1982 musical that brought Corman's two-day movie back into the public eye. The story, as recounted in John McCarty and Mark Thomas McGee's *The Little Shop of Horrors Book* (1988), is that both lyricist Howard Ashman and puppeteer Martin Robinson saw the Corman picture as children; both grew up determined to make it into a stage play. The musical version, written by Ashman in collaboration with composer Alan Menken, premiered at New York's WPA Theatre on May 6, 1982. After twenty-four performances it reopened at Off-Broadway's Orpheum Theatre;

the move was financed by David Geffen, Cameron Macintosh, and the Shubert organization, all of whom knew hit potential when they saw it. In 1983 the show won the New York Drama Critics' Circle Award, the Drama Desk Award, and the Outer Critics' Circle Award. And soon a major motion-picture was in the works.

McCarty and McGee detail how, before the play was launched, its producing team secured adaptation rights from Corman, even though his film was actually in the public domain at the time. Despite the fact that Chuck Griffith's original story was largely retained, he was not asked to be part of the financial agreement. Corman has called this mere oversight, but Griffith, whose recollections may be colored by years of growing animosity, remembers things differently. From Australia, Chuck e-mailed me on December 5, 1998, his account of Roger seemingly trying to monopolize the proceeds from the stage and film musical versions. Griffith claims that Ellen Greene, the play's female lead, opened his eyes to Corman's tactic of swearing that such key players as Jonathan Haze, Mel Welles, and Griffith himself were all deceased, "and therefore there was no point in inviting us to New York for the opening, or for offering us anything. Now, that bought him a bit of bitterness from his old mates."

Everyone who was around when the stage musical became a hit has a different account of Griffith's efforts to be compensated for his work on the original. Veteran crew member Beach Dickerson disclosed to me in October 1998 his belief that Corman would have given Griffith a share of his windfall *if* Griffith hadn't been so aggressive in demanding it. At any rate, Griffith, who was paid about $800 for his script when the Corman film was first made, ended up retaining a New York attorney to sue Menken, Ashman, Geffen, and everyone involved. According to Griffith, "It took forever, but the Warner Bros. [film] remake was held up by the case, so they settled. I get one-fourth of one percent, and it has kept me going since 1983." (Sadly for Chuck, more complications arose in early 1999, causing the deal to lapse. On June 3, 1999, he plaintively e-mailed me that "I was never informed, and have been going downstairs to the mailbox every ten minutes, looking in vain for my checks.")

Griffith's percentage has come solely from the hugely successful stage play, which has spawned some eighteen national and international touring companies, while becoming a staple on the community-theater circuit. The Warner Bros. full-color film extravaganza (1986), featuring Rick Moranis, Steve Martin—and Bill Murray in the old Jack Nicholson role—was treated as a potential blockbuster. Instead, this bloated enterprise, which most agree lacks the charm of the stage version, has yet to go into profit. Chuck finds this very ironic: "The original cost $27,000 and broke even in the first hour of release. The [movie] musical cost $33 million, and they never got it back. The next time I saw Roger, after the settlement, he said wistfully, 'Gee, why didn't you just ask me for a share?' Then we both laughed."

The volatile relationship between Griffith and Corman stems partly from the years in which Chuck felt his work was unappreciated or undermined by others. He cites, for instance, his discarded screenplay for *The Trip* (for which Jack Nicholson was eventually credited as writer), and an unproduced comedy version of Edgar Allan Poe's *The Gold Bug*. But Mel Welles, ever the peacemaker, maintains that despite Griffith's undeniable talent, he was a free spirit who lived life as he chose, wrote at his own pace, and could not always be counted on to fulfill Corman's instructions. Though sympathetic to Griffith's hurt feelings, Welles is convinced that Roger was remarkably tolerant of Chuck's foibles. Thanks to Corman, Griffith has accumulated some fifteen writing credits, and has also had opportunities to direct, as he did as late as 1988 on a Corman quickie, *Wizards of the Lost Kingdom II.*

Griffith may feel he has been taken advantage of by Corman, but Welles holds to the position he articulated for me on February 1, 1999: that Roger is "an honest, forthright, truthful businessman, who has a little bit of Scrooge in him, a lot of Rupert Murdoch in him, and whose milieu is extremely low budget product, which involves a lot of people getting cut rates on their salaries, getting overused and in some cases abused, thereby creating a little bit of—or a lot of—resentment."

•   •   •

The fact that much of the resentment toward Corman comes from screenwriters is one hint that Roger—despite his statements to the contrary—has no great regard for them and their work. (Of course, the low status of writers has long been a common complaint in Hollywood.) Most authors of Corman screenplays have vivid gripes about character development being ignored, plots recycled ad infinitum, and pages torn from scripts because they're "just dialogue." Says Paul Almond, head of business affairs at Corman's New World in the early 1980s: "I don't think he respects writers. He respects directors and editors. In his mind, the script is just the basepoint to start out from and you make the picture in the making of it, not by getting a great script."

Frances Doel, who has spent years as Corman's story editor, agrees that Roger (like virtually everyone in the motion-picture industry) always speaks of the fundamental importance of a good script. She also insists that Roger himself has an excellent sense of story and structure, though these are offset by his impatience about the whole laborious process of writing and rewriting a screenplay. Doel remembers him saying, during a period of frustration over the scripting of *Gas-s-s-s!* (1970), that he favored the notion of getting together with a group of his favorite actors and improvising a movie over a weekend. "I think he really meant it. I think he really would have liked to have done it, to bypass completely the annoyance and horror of the ever-offending script."

Script frustrations notwithstanding, Corman was moving into one of his most fertile periods. His pace was so dizzying (he had six movies in release in the year 1960 alone) that the thirty-four-year-old filmmaker had little time for a personal life. After *The Little Shop of Horrors* he made *The Last Woman on Earth* (1960), in which the young Robert Towne played a leading role while pounding out the script on the set. Among Roger's other offerings in that period was a fifteen-day sword-and-sandal epic, *Atlas* (1961), filmed on location in Greece in color and Vistascope, in a vain attempt to emulate Joseph E. Levine's lucrative Italian import, *Hercules* (1959).

Because its Greek investor backed out at the last minute, *Atlas* became a film that Roger himself has described to Ed Naha as "a total disaster." Far more important for his long-term reputation was his return to serious horror screen fare. In 1960 Corman made his first Edgar Allan Poe film, *House of Usher.*

THE RISE OF THE HOUSE OF CORMAN

Don't expect [Edgar Allan] Poe. But the taste here for poisonous cake with rich, ice-cold frosting probably would have pleased him.

HOWARD THOMPSON, *New York Times,* August 24, 1961

ON THE SET of *House of Usher* (1960), Vincent Price was baffled. He could not grasp how to read one of his lines: "The house lives. The house breathes." Approaching his director, he asked in great bewilderment, "What does it mean?" Roger Corman's own account (which I helped him compile after Price died in 1993 at the age of eighty-two) notes that he told his veteran star, "It means that we're able to make this picture." It seemed that the good folks at American International Pictures were worried that Corman was in the process of making a horror film that didn't include a monster. To win them over, Corman had promised that the house itself would be the monster. Now, with Price's help, he had to make good on his promise. Once Price understood what was needed, Roger recalled that "he went on to deliver the line with a subtle intensity that became for me one of the high points of the entire film."

In a sense, *House of Usher* was Corman's reward for the profits he had brought AIP in the past. It was also, says Mark McGee in his book, *Roger Corman: The Best of the Cheap Acts* (1988), Jim Nicholson and Sam Arkoff's desperate attempt to keep their company afloat by investing in a bigger, better production. They financed the movie to the tune of $250,000, which allowed it to be filmed in CinemaScope and color on a "luxurious" fifteen-day shooting schedule. One-third of the budget went toward the hiring of Price, a big-name leading man whom Corman judged to be suitably refined, intelligent, and attractive for the role of Roderick Usher, the gentle aristocrat who descends into madness. One advantage of starting with a classic nineteenth-century story was that its title was well known to moviegoers; another was that the works of Edgar Allan Poe were in the public domain, and thus cost nothing. To write his screen adaptation, Corman hired an established fantasy writer, Richard Matheson, offering him $5,000 and a small percentage of the net profit.

The gamble paid off. Critics commended Price's acting and the movie's stylized use of color. *Variety*'s laudatory review was typical: "It is a film that should attract mature tastes as well as those who come to the cinema for sheer thrills. It's also a potent, rewarding attraction for children. All things considered, pro and con, the fall of the 'House of Usher' seems to herald the rise of the House of AIP." According to the *Weekly Variety* tabulation of January 4, 1961, the 85-minute feature made nearly $1 million in domestic rentals in its first six months of release. ("Rental" figures, which indicate the portion of box-office revenues paid by theater owners to distributors, were the standard means of reporting a film's financial success until the early 1980s. Because distribution contracts specify that exhibitors may keep about 45 percent of the money they take in at the box office to cover their own expenses, rental amounts reflect approximately half of what we would consider today a movie's total gross.) Arkoff and Nicholson were justifiably thrilled by their fiscal returns on *House of Usher*, and so AIP's long-running Poe cycle was born.

Having convinced AIP that the house was his "monster," Corman seems to have convinced himself as well. In Christian Blackwood's 1977 feature documentary, *Roger Corman: Hollywood's Wild Angel*, Roger airs a Freudian theory of horror in which a house comes to symbolize a child's fear of the unknown. He imagines a tiny tot alone in the darkness, facing possibilities that are both attractive and frightening. This child, says Corman, is confused by the mystery of what's happening behind the locked door. While Corman feels that adults understand the answers on a conscious level, he's convinced that childhood's anxieties are still present within grown-ups, and that the job of someone working in the horror medium "is to break through the conscious mind and tap for a moment those unconscious fears."

Discussing his second Poe thriller, *The Pit and the Pendulum* (1961), in a 1970 article by Digby Diehl for *Show* magazine, Roger went even further in probing the mythic implications of his protagonists wandering down dark corridors in eerie old manors. For him the mystery of the closed door, which was to be a prominent factor in his horror films of this period, resides in the basically Oedipal question of what Father is doing to Mother. "It could be murder—because it sounds pretty violent: the bedsprings are bouncing around, the child hears cries, and that's pretty frightening to him because his parents represent the only security he has in the world."

Given such Freudian pronouncements, it's not surprising to learn that while making the Edgar Allan Poe movies Corman was deep into psychoanalysis. He was therefore a rather different person than he had been in his exuberant. "Let's put on a show" period (1954–60) when the idea was to make movies fast and cheap just for the fun of it. In the 1950s, Corman had never sought to discover profound messages in his screen work. He himself would admit to Diehl with what sounds like nostalgia that "there was less 'artiness' and 'significance' " back then. By contrast, his Poe entries were deliberately imbued with symbolic meaning.

In these ambitious new features, director Corman took what most critics have regarded as a great leap forward. Partly it was a matter of increased technical proficiency. As he was to note during Adam Simon's 1997 TV documentary, the allotted three-week shooting schedules felt like "nirvana." He could use the additional time to experiment, and to set up more interesting and intricate shots. Moreover, as his reputation grew, his projects attracted such mature stars as Peter Lorre (1904–1964), Basil Rathbone (1892–1967), and Boris Karloff (1887–1969). These legendary screen veterans brought their own distinctive personalities to the Poe pictures.

Corman shot seven Poe adaptations between 1960 and 1964. (*The Haunted Palace* is sometimes considered part of the cycle because its title comes from one of Poe's poems, but the plot line is borrowed from H. P. Lovecraft [1890–1937], another famous American writer of spooky tales.) The impact of the Poe features on young adolescents, quietly struggling with their own emerging sexuality, was enormous. Writer-director Larry Brand told me he still has vivid recollections of *The Premature Burial* (1962): "It's thirty-five years ago, and I remember that film better than some films I've seen last year. It's amazing how I remember that film." John Sayles and Martin Scorsese are among the modern-day auteurs who grew up watching Corman's period horror thrillers with their friends in drive-ins and smaller movie houses. (In Christian Blackwood's 1977 documentary, Scorsese discloses that *The Tomb of Ligeia* [1964] was his favorite.)

With the Poe films, Corman effectively captured the youth market, or at least that segment of it that disdained frothy beach-party movies like William Asher's 1965 AIP hit, *Beach Blanket Bingo*. Still, Roger was not content to rest on his laurels. In 1961 he turned from Freudian costume dramas to a project that was fraught with contemporary significance.

•   •   •

The early 1960s was a time when the desegregation of schools in the American South was making headlines. In 1957 Governor Orval Faubus had called out the Arkansas National Guard to forcibly prevent black students from attending the then all-Caucasian Central High School in Little Rock. Corman viewed such episodes with disgust, and became increasingly determined to tackle the issue of school integration on film. His opportunity came when he discovered Charles Beaumont's novel *The Intruder*. Written in 1958, it was a fictionalized account of an actual white rabble-rouser, John Kasper, who turned up in a small Tennessee town to fan the smoldering flames of racial hatred. Hollywood showed some interest in filming Beaumont's work, but then decided it was too controversial for its era. When Corman and his brother Gene became involved, they thought they'd be making the movie adaptation for producer Edward Small, who was working through United Artists. An item in *Variety* for June 16, 1961, states that Tony Randall was in negotiations to play the leading role, and that the budget would be $500,000.

Soon, however, it became apparent that the Corman brothers were basically on their own. They made a deal with Pathé American to distribute the film, but most of the production costs (in the neighborhood of $70,000) came out of their own pockets. For reasons of authenticity as well as cost control, the feature was shot entirely on location, primarily in Sikeston, Missouri, near the Arkansas border. William Shatner, then a young Canadian actor best known for his stage work (and later to be made famous in his role as Captain James T. Kirk of the starship *Enterprise* on TV's *Star Trek*), was signed to play the role of the charismatic demagogue Adam Cramer. Getting other actors to commit to the project was not easy. Author Charles Beaumont, who adapted his own novel for the screen, stepped in without salary to play the courageous schoolteacher, and many parts (including that of the black high-school student who sparks the film's crisis) were taken by non-professionals living in the region.

Everyone involved agrees that by lensing this story in towns where it could have happened, Corman and crew were courting real danger. For three weeks they dodged sheriffs, eluded threats of violence, and side-stepped accusations that they were communists. Gene Corman, who was on the set in his capacity as executive producer, is credited by Roger in his 1990 memoir with fast-talking the troupe out of many legal jams while Roger concentrated on directing the project. This entailed shooting crowd scenes in such a way that Shatner made his most incendiary speeches after the majority of the extras had gone home. Shatner, whose performance won high praise from critics, e-mailed me on February 3, 1999, that as a director Corman was "wonderfully quick and efficient. He knew exactly what he wanted." Shatner remembers the making of *The Intruder* (1962) as "harrowing, stimulating, enabling, and frustrating. Because we shot the film on location in the South, we weren't able to do a lot of the controversial things contained in the script."

Nor were all the problems solved once the 80-minute black-and-white feature was in the can. Because its dialogue contained some ugly (though realistic) racial epithets, the movie was at first denied the Code Seal of Approval by the powerful Motion Picture Producers Association. This refusal prompted a press conference at which Roger Corman cited endorsements of his movie by such groups as the National Association for the Advancement of Colored People (NAACP), the Anti-Defamation League, and a U.S. Senate subcommittee on constitutional rights. Given that major studio products like *The Defiant Ones* (1958) had gotten away with similar language, Roger made the claim, not for the last time in his career, that the Hollywood establishment was biased against the small independent. Corman eventually got his seal, but when race riots broke out in September 1962 over James Meredith's enrollment at the University of Mississippi, an invitation to the Cannes Film Festival was withdrawn. As film historian Mark McGee recounts, the Corman brothers were informed that it was not "in the best interest of Hollywood" for their movie to appear at Cannes.

Still, there was serious recognition for *The Intruder,* notably a prize at the Venice (Italy) Film Festival. American critics viewed the work with respect, though many pointed out its flaws. Stanley Kauffmann, in *The New Republic,* spoke of "a chilling veracity, which is finally dispelled by a totally incredible happy ending." The often curmudgeonly Bosley Crowther of the *New York Times* gave the film credit for "good intentions and a great deal of raw, arresting power." *Variety* hailed it as "a sign of a new maturity on the part of the U.S. motion-picture industry."

None of which meant that *The Intruder* scored at the box office. Corman's distribution deal with Pathé American ultimately fell through, and the film languished. Later reissues of *The Intruder* under such titles as *The Stranger* and *I Hate Your Guts* hardly helped. At the time of the picture's May 1962 release, Corman had told *Show* magazine, "I didn't make *The Intruder* to make money or lose money. I believe in the subject. I'm just hoping for a good public response. If I can only get back what I put in, why, then I'll make more pictures like this. If not, there's always horror." These words proved to be prophetic. As Corman has often said, *The Intruder* was the first film on which he ever lost money. Stung by the experience of going into the red with a message movie, he immediately returned to the safe territory of horror. His next project was *The Premature Burial* (1962).

This 81-minute drama, unique among Corman's Poe films in featuring Ray Milland in place of Vincent Price, was a direct result of the Corman brothers' business relationship with Pathé American. Pathé's owner, William Zeckendorf, had originally agreed to distribute *The Intruder* in exchange for Roger's promise to shoot a Poe adaptation for his company. When Sam Arkoff got wind of this arrangement, which threatened the AIP monopoly on the highly lucrative Poe films, he warned that AIP would retaliate by withdrawing its business from Pathé's respected film laboratory. Zeckendorf capitulated, and Corman was surprised to see Nicholson and Arkoff show up on the set of *The Premature Burial,* cheerfully informing him that he was once again working for them. Such shenanigans on both sides would eventually set the stage for Corman's departure from AIP in 1970.

Writing in 1993 to Professor Susan Madigan of Michigan State University, Corman explained that after *The Intruder*, he retreated from the personal-statement film to concentrate on motion-pictures that would be more obviously commercial, but that might contain some of his thoughts and feelings on subtextual levels. There's a debate among latter-day Corman writers and directors as to whether a covert social message is something Roger Corman still expects in his pictures. Fred Bailey, who wrote a dozen screenplays for Concorde in the mid-1980s, says that Corman would explicitly remind him that "the movie's got to have action, humor, sex, and social relevance underneath. Don't shove it down the audience's throat." Robert Rehme, Corman's head of sales in the 1970s and now president of the Motion Picture Academy, has noted to me that "there's an aggressive, independent spirit of social concern and progressive thinking that runs through his work. I think he can take pride in that."

Yet Deborah Brock, who led Concorde's post-production team for several years, feels Corman's attitude has gradually altered. She recalls that early in her tenure Roger let her know that "we can make some money doing something fun, and we'll also say something a little subversive or liberal or interesting." Brock stresses, "I think that's where he was during the sixties through the eighties. But at some point he quit caring about [social messages] very much."

At any rate, the failure of *The Intruder* was a professional watershed for Corman. According to producer Gale Anne Hurd *(The Terminator, Aliens, The Waterdance)*, who was a Corman assistant from 1978 to 1981, this was probably the point at which he began to divorce his personal feelings from his work. It may also have been, as far as his directorial career was concerned, the beginning of the end.

•   •   •

During 1962 Corman was doing more than making Edgar Allan Poe movies. In keeping with his reputation as a master recycler, he also purchased a clumsy Russian science-fiction film on the strength of its special-effects scenes, then hired a bright young man to add monster footage and dub in new dialogue. The revamped film was *Battle Beyond the Sun* (1963). The young protégé, fresh out of UCLA film school and eager to do great things, was Francis Ford Coppola.

Coppola (b. 1939) went along as a very novice soundman when Corman took a troupe to Europe to film a Grand Prix drama, *The Young Racers* (1963), starring William Campbell and Luana Anders. Typically, Corman couldn't resist the opportunity to produce a follow-up European film with the same crew. When Coppola suggested a *Psycho*-type premise, Corman entrusted him with $22,000 and sent him to Ireland to make what turned out to be *Dementia 13* (1963). This lurid horror film, once again featuring Campbell and Anders, was tricked out with a catchy marketing gimmick: If you failed a "scientific" test determining your ability to withstand shock, you were (theoretically) not allowed into the theater. Critics were not impressed. When the picture appeared on the lower half of a bill featuring Corman's *X—The Man with X-Ray Eyes* (1963), which starred Ray Milland, the *New York Times* remarked that the release stressed gore rather than atmosphere. The newspaper labeled Coppola's directing debut as "stolid."

Corman, of course, knew that fledgling directors work cheap. By the same token, he has always enjoyed finding and developing fresh talent. He allows them unprecedented freedom, which is not to say that his is a total hands-off approach. In 1970 Coppola described to *Show* magazine's Digby Diehl his experience with Corman on *Dementia 13*. Though Roger left him alone during the shooting, they disagreed in the editing room, with the boss insisting on adding voice-overs to simplify some scenes. Even worse, said Coppola, "he wanted some extra violence added, another ax murder at least, which he finally had shot by another director named Jack Hill. But I must say I like Roger (who doesn't?), and I am grateful for the chance he gave me."

Coppola was one of several uncredited directors on the film project that would prove to be Corman's wackiest. This was *The Terror* (1963), a movie that was largely made up on the spot, taking advantage of sets left over from *The Raven* (1963), as well as the services of *The Raven*'s star, Boris Karloff. Corman himself shot two days' worth of interiors, after which such young directors as Coppola, Monte Hellman, and Jack Hill did various bits of location work to try to make sense of a plot that was virtually nonexistent. Jack Nicholson got into the act, too, though the extent of his directorial contribution has long been debated. In 1975 Nicholson described the film to Bill Davidson of the *New York Times* as "a lot of separate components pasted together with Band-Aids." But, said Nicholson, "it was scary-funny, and it made a potful of money."

Actor Dick Miller described *The Terror* to me as "the longest movie ever made," because twenty-eight years later he was approached by Roger to reprise his featured role as Karloff's servant. It seems that in 1991 the lack of a copyright was again apparently causing problems for the Corman legal staff. Concorde head of production Rodman Flender and veteran Corman director Mark Griffiths were given the daunting task of working around the absence of Karloff (who had died in 1969), Jack Nicholson, and others. By adding twelve minutes of new footage to the 81-minute original, they effectively removed the film (now called *The Return of the Terror*) from public domain. *The Terror* remains an interesting testament to Corman's ability to shrug off the need for a coherent screenplay. It also makes a striking contrast to the seriousness of purpose that actress Beverly Garland saw in Corman's early films and that he displayed so unflinchingly in *The Intruder*. By this point, however, his legion of fans regarded any new Roger Corman film as cause for rejoicing.

•   •   •

Now that Corman was making a name for himself with the general public, the big studios came calling. *The Secret Invasion,* shot in 1964 for United Artists with Gene Corman as producer, was a World War II drama that anticipated the plot line of *The Dirty Dozen* (1967). Stewart Granger, Raf Vallone, Mickey Rooney, and teen heartthrob Edd Byrnes were among its stars. Reviews were fairly respectful. In the *New York Times,* Howard Thompson commented that "since Roger Corman, the director, and Gene Corman, the producer, specialize in horror films, [there's] a rather surprising amount of brisk muscularity and panoramic color, if not always credibility." (Despite its accolades, the film died at the box office.) Three years later, Corman directed Jason Robards Jr. in a $1.5 million gangster epic, *The St. Valentine's Day Massacre,* for Twentieth Century–Fox. This brutal film, which some critics consider among the director's best, grossed over $3 million in North America. In between, there was to be a multipicture deal at Columbia Pictures, commencing with a $2 million western, *The Long Ride Home,* from a script by

Robert Towne. It was to star Glenn Ford and Inger Stevens, and feature the very young Harrison Ford.

But after shooting began, Columbia replaced Corman with director Phil Karlson. Towne, who was later to become a noted Hollywood screenwriter (*Chinatown, Shampoo, The Firm*) told Corman's assistant Frances Doel he suspected that the ouster occurred "because Roger insisted on saving money. Roger didn't understand that, unlike Sam Arkoff or AIP, [Columbia] wouldn't think any better of him for saving money. In fact, they would think the opposite. They would think that he was going to make them a picture of lesser quality than they were used to." Doel recalls that when Columbia executives sent Corman lists of equipment they were planning to ship to his Arizona location, he would cross out items he felt weren't needed. If, for instance, two generators were listed, he would eliminate one, figuring that the remaining generator would work adequately for the length of the shoot. Presumably, this thrifty behavior raised the suspicions of the Columbia brass, who feared getting a cheap-looking product.

So Corman's intrinsic compulsion to save money ended up costing him a job. Ironically, the finished film, retitled *A Time for Killing* (1967), quickly disappeared upon release, and there's no evidence that Roger's own reputation suffered after he left the project. At this point in his career, he continued looking to the major studios to fund his more ambitious pictures (like the Civil War epic *Robert E. Lee*, which was to be part of a deal with United Artists but ultimately never got made). Still, there's no question that his experience on *The Long Ride Home* contributed to his deep-seated mistrust of the major-studio system. While he has resorted to the occasional studio co-production over the years, Corman is always happiest when he's calling the shots himself.

Brad Krevoy, in contrast, learned from Corman in the early 1980s how to be an independent producer, but has built his own career on finding studio backing for his features. The producer of the enormously popular *Dumb & Dumber* (1994) has often pondered why his old boss has largely steered clear of the majors. Krevoy speculates that "part of the reason [Corman] didn't enjoy the studio process very much is because he's so independent-minded and so visionary that it was hard for him to have the patience to deal with people who didn't know as much as he did. . . . He'd

have to take these endless development and production meetings with people that didn't really know their trade as well as Roger did." Krevoy believes
that the frustration generated by such encounters kept Corman an independent. He fantasizes, though, about Corman someday running a big
Hollywood studio. "He would revolutionize studios, even today. He'd take all
the production overseas and not deal with the unions. He'd cut costs by 40
percent. I think it would be great to see."

· · ·

In 1964 the thirty-eight-year-old Corman could boast of ten successful
years in the movie industry. His relationship with the Hollywood studios still
looked promising. His reputation among the cinéastes of Europe was soaring. *The Masque of the Red Death* (1964), the most sumptuous of the Edgar
Allan Poe pictures, opened to highly respectful reviews. Once again starring
Vincent Price, the film was shot on London soundstages on a leisurely five-
week schedule. Its talented cinematographer, Nicolas Roeg, introduced a
wildly stylized use of color photography that was much admired. (Roeg
would go on to direct the groundbreaking 1973 feature *Don't Look Now*, as
well as *Performance* [1970] and 1976's *The Man Who Fell to Earth*.) Even the
New York Times praised *The Masque of the Red Death*, saying, "On its level,
it is astonishingly good."

There was one more landmark event in 1964: While looking for an
assistant, Roger interviewed Julie Halloran. Corman, in his memoir,
describes the situation vividly. He was impressed by Halloran, a dark-haired
UCLA graduate in her early twenties with a degree in English. But another
candidate for the job was Stephanie Rothman, who had earned a master's
degree from the USC Film School and an award from the Directors Guild of
America for directing a student film. As Corman puts it, "There was no way
I could not hire Stephanie. So I offered her the job and I asked Julie for a
date. Both said yes."

Rothman went on to write, produce, and direct low-budget features. In
1970 she co-wrote and directed *The Student Nurses*, kicking off the "nurse
movie" cycle that was to become a New World Pictures staple. Julie Halloran
became a market researcher for the *Los Angeles Times*, held various jobs in
and around the film industry, and continued to date Corman. Eventually
they would be married.

The union of Roger and Julie Corman was by no means inevitable, even though she—intelligent, well-educated, and slightly patrician—seemed an ideal match for him. Dick Miller confided to me in September 1998, "I always got the idea that, down deep, Roger was a good Catholic boy, and he was looking for a good Catholic girl. And he wasn't going to get involved with anybody who wasn't. He may have been very much in love or very much involved with a number of ladies in his life, but they didn't fit the pattern. They didn't fit who they were supposed to be in that time and place, and Julie did." She would also bring stability and domesticity into a life that was sorely lacking in these departments. Veteran director Monte Hellman claims that "until Roger met Julie, his food every night was a TV dinner that he would eat on a little TV dinner table." So Julie may have been just what Roger needed. However, in the years that followed that job interview in 1964, Corman also courted others.

According to screenwriter Chuck Griffith, Corman saw himself as "the Sody-Pop Kid." (The reference is to the hero admired by the young boy in one of Corman's favorite films, the 1953 western *Shane*.) The Kid was described to Griffith by Corman as a likable fellow who never got the girl. In turn, Griffith eventually borrowed this concept for Ron Howard's character in *Eat My Dust!* (1976). The hint that Roger could view himself as a failure when it came to romantic relationships surfaces again in Corman's own 1990 autobiography. Describing his state of mind in the wake of 1962's *The Intruder,* he writes that psychoanalysis had led him to question his own motives: "I was in my mid-thirties. Most of my friends were married. I wondered why I had not made that kind of full commitment." His younger brother was the obvious contrast. In 1964, Gene had been a married man for almost a decade, and he and wife Nan had two lively sons, ages six and four. It took Roger six full years to commit himself to Julie. By the time they finally wed, he was forty-four years old, and his days of making films for others were behind him.

•   •   •

Like Julie Halloran, Stephanie Rothman, and Kinta Haller, most candidates for the position of Corman's office assistant have been women. This was especially true in the 1960s, when an assistant's duties might include scrambling eggs for the boss's breakfast. Though such tasks might sound lowly,

Roger was a kindly and fair-minded employer. He may have paid rock-bottom wages, but he gave these young women unprecedented opportunities to learn all aspects of the motion-picture business. Talia Shire, who started with Corman before gaining fame as an actress in her brother Francis Ford Coppola's *The Godfather* (1972), told *People* magazine in 1980 that Roger's assistants typically begin by answering the telephone, and two weeks later progress to reading scripts and scouting for locations—"It beats hell out of going to the Yale School of Drama."

Corman offered young women a chance for professional advancement that they would not have found elsewhere in the Hollywood film industry (especially in the pre-feminist 1960s). He also took an interest in their lives. If you worked for him when his company was still tiny, he could regard you at times almost paternally. At my own job interview in 1973, Corman asked whether I was married. Upon hearing that I was a newlywed, he looked slightly disappointed. Then, smiling proudly, he said, "All my previous assistants have married directors." The earliest assistant, Kinta Haller, clarified for me on January 5, 1999 that "the people that worked for him, like his family, were an extension of his ego. So he took particular interest in knowing what their IQs were, and how competent they were, and what they could do, and the kind of people they were going to be with, and the way they were going to live their lives. . . . He didn't want people around him, I don't think, that he felt uncomfortable with in any sense."

Former staffers all agree that, in business settings, Corman seemed to be most at ease with females. He respected women's abilities and enjoyed their company. On October 29, 1998, director Steve Barnett put it to me colorfully: "Roger, I think, tended to glow a little more around women. At the same time, he exploited the hell out of them 'cause he's paying them no money. But he pays nobody any money, so there's equal-opportunity exploitation there."

The idea of Corman "glowing" around the opposite sex is borne out in a fascinating anecdote conveyed to me by Tina Hirsch. At the time of this incident, in the mid-1970s, Hirsch was a film editor, very young and very attractive. She happened to be at his Sunset Strip office one afternoon, and was about to leave for home when Roger suggested she have a drink with him. When she agreed, he told her to meet him out by the elevator. He then made a full circuit of the office, passing by the entire staff as though to imply that he had important business somewhere within the office suite. Having covered his tracks, says Hirsch, "he was out the door and in the elevator and across the street to this bar where we sat for forty-five minutes or an hour and talked. When he came to join me at the elevator, it was just like he was a kid sneaking out of school. He had this mischievous twinkle about him. He just wanted to get away for the afternoon. He couldn't say, 'I'm going out.' He had to *sneak* out."

To Hirsch, the episode shows that Corman is "afraid not to be working, afraid not to be productive. [There was] that extremely strong puritan work ethic in him which I think all of us related to, because I think we all had that, too." Hirsch is right about the work ethic, but her anecdote has other implications as well. It shows a shy man's ongoing fascination with attractive women, with whom he wouldn't dream of behaving improperly. Somewhere within Roger was a boldness and an eagerness to flout social convention by doing something forbidden. But he saved the outlaw side of himself mostly for his movies.

Chapter 6

ANGELS AND ACID

I was always the squarest guy in a hip group.

ROGER CORMAN, 1990

"WE WANT TO be free to ride our machines without being hassled by the Man! And we want to get loaded!"

This deathless dialogue comes from *The Wild Angels,* a movie that was to turn Roger Corman into a spokesperson for the anti-establishment. It was 1966, the Vietnam War was raging, and young people across America were searching for heroes in unlikely places. The film's outlaw biker gang— whose members were played by such rising Hollywood talents as Peter Fonda, Bruce Dern, and Diane Ladd—gave youthful moviegoers what they were looking for.

In *The Wild Angels,* Corman, who had taken his inspiration from a magazine photo of a biker funeral, captured the public's fascination with misfits and the socially expendable. Filming in a cinema verité style and incorporating the Venice, California, chapter of the Hell's Angels into his cast, he achieved a raw realism nearly impossible to ignore. Reaction to the 93-minute picture was largely along generational lines. In the *New York Times,* Bosley Crowther dismissed it as "an embarrassment," but his younger colleague Vincent Canby wrote a major Sunday profile of the man he called "a filmmaker with a highly personal cinematic style." *The Wild Angels* was invited to the Venice (Italy) Film Festival, where Europeans cheered it for thumbing its nose at bourgeois American values. More important, the domestic box office soared. *Variety* for January 4, 1967, indicates that in its first six months *The Wild Angels* accrued rentals of $5.5 million on a $360,000 investment, far exceeding Roger's previous successes. It is not surprising that the Corman publicity machine began working overtime at once. Jack Bradford's column in the *Hollywood Reporter* for May 12, 1967, reports that "Roger Corman opens his own Swiss bank with a million plus deposit, courtesy of *The Wild Angels*."

AIP was of course delighted that its investment in the color feature had paid off so handsomely. At the same time, however, Roger's radical new approach made Sam Arkoff and Jim Nicholson squirm. Corman complained to *Take One* that prior to the movie's orgy sequence, the two AIP bosses inserted an establishing shot that turned his church location into a funeral home. In Corman's words, "The insert was badly exposed and grainy, which I thought was good, because the thing looked so ridiculous that anybody who saw it would know instantly that it had been done by an idiot."

Corman had endured his share of problems on the set, as assistant director Paul Rapp attests. There were fears of pot busts, the near asphyxiation of a cast member, and motorcycles that refused to stay in working order. The California Highway Patrol lurked, waiting to arrest bikers who had outstanding warrants. Frank Sinatra, then at the height of his powers, let it be known that if anything happened to his elder daughter Nancy, who was playing the female lead, there would be major hell to pay. In the thick of things was young Peter Bogdanovich (b. 1939), who acted as Corman's production assistant, rewrote Chuck Griffith's script without credit, directed second unit, and was beaten up by the Hell's Angels for real when he served as an extra in an on-camera fight scene.

Corman had met Bogdanovich initially back in 1964, when Peter was a young writer for *Esquire* magazine. As chronicled in *Films and Filming* (June 1972), Corman first proposed that Bogdanovich emulate some of the great award-winning epics of that era: "I'd like you to write me a combination of *The Bridge on the River Kwai* [1957] and *Lawrence of Arabia* [1962]— but inexpensive to produce." After *The Wild Angels*, however, Corman resolved a longstanding contractual dispute with Boris Karloff by asking

Bogdanovich to write and direct a movie that gave Karloff two days' work while also incorporating footage from *The Terror* (1963). The result was *Targets*, an inventive contemporary horror offering about an aging actor who encounters a sniper at a drive-in movie theater. Released in 1968, *Targets* quickly established Bogdanovich as a filmmaker to watch. In 1971 he would direct *The Last Picture Show*, which won two Academy Awards.

Years later, when Bogdanovich's career was threatening to derail, he was the rare beneficiary of Corman's largesse: Roger agreed to back his upcoming project, *Saint Jack* (1979). As Joe Dante confirmed, "The thing about Roger is that you meet him on your way up, and if you're not lucky you meet him again on your way down. And Peter was particularly lucky because when he was on his downward spiral Roger hired him to do this picture. I know they had a lot of fights about it, but it turned out to be a good picture, and it put him back on the road."

The Wild Angels had an enormous impact on the motion-picture industry, with AIP quickly gaining a new reputation as the home of rebel filmmaking. Along with other independent companies, AIP immediately began to exploit a new subgenre: the biker film. Between 1967 and 1972, at least two dozen low-budget motorcycle quickies emerged, with titles like *Devil's Angels* (AIP, 1967), *Angel Unchained* (AIP, 1970), and *Hell's Angels on Wheels*, made in 1967 for Joe Solomon's Fanfare Films. Once he founded New World Pictures in 1970, Corman jumped on his own bandwagon, producing such biker flicks as *Angels Hard as They Come* (1971), which marked the screenwriting debut of future director Jonathan Demme.

•   •   •

After *The Wild Angels* established his credentials as a radical filmmaker, Corman joined forces with actor Peter Fonda to explore the drug culture in *The Trip* (1967). The original script was by Chuck Griffith, himself a passionate believer in the powers of the hallucinogen LSD. Looking back, actor Mel Welles remembers that Corman "didn't have the nerve to make it" the way Griffith wrote it, and Jack Nicholson was credited with the rewrite. In Christian Blackwood's documentary film *Roger Corman: Hollywood's Wild Angel* (1977), Peter Fonda describes initiating the fundamentally straitlaced Corman into the counterculture. Fonda had demanded that Roger take LSD before directing *The Trip*, as a way of proving his connection to the material. In his usual methodical way, Roger researched LSD, and then arranged to sample it himself. On July 19, 1967, at a New York press conference covered by *Weekly Variety,* he claimed his experiment with acid had taken place under strict medical supervision, with a stenographer on hand to record the episode.

In fact, Roger's grand experiment occurred on a picturesque seaside cliff in Big Sur, California. There was no doctor in sight, and the "stenographer" was Frances Doel, who had been told to prepare for the big moment by boning up on the ancient Tibetan Book of the Dead. As recorded in his 1990 memoir and elsewhere, Corman's own account of his experience is magical. He lay facedown on the ground, and saw spellbinding images, including a jewel-laden clipper ship that turned into a woman's body. He also believed he had discovered a brand-new art form, one that could be transmitted through the earth from the mind of its creator directly into the mind of the audience. "To this day," says Corman in his autobiography, "I'd like to think this could work and it would be wonderful. I think of all the costs you could cut in production and distribution alone."

To convey such mind-bending experiences through the motion-picture medium, Corman relied on hallucinatory visual images in dazzling color. Crew member Sharon Compton wrote me that one of her jobs on the picture was painting a brown horse black. "The dream sequence we had made up featured a mysterious hooded rider in a black cloak. He relentlessly pursues our hero [Peter Fonda] and when he corners him and throws back his hood, we see that the dark rider is the hero himself. This satisfied not only the dramatic need for a chase sequence and suspense, but also smacked of deep (if incomprehensible) psychological meaning. It just didn't seem right that this dark rider from the paranoid subconscious should be riding a bay . . . but a bay was what we had." Compton wryly noted that "these artistic details seemed important at the time, but I realize now that it was [a] naive and unnecessary gesture. What can I say, our hearts were young and gay, and we were makers of film."

Once again, in *The Trip,* Corman had seized on the mood of the time. *The Trip* was the first mainstream American movie to explore the drug culture; many called it the quintessential sixties psychedelic film. As public controversy over the picture continued to rage, the AIP brain trust found itself both delighted and appalled by its new cult hit, which earned more than $4 million in North American rentals (according to *Weekly Variety* for January 3, 1968) and was featured at the Cannes Film Festival.

Corman had always respected Jim Nicholson, whom he regarded as the creative force behind the Nicholson-Arkoff team. But he could not lightly forgive what Jim Nicholson did to his movie. In this era, the fifty-six-year-old Nicholson was growing increasingly conservative at the same time that Corman, ten years younger, was flirting with radicalism. As Corman recounts in his memoir, Nicholson actually stepped in to add an opening disclaimer that warned audiences about the dangers of drug use. The studio executive also re-edited the final shot of the film, putting a jagged crack over the image of Fonda's face, thus undoing Corman's own nonjudgmental ending by suggesting a shattered life. Roger was furious. Soon, with the production of *Gas-s-s-s!* (1970), Corman's relationship with his longtime backers at American International Pictures would be strained beyond repair.

• • •

Despite his unhappiness with Jim Nicholson and Sam Arkoff, Corman next made for AIP a gritty little gangster thriller that was intended to capitalize on the success of Arthur Penn's *Bonnie and Clyde* (1967). Roger's film, *Bloody Mama* (1969), gave him the chance to work with an Academy Award–winning actress, Shelley Winters. The story, set in the rural South during the Great Depression, was that of Ma Barker and her dysfunctional brood of sons. Winters helped Corman assemble a cast of promising young stage actors, including Robert Walden, Don Stroud (for whom Corman and Winters had the highest hopes), and Robert De Niro. Though Corman generally dislikes movies containing in-jokes, one scene in *Bloody Mama* may have given him a quiet smile. In it, Winters confronts De Niro, playing the son who starts out sniffing glue and then graduates to harder substances. Her words to him are, "When you are workin' on those model airplanes, you get to actin' awful silly." Surely when young Roger spent hours on his own model planes, glue was not the major attraction.

The year that Corman shot *Bloody Mama*, several of his former actors made a movie that became the ultimate 1960s statement, fully evoking the romantic nihilism of the era. Peter Fonda described the genesis of *Easy Rider* in a 1969 issue of *Take One* magazine: Staying at a Canadian hotel for a motion-picture exhibitors' convention, he happened to study a publicity picture of himself and Bruce Dern riding their choppers in *The Wild Angels*. Staring at the iconographic photo, Fonda got an idea: "Man, yeah, that's the image . . . a dude who rides a silver bike and turns everybody on and rides right off again." As the movie's plot evolved in his head, he decided, "Let's get to Mardi Gras in the film, great time, we'll have a lot of free costumes and shit like that, a real Roger Corman number where we don't have to pay." *Easy Rider* was produced by Fonda in 1969. He and Dennis Hopper (a longtime friend who had been featured in *The Trip*) wrote the screenplay, along with novelist Terry Southern; the roles played by Fonda, Hopper, and Jack Nicholson were to make them all stars. Corman, aware of the developing project, tried to help get it AIP backing.

Sam Arkoff admits, in his autobiographical work, *Flying Through Hollywood by the Seat of My Pants* (1992), that AIP was ready to invest $340,000 in *Easy Rider*, but balked at Hopper's plan to direct the film himself. Arkoff and Nicholson believed that Roger Corman, with his long track record, would be the best man for the job. Hopper, of course, proved them wrong. But though Corman had no part in the finished film, it very much reflects his spirit and style.

● ● ●

Gas-s-s-s!, made in 1969, was Roger Corman's last attempt at a countercultural manifesto. Paul Bartel, the director of New World's comically macabre *Death Race 2000* (1975), finds *Gas-s-s-s!* an interesting example of what Roger thinks is funny. The premise of the movie (whose full title is *Gas-s-s-s! or: It Became Necessary to Destroy the World in Order to Save It*) is that a mysterious airborne poison has killed off everyone in the United States over the age of twenty-five. Corman's youthful characters—played by such rising young actors as Bud Cort, Talia Coppola (Shire), and Ben Vereen—form into family units and begin a strange odyssey through the American Southwest. The film, made at the height of the anti-Vietnam protests, takes potshots at God, organized religion, and most mainstream social institutions in America.

Shot largely in Texas, *Gas-s-s-s!* is a model of Roger's brand of guerrilla filmmaking. For a scene set on a highway littered with broken-down automobiles, production manager Paul Rapp recalls that the Corman crew gained access to Dallas's barely completed LBJ Freeway, then had junkyards tow jalopies onto it at minimal cost. Fred Bailey, who had a small role on-screen as a rabble-rouser, told me in late 1998 how Roger staged his big scene (without permits) on the Southern Methodist University campus, waiting until classes let out to get the effect of a large crowd. But for the last shot of the movie, filmed at Acoma Pueblo in western New Mexico, Corman tried for something uncharacteristically fancy. Using both a zoom lens and a crane, he began with his leads, Elaine Giftos and Robert Corff, kissing in a tight two-shot, then pulled back to show the entire Acoma tribe, the marching band of a local high school, a Hell's Angels chapter, and a gaggle of actors impersonating U.S. presidents, all of them dwarfed by the desert landscape. Once again, AIP stepped in. As the financiers of the film, Arkoff and Nicholson felt entitled to improve upon it, in collusion with Corman's own editors. Not only did they end Roger's spectacular shot on the kiss, but they also removed from the movie the character of God, whose presence Corman would later describe to filmmaker Adam Simon as "funny and hip and somewhat meaningful." Roger has complained that Sam Arkoff also limited the film's distribution, which contributed to its failure both with critics and at the box office. It was the last time he would ever direct for AIP.

In his 1992 autobiography, Arkoff looks back fondly on his years with Corman: "Roger and I had a great relationship, probably unmatched in this business, particularly considering the number of pictures we made together. It was an informal and cooperative relationship, and although we have not worked on a picture in many years, our personal friendship has continued." This gracious quote sidesteps the tensions inherent in the Corman-Arkoff connection; witness the case of *The Premature Burial* (1962), when Corman tried to go his own way until the AIP honchos reminded him who was boss. Film historian Mark Thomas McGee notes that between Arkoff and Corman, one-upmanship was often the name of the game. In fact, says McGee, it was the swirl of publicity that greeted Corman's 1990 autobiography that prompted Arkoff to begin writing his own. After Corman got his Hollywood Walk of Fame star in 1991, Arkoff wanted one too. (His was unveiled in 1993.)

During my long conversation with moviemaker Adam Simon in October 1998, he compared Roger's treatment at the hands of Nicholson and Arkoff to the way Corman himself treats today's young directors, recutting their work and seeming to renege on pledges he's made them. In 1993, when Corman asked Simon to scoop *Jurassic Park* by shooting for Concorde Pictures a quickie dinosaur film called *Carnosaur,* Simon took the difficult assignment because he was guaranteed a budget of at least $3 million. Then, three weeks before photography commenced, the budget suddenly shrank to $850,000, a figure Simon is now convinced was part of Corman's plan all along.

From Simon's point of view this was betrayal; he sees it as Corman taking advantage of an eager young filmmaker who would work his hardest to make a good picture no matter what promises might be broken along the way. Simon told me he now regards *Carnosaur* as a valuable lesson in self-preservation. When Roger invited him to do another feature, he was able to turn him down flat; and he has learned since to fight tooth and nail to protect his creative efforts. Simon views Corman's behavior toward fledgling directors as part of a recurring pattern: "Roger reenacts this time and time again with filmmakers. Where the experience he obviously had with Arkoff and Nicholson—where they gave him all these opportunities, and then limited him or screwed him or hurt his work—forced him to go out on his own. But he inevitably became what they were. He's had to."

Simon, of course, knows that Corman's behavior toward underlings is typical of those on the top rungs of the corporate ladder, in Hollywood and everywhere else. But he feels that in Corman's case there is a mythic dimension as well. In Simon's terms, Roger had to reenact the Jungian drama of killing his AIP father figures (Arkoff and Nicholson) before he could hope to gain his personal independence. Now that he himself is a company head, several generations of young filmmakers instinctively regard him as a cinematic father of sorts. Directors try to please him, going to great lengths to give him what he wants. If Simon is correct, the only way for them to find artistic maturity is to pull away from Corman's influence—to symbolically slay him—and move on within the industry. In Simon's own case, this process was genuinely painful. It is only now that he can look back on his Concorde days (1989–93) with nostalgia and gratitude: "God designed us in such a way that our memory for pain is very, very short. So that ten years later you can not really remember how much it hurt to do some of those things; you just remember that you did them and that it got you to a certain place in yourself, and that he's the guy who did that."

In Simon's opinion, part of what Corman faced during the shooting of *Gas-s-s-s!* was his impending mythic confrontation with those who had spawned him. But there were other stresses, too, including the film's offbeat subject matter and its attempt at avant-garde style. Then, probably, Roger was starting to feel a bit old as well. Though making a film based on the premise that youth meant survival, he himself was now forty-three. In addition, although *Gas-s-s-s!* may have ended on a romantic fade-out, Corman still remained unattached in his personal life. Several who worked on this project have mentioned his noticeable state of agitation at the time. Production manager Paul Rapp recalls that during the making of *Gas-s-s-s!*, as they shared a taxi in a blizzard, Roger turned to him and asked with great urgency, "Paul, should I marry the blonde or the brunette?" Later Rapp was to realize that the blonde in question was a young woman from Newport Beach, California. And the brunette was Julie Halloran.

Rapp's recollection, which he shared with me on October 21, 1998, seems hard to buy. But Frank Moreno, who has known Corman since long before he became New World's sales manager, confirmed Rapp's account when we spoke a few weeks later. "Actually," says Moreno, "[Roger] went around asking people who he should marry. He had a list of two or three people that he was considering marrying, and he wanted a family." No one has ventured to pinpoint exactly how Julie won out in this seemingly eccentric selection process, as Roger polled those around him in order to validate the promptings of his own heart. Suffice it to say that Corman, well known for his decisiveness, actually applied his title-testing strategy to the choice of a mate. And he would use it again when it came to naming his children.

• • •

In the aftermath of the rift with AIP over *Gas-s-s-s!* in 1970, Corman was ready to try another big studio film. The Corman brothers made a deal with United Artists for an ambitious World War I flying drama, *Von Richtofen and Brown* (1971), starring John Phillip Law and Don Stroud. Gene functioned as his brother's producer on location in Ireland, where Roger thoroughly enjoyed the chance to stage aerial dogfights in period biplanes. Julie visited him on the set, and stayed on to work as a production assistant. The people of Ireland were friendly, and the countryside near Galway beautiful. Thus, Roger should have been happy, but once again he found himself chafing under the outside pressure exerted by studio brass. When the film was redubbed, against his wishes, by actors using phony German accents, he had had enough. This was to be the last movie Corman directed for almost twenty years.

Von Richtofen and Brown clearly has special meaning for Roger. Though he is not naturally prone to self-analysis, he does refer to this work in admitting to the contradictory drives within him. At the end of his memoir, mulling over those Corman films that give clues to his personality, he declares that "the Baron von Richtofen, the proud, fearless aristocrat in a passing age of warfare, and Roy Brown, the nervous factory worker with superior reflexes and cunning who shoots him out of the skies in World War I, both reflect 'warring' aspects of my character, the elitist-artist and the hustler-maverick destined to defeat him."

Just prior to making Von Richtofen, Corman spoke with journalist Digby Diehl about his career, which at that point amounted to some 110 pictures in fifteen years. His fatigue is apparent in his words. As quoted in Show (May 1970), Roger explains to Diehl that in the early days, his strong urge to create was not hampered by the scrutiny of critics. But as "the critical evaluation grew, probably the creativity itself has withered a little. . . . I'm not so sure that the pictures I'm making now are any better than the pictures I made six or seven years ago." Citing the Italian director Federico Fellini (1920–93), who liked to work out his personal fantasies on film, Corman muses that his own current lack of artistic zeal perhaps stems from the fact that he's running out of fantasies. If a screen director explores a hundred fantasies over a lifetime, he's accomplished a fair amount of work. But, says Corman, "I've done that much in twelve years. Well, how many fantasies can I have left?"

This was Corman's state of mind before going into Von Richtofen. So it's no surprise that, once United Artists' tampering had driven him off the project in post-production, he was ready to make some professional changes. By the end of 1970, he had formed his own company, through which to make and sell films on his own terms. Promotional spots for Gas-s-s-s! had contained the catchline, "Old-timers are on the way out. The new world's taking over."

It may have been coincidence, but Corman decided to call his fledgling film company New World Pictures.

. . .

In 1970, at the time he formed New World Pictures, Roger Corman had no plans to quit directing for good. He told the media he was merely taking a brief hiatus, and he most likely believed this was so. But for some colleagues who had long known him, it stood to reason that he might not return anytime soon. Filmmaker Monte Hellman, for one, believes that Corman was never entirely at ease as a director. Hellman explains that it was "not that he didn't have ideas or didn't know what he wanted visually, but I don't think he was ever comfortable talking to actors. He asked me to be dialogue coach on *The St. Valentine's Day Massacre* [1967], and there was no need for a dialogue coach. The only reason he hired me was because he wanted someone to act as an intermediary, who could talk to the actors in a language that they understood. . . . He felt, I think, in awe of actors like Jason Robards. He didn't feel that he knew the language."

Nor, perhaps, was Corman ever quite comfortable with the degree of emotional investment that the director's job demands. He was to tell Charles Goldman in a 1971 interview for *Film Comment,* "Directing is very hard and very painful. Producing is easy. I can do it without really thinking about it." Corman here surely underestimated the difficulties he would one day face as a full-time producer, but the sense of creative burnout expressed in this quote is unmistakable.

In Christian Blackwood's 1977 film documentary, Corman firmly states that "directing is a young man's game." He describes a fulfilling, though less fatiguing life as the boss of New World Pictures, telling Blackwood he finds his excitement in devising a concept for a film, working with the writer on the script, helping the director and the production manager during the planning stage, then collaborating with the director and the editor in post-production. He admits he's not sure he still has the energy to direct a feature, because "getting up at six o'clock in the morning as a director is a very difficult thing."

The Roger Corman who spoke to Blackwood in 1977 was the doting father of three very young children, so he hardly needed the additional physical and mental strain of a directing career. But filmmaker Joe Dante speculates that Corman never has been quite the same since his directing days ended. "I think when Roger stopped directing and started only producing, he missed something—some piece of himself he used to use when he was directing." Dante may be right. It's poignant to read Digby Diehl's 1970 article for *Show* magazine in which Corman clearly misses the fun of grinding out fast, cheap films without worrying about critical respect. Diehl's piece ends with Roger citing a story from the late 1930s, Irwin Shaw's "The Eighty Yard Run." In it, a middle-aged man whose greatest life achievement was a long touchdown run, returns to the old high-school field and tries to relive his moment of gridiron glory. In that spirit, Corman sheepishly acknowledges to Diehl, "I want to make a film in five days again."

• • •

The first notable book on Corman was published in 1970. *Roger Corman: The Millennic Vision*, a tiny volume of essays edited by British critics David Will and Paul Willemen, was a by-product of the Corman retrospective that year at the prestigious Edinburgh Film Festival in Scotland. The book was yet another sign that Corman's true enthusiasts, particularly those in Europe, took his filmography seriously indeed. Because it was published in the same year that Roger was winding down as a director, its adulation of his movie work must have given him pause.

But 1970 was a time for Corman to look forward as well as back. He had his new company to build. And on Saturday, December 26, 1970, he and Julie Halloran were finally married, in a small family ceremony at St. Paul's Chapel in Westwood, California, adjacent to Beverly Hills. The nuptials were moderately Catholic, in deference to the wishes of Julie and her parents. Gene served as his brother's best man; Gene's wife Nan and Julie's two sisters were also in attendance. The forty-four-year-old Corman was dressed for the occasion in a business suit; his bride (age twenty-eight) held a colorful bouquet of flowers, and wore a long white dress but no veil. Following the wedding, a large reception was held at the nearby home of Danny and Kinta Haller. Frances Doel remembers that the champagne ran out, and actor Jack Nicholson went for another case. The mood was jubilant: Corman's new world had truly begun.

Part Three

NEW WORLD PICTURES

(1970–83)

Chapter 7

SUNSET BOULEVARD

A little bit of statement, a little bit of sex.

ROGER CORMAN, 1972

IN 1970 NEW WORLD PICTURES was something new on the Hollywood scene: a small independent film company completely financed by, and run by, a bona fide moviemaker. It gave Corman the opportunity to be an auteur producer, controlling every phase of his films' production and distribution. At New World, Roger would be able to combine his creative vision with his commercial savvy.

This is not to say that Corman's was the only small company head-quartered in Hollywood in the early 1970s. But the mini-moguls of the past were changing their strategy. After Jim Nicholson departed from AIP in 1972, Sam Arkoff began edging toward the production of bigger-budget films like *The Island of Dr. Moreau* (1977). Joseph E. Levine, the one-time exhibitor who first made a splash by importing *Godzilla* (1954) from Japan and *Hercules* (1959) from Italy, had moved into the mainstream as the backer of such star-studded features as *Carnal Knowledge* (1973) and *A Bridge Too Far* (1977). Sam Katzman, long known for teen movies like *Rock Around the Clock* (1956) and *Riot on the Sunset Strip* (1967), died in 1973.

Corman's more immediate rivals included Crown International, among whose titles were *Chain Gang Women* (1971) and *Pom Pom Girls*

(1976). Like Crown and the other small companies of the era, New World chiefly released conventional exploitation fare. However, on looking back, producer Thom Mount insists that Corman's films always have had something else to offer: "Roger specialized in elevating exploitation. And starting with what other people in that world—the Arkoffs and others —would have been happy to leave as pure exploitation, Roger upgrades it, and is always willing to reach for something that's smarter, and a script that's a little better, and a writer that's a little more interesting, and a director that's a little riskier, and an actor that has a greater chance of breaking out. As long as it doesn't cost more."

The New World slate of films, always shaped by the boss's intuitive sense of the marketplace, was developed and produced almost entirely in-house. Corman's operation has been likened to a scaled-down Hollywood studio, but this does not mean he had access to sophisticated production facilities. Most New World movies were shot (invariably in color) on location in or near Los Angeles—soundstages were considered an unnecessary luxury, one that might detract from the sense of immediacy captured by the best of the films. The company's pictures covered a widening array of popular genres, including thrillers, action flicks, and sexy comedies. Because New World audiences were mostly teens and young adults, the films were generally designed to earn what Corman called a "hard-R" from the Motion Picture Association of America (MPAA), which had instituted its ratings system in 1968.

From the beginning, the commercial side of Corman's equation paid off. An article published in the *Independent Film Journal* on May 25, 1972, sums up the successes of New World's inaugural year: eleven films in distribution, and $3.2 million in profits. Corman explained his modus operandi to the *Journal's* Judy Raskin—in contrast to the studios' million-dollar pictures, he makes $250,000 films "that look bigger because many of the writers, producers, and directors were in for profit participation, sometimes the actors too." Despite Corman's boast, profit-sharing was normally not in the cards for his creative teams. As before, he continued to hire young unknowns who would work for almost nothing in exchange for the chance to learn their craft. Writer Howard R. Cohen told me he once griped to

Roger that it was hard to live on what he paid. Corman's matter-of-fact reply: "I get the money; you get the career."

Corman's headquarters in the early days of New World was a rather run-down penthouse suite near Doheny Drive in the heart of the Sunset Strip. The four-story building, complete with outdoor glass elevator, was situated across Sunset Boulevard from a burlesque joint, The Classic Cat, and it was just down the block from a legendary music club, the Whisky-a-Go-Go. The office atmosphere was informal. Though New World's dozen employees were quite accustomed to the boss prowling the halls with his shoes off, his habit of putting his feet up on his large and nearly bare desk surprised visitors who spotted the holes in his socks. The furniture was cut-rate modern, but the inevitable framed movie posters were augmented, in Corman's own office, by large placards given to him by a French producer after the 1968 student revolts in Paris. They were emblazoned with revolutionary slogans like *Salaires légères, chars lourds* ("Light Salaries, Heavy Tanks") and *Le patron a besoin de toi, tu n'as pas besoin de lui* ("The Boss Needs You, You Don't Need the Boss").

These sentiments may have been fitting when Corman took on the establishment with *The Wild Angels* (1966), but they seemed curiously out-of-place as decor for a rising film producer known for his skinflint ways. A sketch of a fist smashing through a brick wall, accompanied by the slogan *La lutte continue* ("The Struggle Continues") could be seen as an ironic reminder of the day when Gene Corman, whose own offices adjoined the New World suite, legendarily got mad and put his fist through the wallboard after arguing with Roger. It was neither the first nor the last time the Corman brothers would skirmish over turf in the 1970s, though generally they remained cordial.

· · ·

New World's early product line did big business in downtown "grind houses," in triple-bill theaters, and in out-of-the-way spots like the Dogwood Drive-In in Palestine, Texas, and the Roxy in Salmon, Idaho. Because Gene, in 1970, was too busy with his own projects to join in the running of New World, Roger at first partnered with Larry Woolner, who had once owned a chain of drive-in theaters throughout Louisiana. Woolner's expertise in distribution proved helpful, but a rift soon developed, and after a year Woolner moved across the street to form a rival company, Dimension Pictures. Yet, in his 1990 memoir, Corman credits Woolner with the idea for New World's first feature, *The Student Nurses* (1970).

This 89-minute, R-rated release inspired a formula that was much copied: a trio of beautiful "babes in uniform" (one blonde, one brunette, one racial minority) have on-the-job adventures, find romance, and face endangerment from rapists and bureaucrats. The nurses' social crusades—against the doping of athletes, or for better treatment of the Hispanic community—are always taken seriously, as well as the "necessity" that each nurse disrobe at some point in the story. Jonathan Kaplan *(The Accused)* told documentary filmmaker Christian Blackwood that when he was asked to direct the third in the series, *Night Call Nurses* (1972), his first meeting with Corman consisted chiefly of the directive "to get frontal nudity from the waist up, total nudity from behind, no pubic hair, go to work!"

Kaplan did so well (Julie Corman phoned him with the news that the movie had played five weeks in Chattanooga) that he was rewarded with an assignment to direct *The Student Teachers* (1973), in which Dick Miller played a gym teacher–turned–rapist. To broaden the professional spectrum, New World also released a stewardess film, *Fly Me* (1973), shot on location in the Philippines. Surprisingly, these movies have had staying power over the years. Among their fans was the young Quentin Tarantino, who snuck out of his mother's house in suburban Torrance, California (twenty miles south of Los Angeles), to watch them on late-night double bills at the seedy Carson Twin Cinema. Wensley Clarkson's book *Quentin Tarantino: Shooting from the Hip* (1995) reveals that the future filmmaker was enough of a connoisseur to have favorites: He preferred Kaplan's *Night Call Nurses,* which he describes as "a classic mix of sex, nudity, and political consciousness."

An important aspect of the so-called "three-girl movies" is that, in an era when female directors were almost nonexistent, two of them were directed by women, Stephanie Rothman and Barbara Peters. Julie Corman was also earning her producing spurs on the nurse features, beginning with *Night Call Nurses.* Roger Corman has always prided himself on giving opportunities to capable young people, regardless of gender. Over the years he has relied heavily on female attorneys, female sales executives, and female studio heads. As director Linda Shayne attests, "Roger has promoted more women to positions of power than probably any person I know."

Just why was Corman so far ahead of the rest of Hollywood in terms of hiring women? This question came up on October 15, 1998, when I spoke to Clark Henderson, now head of post-production at Miramax Films. Henderson was once told by Corman that women negotiate better deals than men and generally manage better in an office setting because they don't have "that rooster thing going on all the time." Unlike men, who tend to view business as a turf battle, women are good at using diplomacy to get their way.

One prime example of a trusted Corman employee with the smarts to rise through the industry ranks is Barbara Boyle (b. 1935). Boyle came to New World in 1974 as a youngish attorney; by the time she left in the early 1980s she was the company's chief operating officer and executive vice president for business affairs. She has gone on to become a successful producer (1996's *Phenomenon*, 1999's *Instinct*), and she and Corman share a strong mutual respect. On June 12, 1991, when Corman received his star on the Hollywood Walk of Fame, Boyle got a knowing laugh from the invited luncheon guests when she explained Roger's preference for hiring women. The phrase she used was almost identical to one cited for me by the very mainstream producer Gale Anne Hurd, another Corman success story. Hurd noted that Roger said it often: He preferred female employees because "women worked harder, were paid less money, and were more loyal."

Thus, behind the scenes, Corman put the opposite sex in power positions. Still, on-screen there's no denying that New World's movies put actresses in compromising positions. The nurse pictures were always marketed on the basis of their heroines' sex appeal. In 1974 the last of the nurse features used as its catchline the suggestive phrase, "Keep abreast of the medical world with the *Candy Stripe Nurses.*" Even more outrageous were the ad campaigns for the "women in prison" series that kicked off in 1971 with *The Big Doll House* (which according to *New York Times Magazine*'s Bill Davidson grossed $3 million), followed by *The Big Bird Cage* (1972), and, inevitably, *The Big Bust Out* (1973). Most of these features were shot in the Philippines with a hardy and voluptuous cast made up of the likes of Roberta Collins and Pam Grier. Statuesque Grier, who quickly became a symbol of strong black womanhood, was soon to play a major role in Hollywood's "blaxploitation" phase.

Among enthusiasts, the "babes behind bars" movies have been hailed as feminist in nature: the women are brutally subjugated for several reels, then spend the rest of the film turning the tables on their oppressors. Yet this is feminism of a rather specialized sort. Onetime Corman assistant Laurette Hayden, now a vice president at the Lifetime Television Network, joked with me on October 30, 1998, about how the female lead is inevitably falling out of her clothing while running through the jungle: "I think the faster she runs, with the machete in her hand, the more quickly the clothes fall away."

A producer, and sometimes director, on these films was Cirio H. Santiago. Roger had discovered Santiago (b. 1936) when passing through Manila. An affable man who loves golf and playing the horses, and who has access to the Philippine army for on-camera stuntwork, Santiago is legendary among Corman's actors for his carefree attitude toward basic safety precautions. By January 1972, Corman was so committed to shooting in the Philippines that, as chronicled by Will Tusher in the *Hollywood Reporter*, he negotiated a deal to build two soundstages outside Manila, in exchange for lucrative tax advantages. Over the years Corman and Santiago have continued to work together, despite major political upheavals in the island nation. Roger, moreover, has happily branched into other Third World countries (among them Mexico, Argentina, and Bulgaria) that offer exotic scenery, cheap labor, and an absence of union regulations.

• • •

Like most independent filmmakers, Corman has always looked for ways to dodge the strictures of the pervasive Hollywood trade unions. Though his casts are composed of Screen Actors Guild members, he still largely avoids working with the Writers Guild and the Directors Guild; craft union members generally have no place on Corman crews. It is ironic, therefore, that Roger's last picture for Arkoff and Nicholson had a union organizer for its hero. The picture was *Boxcar Bertha* (1972), starring Barbara Hershey and David Carradine, and it was distributed by American International Pictures (AIP) because of lingering contractual obligations. (Speaking to Wayne Warga of the *Los Angeles Times* in 1975, Corman would confess, "I have this recurring nightmare where I think I've made some picture for AIP long ago and they still owe me money. The trouble is I can't think of the name of the picture.") Carradine, for whom *Boxcar Bertha* was to be the first of many Corman screen assignments, told me he remembers Roger's press statements pointedly emphasizing the film's lovers-on-the-lam plot to deflect attention from its pro-union political message.

At first Corman indicated he wanted to direct *Boxcar Bertha* himself, but then he turned it over to an intense, long-haired young filmmaker named Martin Scorsese (b. 1942). Though Corman observed to me on April 13, 1998 that "Marty was as much a New York man as I've ever met in my life," he spoke admiringly of Scorsese's convincing depiction of outlaw life in the rural, Depression-era South in the movie. Scorsese still had much to learn in the editing room. Before releasing *Boxcar Bertha*, Roger worked closely with the film's editors to trim it from two and a half hours to a brisk 88 minutes. Since his own rise to fame, Scorsese has had nothing but praise for the Corman aesthetic. He revealed to Bill Davidson of the *New York Times Magazine* that on his 1973 breakthrough film, *Mean Streets* (starring the young Robert De Niro and Harvey Keitel), "I used a Corman crew and shot it in the Corman style—doing nearly everything on location to get the totally realistic seaminess I wanted."

Another major Hollywood director-to-be started out as a publicist (on 1971's *Von Richtofen and Brown*) and screenwriter (for New World's 1971 biker flick, *Angels Hard as They Come*). After only a brief stay at what Hollywood hopefuls had begun to call the Roger Corman School of Film, Jonathan Demme (b. 1944) was directing his first feature. *Caged Heat* (1974) hardly seemed an auspicious project. This 84-minute picture, starring Roberta Collins and Barbara Steele, was yet another women-in-prison entry, shot locally on a $180,000 budget. The marketing campaign was typically lurid—the ads screamed out, "White Hot Desires Melting Cold Prison Steel!"—but Demme's work actually earned some respectful press. The *Los Angeles Times*'s Kevin Thomas, one of several critics nationwide who would admit to enjoying New World products, described *Caged Heat* as having "wit, style, and unflagging verve. . . . [It] sends up the genre while still giving the mindless action fan his money's worth."

Demme told documentary filmmaker Christian Blackwood that he was proud that, two years before the more highly touted *One Flew Over the*

Cuckoo's Nest, Caged Heat dramatized the abuse of psychosurgery in American prisons. He admits, however, that Roger liked the work because its heavy violence quotient appealed to his target audiences. Demme learned from Corman the need to respect the commercial side of filmmaking. In a 1998 television interview with talk-show host Charlie Rose, Demme quotes an emphatic Corman: "As a director, you're 40, 45 percent artist and 60, 55 percent businessman. Never forget that." Part of the filmmaker's job, in other words, is to repay his financial backers. Roger warned Demme that "as soon as you let the arty part get carried away, you're gonna find yourself out of work." In the course of Demme's career he has balanced commerce and art most successfully in his 1991 megahit, *The Silence of the Lambs.* The fate of 1998's *Beloved,* which was highly praised by some critics but died at the box office, perhaps reinforces the validity of Corman's advice.

Back in the early 1970s, when Demme roamed the halls of New World Pictures in his trademark brown-and-white saddle oxfords, he was quite willing to be commercial. I vividly remember a story conference at which he used a large chart to analyze three low-budget hits of the day: *Billy Jack* (1971), *Walking Tall* (1973), and *Dirty Mary, Crazy Larry* (1974). Demme noted that these rural action thrillers had significant elements in common: a hero with an odd weapon, an offbeat mode of transportation, and an unusual sidekick. So, as Corman grinned appreciatively, Demme proposed his own screen project, in which his leading man wielded a crossbow, traveled on an old Indian motorcycle, and hung out with his toddler son. This evolved into the quickly forgettable *Fighting Mad,* a 1976 co-production between New World and Twentieth Century–Fox, with Peter Fonda in the leading role.

Corman could be a generous teacher, willing to share with his protégés the industry secrets he'd learned over the years. Demme was one of the first to hear the "director's speech" that Roger gave to several generations of eager young filmmakers. Depending on the era and Corman's mood, it ranged from a lengthy disquisition over lunch to a brief pep talk. In any case, most directors remember it as a common-sense rundown of moviemaking fundamentals: prioritize your shots; rehearse while the crew is lighting the set; chase the sun; use foreground objects to enliven a dialogue scene; bring in movement to stimulate the eye; and, above all, wear comfortable shoes, and sit down a lot. Both Jonathan Demme and Ron Howard told documentarian Blackwood that they rely on Roger's principles to this day. I know at least one up-and-comer who reviews them before every directing gig.

．　．　．

Part of the Corman stock-in-trade was keeping up with the latest Hollywood trends. For instance in 1971, MGM's *Shaft* effectively launched the "blaxploitation" craze by using an African-American private eye as its tough-talking, hard-hitting hero. The movie was a huge box-office hit, and awakened American filmmakers to the potential ticket-buying power of African-American movie fans. Gene Corman quickly jumped on the bandwagon, producing a trio of black action features (including 1973's *The Slams*) for MGM.

Not to be outdone, Roger released *The Final Comedown* (1972), a black-themed political thriller starring Billy Dee Williams and Raymond St. Jacques that began life as an American Film Institute project written and directed by Oscar Williams. When the film's implicit anti-white bias kept most moviegoers away, Corman tinkered with the ad campaign to make it seem more enticing. The much-publicized kidnapping of heiress Patty Hearst by the radical group known as the Symbionese Liberation Army encouraged him to retool the feature as *The Battle of the Liberation Army*. This brainstorm never went beyond an announcement in Hank Grant's column for the *Hollywood Reporter*, but ultimately four days' worth of new footage was added, and *The Final Comedown* reappeared in 1976 as *Blast!*

Despite the movie's failure under all of its release titles, Corman kept looking for a black action vehicle that could attract significant crossover audiences. *The Arena* (1973) was a quixotic attempt to cross *Spartacus* with *The Defiant Ones*: Pam Grier and Margaret Markov played female gladiators in ancient Rome who are forced to overcome racial differences in order to fight for their freedom. The ads, which showed dusky-skinned Grier forcing blonde Markov to her knees with the help of a steel trident, promised that the viewer would "See Wild Women Fight to the Death!" But although the statuesque Grier in abbreviated gladiator garb was an awesome sight, Corman cagily revamped his advertising art for the Southern market by redrawing the black beauty as a Caucasian.

The Arena was to be Grier's last film for Corman. Her performances in *Coffy* (1973) and *Foxy Brown* (1974), two black revenge dramas made for AIP by Corman alumnus Jack Hill, quickly turned her into a low-budget cinematic icon. (In 1997 Grier's image was still potent enough to inspire Quentin Tarantino to build his heist thriller *Jackie Brown* around her.) So when Corman decided to combine blaxploitation with Bruce Lee–style martial-arts moves, he had to find a new African-American female star. His search produced Jeanne Bell, a petite Playmate of the Month with limited dramatic abilities, who was tapped to play the title role in *TNT Jackson* (1974).

Corman, always a believer in recycling screen stories, decided to borrow the plot line of Sergio Leone's western *A Fistful of Dollars* (1964), which itself derived from Akira Kurosawa's Japanese classic, *Yojimbo* (1961). Starting with this tale of a loner playing both ends against the middle, Roger sought to graft it with the story of a young black woman, adept in kung fu, who comes to Hong Kong in search of her missing brother. Corman instructed Frances Doel to write a quickie first draft over a weekend; he then hired actor Dick Miller to make this into a shootable screenplay. Accounts differ as to what happened next. Miller felt that one too many rewrites had been demanded of him; the office scuttlebutt was that Dick incurred disfavor by padding his own screen role. In any case, there was a shouting match, during which Corman ripped up Miller's submission. Miller has described for me his version of what happened next: "I finally said, 'Shove it!' He got up— without his shoes—and kicked a lamp, and broke it. I heard years later that his biggest bitch was that he had broken the lamp." Miller's audacity swiftly won him respect among all the Hollywood underlings who had been dying to tell their producers to go to hell. But it came at a price: for years afterwards, the two men barely spoke.

All things considered, *TNT Jackson* (which was shot in Manila with Cirio Santiago at the helm) was not as bad a movie as it could have been. Which didn't mean that its convoluted plot made much sense. As always, it fell to New World staff editors Joe Dante and Allan Arkush to cut an exciting "Coming Attractions" trailer that would pull viewers in. Creativity was their specialty: They borrowed a shot of somebody pouring sugar to hint that the story hinged on drug trafficking. They also helped devise a litany of doggerel that fans of the movie can still chant today: "TNT Jackson/She'll put you in traction/She's long, she's lean/She's a lip-smackin', bone-crunchin' destruction machine." As a final touch, the press kit devised by Dante and Arkush's colleague, Jon Davison, imaginatively touts Jeanne Bell as the winner of the coveted (and purely imaginary) Ebony Fist Award, bestowed upon her by martial-arts experts for her "expert form, flexibility, and muscle tone."

•   •   •

In the early 1970s, Jon Davison, Joe Dante, and Allan Arkush were East Coast kids who idolized Corman and his films. They won their New World jobs more through enthusiasm and persistence than from any technical expertise. (Arriving in Los Angeles to cut a trailer for *Caged Heat,* Dante—who trained as a cartoonist—had never before worked on a 35mm film.) What distinguished them from later generations of Corman people was the fact that all three joined Roger's staff without preconceived goals. During our Los Angeles reunion in fall 1998, they reminisced about spending their New World days happily going to movies, talking about movies, working on Corman movies, then seeing more movies on the late show. Said Davison, "Nobody had thought about a career." In those days, agreed Arkush, "watching movies and working on movies was plenty."

Not that New World was always an ideal place to work. Though Corman's shrewd precision in the editing room was a lesson in itself, he could also be both demanding and capricious. Both Dante and Arkush recall unexpected mass layoffs at New World, which might come in midsummer or just before Christmas. This was Corman's way of not having to pay his staff for holidays or slow periods. He considered it reasonable to send his workers out to collect unemployment, as they remember Julie Corman doing between her New World projects. According to Arkush, "He would fire us under the guise of giving us a summer vacation. Give us a month off. Then he'd hire us again in September." Such Corman shenanigans led to the creation of the top-secret *New World News,* a crudely-assembled employee newsletter that contained such satiric items as the headline "Roger Fires Everybody" next to a photo of Adolf Hitler captioned, " 'I Vant Zem All Out!,' says Roger."

Although working conditions could be exasperating, true film buffs like Dante and Arkush were also frustrated by something more intangible—

a sense that Roger's long-range cinematic goals did not always match theirs. They belatedly discovered, as Dante puts it, that Corman "wasn't this dedicated maverick filmmaker that was making films against the system. . . . The depth to which he had become corporate was kind of shocking to me." Dante was then young and naive about what it takes to run a successful business venture. Despite certain disdain for what Corman was after, he and the others would ultimately stay on for years, learning every aspect of filmmaking but how to crack through the barricades of the studio system.

Looking back at his New World stint (1973–78), Dante acknowledges that, above all, it helped him discover his professional calling. Like most editors, he habitually kept to himself. But when he unexpectedly became a Corman director on *Piranha* (1978), he suddenly felt the need to relate to people in a more open and outgoing way. Says Dante, "That was very liberating for me. Because I found a personality I didn't know I have. And I was able to use that same one throughout my whole career. If it hadn't been for Roger, I never would even have discovered it."

.   .   .

For some New World employees, the capricious side of Corman's nature was not adequately balanced by the professional opportunities he gave them. On September 11, 1998, Julie Moldo summed up her Corman experience in a simple phrase: "I was fired when my brother dropped the candelabra." Moldo was hired by Corman at $125 a week instead of the usual $100 because of her Phi Beta Kappa key. Her chief job was to track the distribution of New World releases. Later her younger brother Byron came aboard as a part-time mail clerk and general gofer. One day Byron was asked to supervise the men from Bekins Moving and Storage as they packed the contents of Corman's Beverly Hills home to transport them to his new Brentwood digs. Among the items was a brightly decorated clay piece of folk art, worth perhaps $100, popularly known as a Mexican Christmas tree. The movers dropped it; Byron was terminated; and Julie soon heard that her services were no longer required.

Over the years, more than one Corman staffer has been let go for reasons that seem whimsical or unjustified. Sometimes the employee's main fault is simply having been around too long. Roger dislikes breaking bad news personally, so he usually gets someone else to deliver the message when the ax is about to fall. (I'm told that to be dismissed by Roger himself is an honor of sorts.) In recent years he has actually been known to give an unwanted staffer a movie to direct as a way of easing him or her out of the company. The deal is that, if chosen to shoot a film, you surrender your staff position and receive instead a director's fee; after your film is completed, you are on your own. Former production head Rodman Flender marveled to me about the oddity of this method of dismissal, "What a great way to get fired—to direct a movie! It's probably the only place in the world where that's how you lose your job, by getting to do what everybody's dream is."

By way of contrast, the story of one employee from the early 1970s reveals the generous side that Corman usually keeps hidden from public view. Larry Cruikshank had known Roger since the old days, when he was (depending on whom you ask) either Roger's first agent or the man who rented him his first office space. When Cruikshank needed a job, Corman found a place for him on the New World staff. In the mornings he negotiated contracts and performed other business functions; in the afternoons he was a permanent fixture at a local watering hole. Nonetheless, his salary continued unabated. After Larry developed cancer, Roger instructed his staff to keep paying his health insurance premiums. Following Cruikshank's death in the mid-1980s, Roger made sure that the attendant who had nursed him through his final illness received adequate compensation for his labors.

There were other down-at-the-heels Hollywood functionaries, too, whom Corman quietly supported in one way or another, because their association dated back to the early years. Such kindly acts were not for show. Longtime employee Pamm Vlastas, who remembers the entire Cruikshank episode, insists that Roger "never expected credit, or necessarily wanted anybody to know about it."

Corman has also been kind to latter-day employees, generously helping them out of jams with timely loans. Like many bosses, he is normally stingy with raises, but he awarded a young father-to-be a large salary increase as soon as he heard the glad news. He has assisted a Filipina accountant who faced immigration woes, and has co-signed bank loans for those trying to purchase a first home. Former New World head of sales Frank Moreno sounded a common theme in insisting, "If I were ever in trouble . . . I could knock and he would frown and not want to hear it, but he would not deny me. He wouldn't say No, no matter what it was."

For his celebrity alumni, Corman combines generosity with his usual shrewd business sense. Along with distributing Peter Bogdanovich's comeback film, *Saint Jack* (1979), he has invested in actress Sally Kirkland's stage productions. (Kirkland detailed for me how he also taught her to drum up money elsewhere.) Producer Paul Almond recalls Corman making a timely loan to Francis Ford Coppola just prior to the release of *The Godfather* (1972), taking a lien on Coppola's San Francisco–based Zoetrope studio facility as security until the returns on the gangster epic film came rolling in.

Coppola was the first alumnus to hire his former boss as an actor, casting him as a U.S. senator in *The Godfather Part II* (1974). Coppola's logic was that politicians generally look distinguished, speak well, but are slightly uncomfortable when on-camera. For a scene depicting a Senate hearing on organized crime, he lined up a group of friends, mostly Hollywood producers and directors, who would have the requisite dignified awkwardness. Over the years, however, Roger's on-screen comfort level has increased, and he always turns in a creditable performance.

Joe Dante joked to me on November 5, 1998, that part of the pleasure of using Corman in a cameo role is paying him the minimum wage allowable by the Screen Actors Guild. "Everybody wanted Roger to work for them for nothing, because we all worked for him for nothing." When Dante made his own first post-Corman film, the highly successful *The Howling* (1980), he asked his old mentor to do a walk-on in a barroom scene. It was Corman's idea, enthusiastically adopted by Dante, that he spoof his cheapskate image on-camera by checking a pay telephone's coin-return slot for loose change. Most Corman cameos, however, take advantage of his naturally authoritative presence. In Ron Howard's space epic *Apollo 13* (1995), he played a congressman quizzing NASA about cost containment. For Jonathan Demme, Roger was the head of the FBI in *The Silence of the Lambs* (1991), and, memorably, a canny corporate type who takes the witness stand in *Philadelphia* (1993).

Although Howard and Demme now make multimillion-dollar studio films, Roger himself has no such aspirations. (Onetime Corman assistant Anna Roth told me in October 1998 that when she accepted a job with

Coppola, Roger solemnly warned her, "Once you've spent $40 million on a movie, there's no turning back.") The impressive output of Corman alumni shows what they can do after shaking off the constraints of Corman's own self-limiting ambitions. By casting Roger in their films, they are paying tribute to their cinematic roots, to a time when they learned the fundamentals before going on to bigger budgets and bigger rewards. Many of them have enriched Hollywood with films of size and substance, while Corman's own artistic goals have remained small. But Gale Anne Hurd, who since leaving Corman has produced such blockbusters as *The Terminator* (1984) and *Armageddon* (1998), believes he finds his satisfaction elsewhere. Says Hurd admiringly, "He's the only person I've known in the industry who wanted his protégés to succeed and perhaps have even more impressive credentials than his own."

It's true that Roger Corman loves basking in the glow of those he has mentored. Still, he would not want to emulate them. He keeps on making money, while his celebrated progeny must at times face the fallout from ambitious, expensive screen flops.

Chapter 8

ARTISTIC LICENSE

I got a letter from Ingmar Bergman thanking me. He was delighted his film was being seen by a wider audience.

ROGER CORMAN, 1998

ROGER CORMAN AND the Academy Awards are not usually mentioned in the same breath. But on April 8, 1975, many of the big winners at the annual festivities had a Corman connection. Best Film and Best Director Oscars went to Francis Ford Coppola for *The Godfather Part II*. Best Supporting Actor was Robert De Niro for his performance in the same gangster epic. Ellen Burstyn was named Best Actress for *Alice Doesn't Live Here Anymore,* directed by Corman alumnus Martin Scorsese. Other nominees that year: Talia Shire and Diane Ladd, both up for Best Supporting Actress; cinematographer John Alonzo, whose very first film was *Bloody Mama* (1970); and Jack Nicholson, favored to win Best Actor for his starring role in *Chinatown* (the award went instead to Art Carney, for *Harry and Tonto,* leading Roger to joke that Jack's loss had spoiled his personal sweep). Robert Towne, who won the year's Best Original Screenplay honors for his *Chinatown* script, surveyed the glittering multitudes and said, in the presence of reporter Bill Davidson from the *New York Times Magazine,* "This joint looks like a meeting of the Roger Corman Alumni Association."

During that same ceremony, held at the Dorothy Chandler Pavilion in downtown Los Angeles, Federico Fellini's *Amarcord* was voted Best Foreign

Language Film. This was another coup for Corman, whose New World Pictures had served as the Italian entry's North American distributor. The working relationship between Corman and many of the great European auteurs had begun in 1973, when New World snapped up Ingmar Bergman's *Cries and Whispers*, starring Harriet Andersson, Liv Ullmann, and Ingrid Thulin. At the time, none of the studios wanted to take a chance on a delicate chamber piece shot in Swedish. But Frank Moreno, who became Corman's general sales manager after Larry Woolner's departure, loved foreign movies and was convinced they could clear a profit in the United States. Knowing that drive-in theater audiences were starting to disappear, and sensing that prestige pictures would give New World heightened credibility in the commercial marketplace, Moreno suggested they acquire an art-house film for domestic distribution. Corman authorized him to spend a modest $75,000.

Through Max Laemmle, well-known in Los Angeles for his small chain of art theaters, Moreno discovered *Cries and Whispers*, and promptly made the deal. According to Moreno, there was a party that evening at which Corman genially boasted that he had just bought the latest Bergman picture, sight unseen. An indignant man quickly took him aside announcing, "My name is Paul Kohner and I'm the agent for Ingmar Bergman. And you have not bought the film. You have not bought it until you see it." Corman subsequently watched the picture, pronounced it a masterpiece, and the deal went through. But his normal tendency was to leave the entire matter—the acquisition, marketing, and booking of foreign films—wholly in Moreno's capable hands. The fact that Moreno bypassed New World's in-house marketing department is probably why the *Cries and Whispers* ad campaign was a model of good taste.

Remarkably, the film was booked in drive-ins as well as art houses, delighting Bergman, who had always wanted to reach a wider audience. In 1974, when *Cries and Whispers* was nominated for five Academy Awards, including Best Picture, Best Director, and Best Screenplay, Corman rented a tux and went to the Oscar ceremony as Bergman's representative. (Sven Nykvist took home the film's only statuette, for Best Cinematography.) In the end, *Cries and Whispers* boosted the company's respectability, while Wayne Warga of the *Los Angeles Times* records that it also grossed $2 million at the box office.

In the wake of *Cries and Whispers,* Moreno made deals for an offbeat animated science-fiction feature from France, *Fantastic Planet* (1973), and for Federico Fellini's exuberant memory piece, *Amarcord* (1974). Joe Dante and Allan Arkush told me they had only one weekend to pull together the trailer that would sell the Fellini film to American audiences. When *Amarcord* was screened for them, they sat in awed silence. But Roger's instructions quickly brought them back to earth: "I know it's Fellini, but we're still selling sex and violence here. Make sure the car thing is in there, make sure the boys jerking off is in there. . . ." The work that resulted was, in Dante's words, "all boobs and buns." They heard later that Fellini preferred it to the Italian trailer, because of its flat-out vulgarity. Hank Grant's column in the *Hollywood Reporter* soon hinted that Corman and Fellini were on the brink of a five-picture co-production deal, with Jack Nicholson nearly set to star in *Casanova.*

Though no long-range Fellini deal ever materialized, other foreign films were quickly added to the New World roster. These included Akira Kurosawa's *Dersu Uzala* (Best Foreign Film Oscar for 1976), as well as major works by François Truffaut *(The Story of Adele H)*, Volker Schlöndorff *(The Tin Drum)*, and Bruce Beresford *(Breaker Morant)*. Former New World sales executive Bob Rehme notes appreciatively, "We really were the Miramax of the period." Gale Anne Hurd, Corman's assistant at the time, maintains that Truffaut's visits to New World headquarters revealed "a totally different side of Roger—the cinéaste, as opposed to the businessman." Another former assistant, Laurette Hayden, describes "the wonderful schizophrenic balance between these beautiful European movies that we distributed and the low-budget films that we were all frantically working on." Hayden cherishes the afternoon she spent running the projector as Corman and Werner Herzog sat side by side, watching the German director's new feature, *Fitzcarraldo* (1982): "I wouldn't trade that four hours for anything."

Except for the occasional idiosyncratic trim, Corman didn't tamper with great screen art. He was not, however, above buying second-rate foreign films and trying to improve their sales potential through creative editing. Take the case of *Foxtrot,* a 1975 British drama featuring Charlotte Rampling and Peter O'Toole. When it failed to attract American audiences, Corman retitled it *The Other Side of Paradise.* He also had a crew shoot inserts of hands, breasts, and torsos for the love scenes, so the two stars appear to be coupling in the nude, even though the bodies on-screen are not theirs. Describing to me these outrageous additions, director Joe Dante wryly quipped that "in the old days it was thought that nobody really paid enough attention to the movies for anybody to notice."

In recent years, Corman has rarely acquired foreign films for distribution. To a large extent, he was victimized by his own success. Once he showed that these features could turn a profit, the big studios began launching their own classics divisions. And Harvey and Bob Weinstein, two rock-concert promoters who founded Miramax Films in 1979, were soon putting most of their energies into importing bankable art pictures. Whereas Frank Moreno once had the luxury of viewing completed features before deciding whether to buy, acquisitions executives from Miramax, Fox Searchlight, and Sony Pictures Classics today fight over movies that are still in pre-production. So it is highly likely that the next *Life Is Beautiful,* or *Il Postino,* or *Like Water for Chocolate* that comes along will not have Roger Corman's name on it.

• • •

Frank Moreno, the man who put New World in the art-film business, hardly fits the image of the typical Corman employee. Though Corman prided himself on hiring Phi Beta Kappas from first-rate colleges, Moreno never went beyond a high-school diploma. The son of a New York City janitor from Puerto Rico, he lacked the academic honors that Roger usually considered proof of intelligence. During the course of our long chat on November 27, 1998, Moreno maintained that, because he had no scholastic credentials, "Roger would never have hired me to be his assistant or to work in the creative end in any way. But for someone who was going to go out there and fight the masses and get the playdates and get the pictures on the screen, I was acceptable."

Having grown up in poverty, Moreno cannot accept Corman's Depression-era upbringing as the full explanation for his miserly ways: "You get through that. . . . I was raised in a basement, but I got out of that." Whatever its cause, Corman's cheap streak sometimes made Moreno's job more difficult. For instance, Frank used the *New York Times* as a research tool, to help him in booking art-house releases. But one day Corman canceled

Moreno's $10-a-week subscription because he deemed it too costly. Still, when Moreno purchased films (paying as much as $250,000 in the case of *Amarcord*), Corman never interfered. His faith in Moreno's judgment was certainly warranted. Of the fifteen or so motion-pictures acquired by Frank, only one (1981's German-made *Christiane F.*) failed to pay for itself. Not only did the pictures make a modest profit, says Moreno, but Corman "got a lot of press from the art films, well deserved. Because he put up the money. Without the money there are no films. He gave us the freedom to go out there and find these films."

After three years with the company, Frank Moreno left in 1975. The cause of his rift with Corman was financial in nature. Moreno claims Corman had agreed to give him 10 percent of the earnings on the foreign films, but insists he was unable to collect. When Julie Corman learned of Frank's impending departure, she told him, sympathetically, "Next time you'll get it in writing." In his absence, Bob Rehme, Barbara Boyle, and then Paul Almond handled the acquisition of foreign features. Frank returned in 1978 but had learned his lesson: "I got it in writing, but when it came time to collect, [Corman] didn't want to pay. I had to go up there and negotiate and settle my contract with him and get my participation. Behind me came Barbara and Paul, who each had a little piece. And Roger was very upset for about two weeks. His sense was that it was all his, and that we weren't entitled."

Despite Corman's apparent reluctance to uphold his end of a bargain, Moreno today holds no grudge. He speaks with good humor about Corman's more outrageous economizing, like trying to get Moreno and Barbara Boyle to share accommodations on a business trip to save the price of a second hotel room. Gradually, explains Moreno, he stopped being Corman's hireling and became (as very few people do) Corman's friend. When, circa 1980, he left Corman for the second time to strike out on his own, the relationship continued. Corman made a substantial sum by investing in Frank's Florida theater chain, Wometco. He now turns to Moreno for business advice, sometimes phoning him to say, "I just sold this property and I happen to have three million dollars sitting here. . . . Do you have something that you'd like me to put it into?"

Today, though Moreno lives in San Diego, California, he stays in close contact with the Cormans, dining regularly at their home and sharing social outings. Amazingly, Roger always reaches for the tab. Frank marveled to me at the fact that "he'll beat me out of a nickel on any deal I ever make with him, but he'll be very generous with me if we go out together. He won't let me pay unless I insist."

• • •

Throughout the 1970s, while distributing the art films of others, Corman still aimed to make a movie of his own that would please both critics and audiences. In 1974 he had high hopes for *Cockfighter,* based on a novel by Southern writer Charles Willeford. Part of the allure was the intellectual pretension of Willeford's novel, which contained arcane references to Homer's Greek classic, *The Odyssey.* Corman also liked the thought of bringing to the screen the raw vigor of an outlaw sport. And he was convinced, says an employee from that era, that the faint lewdness of the title would give *Cockfighter* added appeal to moviegoers.

Because Corman's heart was in this project, he should probably have directed it himself. Instead he hired Monte Hellman, whose script revisions displeased him. Visiting the production office in Atlanta, Georgia, Roger slammed the shooting script against the wall, then headed for the airport. Hellman mused to me on December 4, 1998, that this behavior says a lot about Corman: "He may have very strong ideas, he may have very strong emotions, but the overriding thing is going to be the bottom line, which is whether he's going to make or lose money. And he's not going to cancel the picture after putting that much money into it."

But *Cockfighter,* despite impressively gritty work by Hellman and veteran character actor Warren Oates, was to be one of Corman's biggest miscalculations. He arranged for a world premiere screening in Atlanta, then discovered that most Georgians view cockfighting as an embarrassment. Vocal opposition by the American Society for the Prevention of Cruelty to Animals to the movie's on-camera treatment of chickens didn't help. The public stayed away, and it was clear that something drastic had to be done immediately. Joe Dante related to me how Corman phoned him with a concrete plan of action: "We're going to take the sex scenes from *Private Duty Nurses* [1971], and we're going to take the dynamite truck chase from *Night Call Nurses* [1972], and we're gonna cut 'em all together in a one-minute montage. And I want you to cut it into the movie right when Warren Oates goes to bed and turns the lights out. And that will be a dream sequence. . . . Put all this stuff in the trailer, and now we're going call it *Born to Kill.*" Later, other titles were tried, including *Wild Drifter* and *Gamblin' Man.* But by any other name, *Cockfighter* remained one of Corman's rare box-office flops. Director Paul Bartel notes, "It cured him of trying to make art films. It was cheaper to buy them from Europe, for very little down."

Big Bad Mama (1974) was less ambitious and more successful. Taking a light-hearted look at the terrain already covered by 1970's *Bloody Mama* with Shelley Winters, the film starred Angie Dickinson as a lusty, luscious Depression-era widow who, with her two nubile daughters, turns to a life of crime. This was Roger's highest-budgeted film to date. Due largely to the cost of its star power, it came in at $450,000. Dickinson's freewheeling nude scenes with William Shatner and newcomer Tom Skerritt drew customers to drive-ins all over the nation. Critics like Alan R. Howard *(Hollywood Reporter)* praised the movie's vitality and visual flair.

Corman's biggest hit by far of the mid-1970s was the outrageous *Death Race 2000* (1975). This began as his attempt to scoop *Rollerball* (1975), a much-hyped, expensive United Artists production starring James Caan, in which a futuristic society is dominated by a lethal game. On December 1, 1998, I spoke at length to Paul Bartel, who explained to me the thinking behind Corman's own project: "It was very important to him to be the David against the studio Goliath, and to come up with a cheap version that could be marketed along the same lines as some megaproduction." First Corman purchased "The Racer," a story by science-fiction writer Ib Melchior in which drivers score points by running over pedestrians. After some false starts by others, Chuck Griffith wrote the script. David Carradine signed on to play a masked national hero named "Frankenstein," and Bartel (b. 1938) was hired for about $5,000 to direct his second feature.

What attracted Bartel to the project was its implicit black humor. The problem was that Corman expected a serious action film. Virtually everyone connected with *Death Race 2000* remembers its original version, described for me by Joe Dante as "a real pop-art masterpiece before Roger got to it." It seems that Corman, according to the account I was told, upon hearing the laughs at the sneak preview, decided the picture was silly and needed to be rescued. Bartel was removed from the post-production process; Corman entered the editing room himself to delete gags and add additional gore. No wonder Bartel sounds bitter today when he generalizes about Corman as producer: "That was an important part of every production—dismissing the director who had betrayed the film, and then saving it. Roger was the one who saved the movies."

When *Death Race 2000* got its first rave reviews from hip critics, Corman merely assumed they were Bartel's cronies. Later, as it racked up $4.8 million in rentals (according to *Weekly Variety* for January 7, 1976), he decided not to argue with success. In 1978 he starred Carradine again in a sequel of sorts, *Deathsport*, directed by Henry Suso and Allan Arkush, which was an action film devoid of intentional humor. Bartel theorizes that he did so "with the idea of showing what *Death Race* could have been." It is *Death Race 2000*, however, that remains the cult classic. The *Hollywood Reporter* for July 13–19, 1999, announced that a high-profile remake is currently in the works. Following negotiations with Corman, director Paul Anderson (1995's *Mortal Kombat*, 1997's *Event Horizon*) is now developing *Death Race 3000* for Paramount Pictures. Superstar Tom Cruise will produce and is slated to play the leading role.

• • •

Aside from the fact that Roger Corman took control of *Death Race 2000* away from him, Paul Bartel has one more reason to be disgruntled. Bartel told me on December 1, 1998, that when their original deal was struck, Roger offered him a profit share. Later, according to Bartel, when he broached the subject, Corman shrugged "that he hadn't been serious when he said that, and that the accounting would be much too complicated." If this story is added to that which New World's sales manager Frank Moreno detailed earlier, a pattern seems to emerge.

Nonetheless, it is true that with Corman, some promises do get kept. For example, David Carradine emphasized to me that he duly got his piece of the financial participation on *Death Race 2000*, though he was wise enough to have this spelled out in his contract. Writer-director Larry Brand, who was paid nothing up front for his services as a director but received a moderate back-end payment when *The Drifter* (1988) went into profit, insists that Corman is frugal but honorable: "He would never attempt to renege on a deal." Still, even though a number of former staffers swear they've always been treated fairly where money was concerned, tales of promises seemingly overlooked and payments apparently forgotten continue to surface. Director Joe Dante puts the matter in perspective: "I'm sure he's reneged on a lot of stuff. But he probably meant it when he said it." Evidently, for Corman, selective memory can be a convenient out.

There's no question that Corman likes being known as a man whose word is his bond. And few would deny that his actions toward those persons he hires are basically well intended. But despite the fact that he's capable of the unexpected generous gesture, he sometimes cannot resist—out of ingrained thrift—trying to keep all the marbles for himself. He seems to be ruled by a reflex that often will not let him share the fruits of his (and everyone else's) labors.

Many Corman veterans agree that, essentially, part of what attracts Corman to money is the gamesmanship involved in getting and holding on to it. Director Paul Bartel affirms this point of view: "I always thought that even more than money, taking advantage of people was the objective for him, [because] that was proof that he was winning and everybody else was losing." This "Gotcha!" side of Corman's personality is also emphasized by a recent staffer, who is convinced that Corman would gladly sacrifice ten dollars if someone else would lose twenty dollars as a consequence. Such sentiments are harsh, but they capture the spirit of the film that Corman has said contains his all-time favorite ending, one that he himself dictated to writer Chuck Griffith. *The Creature from the Haunted Sea* (1961) closes with the monster, still unvanquished, sitting on a chest of gold on the ocean floor. Corman speaks of this as possibly his most personal screen effort. He clearly identifies with the creature, whom he describes in detail to conclude his autobiography: "The skeletons of all the people in the picture are scattered around him and he's picking his teeth. . . . The monster wins."

· · ·

Amassing money may have been Roger Corman's favorite game, but it was not his only interest. During the 1970s he had several opportunities to indulge the engineer side of his psyche through major construction projects. In 1973 he and Julie bought an oceanview lot on San Onofre Drive in Brentwood, just west of Beverly Hills, and then hired noted architect Cliff May to design their new abode. The result was dramatic, though some viewers called it sterile. The nearly 5,000-square-foot house—perched rather precariously on the lip of a canyon—featured large expanses of glass, a fifty-foot living room with lofty ceilings, and clean, contemporary lines throughout.

As a modern-art devotee (he once chose to meet Bob Rehme for a business discussion in a gallery of New York's Guggenheim Museum), Corman oversaw every aspect of the building and decorating process. Yet his enthusiasm for good design did not stand in the way of his passion for frugality. He was constantly asking the builders to cut corners, and when it came time to hang art on the walls, it was not in his nature to pay top dollar. Peter Jamison, the art director on 1974's *Big Bad Mama,* was hired to do huge minimalist paintings for the Corman home; later a UCLA art student executed boldly geometric Ellsworth Kelly–type canvases to decorate the walls of Corman's new office. (Former assistant Ginny Nugent recalled for me in a telephone conversation on March 31, 1998, that, for a special occasion, Julie Corman gave her husband a genuine Ellsworth Kelly. He was furious at the expense involved, but cheered up considerably when it appreciated in value.)

Corman's new two-story office building, on busy San Vicente Boulevard in the heart of Brentwood's commercial strip, was not intended as a showplace. Built for $750,000 in 1976 by Beach Dickerson, the sometime actor who had also served as contractor on the San Onofre Drive home, it is modest and utilitarian, to put it as kindly as possible. Picture a dilapidated structure with a leaking roof, cramped hallways, a steep staircase, and no lobby to speak of. Add a profusion of movie posters, juxtaposing Ingmar Bergman's *Autumn Sonata* (1978) with standard Concorde genre fare like *The Terror Within* (1988). Then imagine decades-old scripts piled carelessly on a once beige carpet that has not been changed in twenty years, and you have a sense of Roger Corman's business surroundings. (In late August 1999, a Concorde staffer shared with me the astounding news that the walls were being painted and that plans were afoot to install new carpeting. This stab at refurbishing the office environment is so out-of-character for Roger that his employees are still pondering what it means.)

I remember attending a meeting with Corman in 1987. It was held on the Sunset Strip, in a brand-new high-rise owned by Carolco Pictures. Carolco was then flush, on the strength of the *Rambo* movie series, and its premises were designer-chic. Roger glanced around at the profusion of marble and glass, then said to me rather wistfully, "I have a building too." On September 25, 1998, I shared this memory with producer Brad Krevoy, who commented, "The great irony of that story is he still has his building. And those guys from Carolco went bankrupt and had to sell theirs." So there's definitely something to be said for frugality in the Hollywood business world.

● ● ●

Beach Dickerson relates that Corman tried to involve his wife Julie in the various building projects, but she wasn't much interested. On May 2, 1975, about the time that their new residence was finished, she gave birth to the first of their children, a daughter. An announcement in *Boxoffice* on May 12 listed the newborn's name as Aimee. This error probably reflects the long, arduous process that went into choosing a name for each Corman offspring. For weeks after the birth, the office staff was polled about possible choices for the new arrival. Legend has it that when the name Catherine Corman was at last unveiled, someone joked that it would look good on a marquee. At this, Roger turned grave, then said, "Let's think of it as a working title."

A year later, on May 18, 1976, Corman finally had the son he'd been hoping for. The moniker eventually selected was Roger Martin (he has always been called by both names). A brief story in the *Los Angeles Herald Examiner* for September 29, 1977, mentions a third child, born on August 3 of that year. This account goes on to explain that the infant is still nameless, because the parents can't agree: " 'But I have to name my son before I start my next production,' laughs Roger." Not until April 24, 1978, did *Variety* formally introduce Brian William Corman to its readers. An endearing profile of the family, full of lively photos of Corman romping with his toddlers, was published in the *Los Angeles Times Home Magazine* for October 22, 1978. Here the filmmaker expounds on his style of intelligent parenthood. He explains that he has assembled a large library of books on child-rearing, and that "I correspond with child psychologists trying to keep up with current techniques of child development." Corman stresses that because he himself was raised in a close-knit family, "an intense, lovingly involved relationship at home seems very natural to me."

But Corman's "lovingly involved" relationship with his progeny would develop over time into something that seemed far more complex: a blend of obsessive interest and cool detachment that hinted at rough sailing when the toddlers became teenagers. From the first, Roger was trying out parenting theories. There was a special crib from Germany, heartbeat tapes, and elaborate sensory-stimulation experiments. Home bedrooms were painted yellow to promote the children's capacity for intelligence, until (according to former assistant Ginny Nugent) Catherine protested at age six. Employees from the late 1970s recall how Corman would scrutinize the kids' early utterings and drawings: he proudly reported to a staffer that "Roger Martin drew a black gun and Catherine drew a pretty yellow flower." At an early age, each youngster was assigned a separate tutor. Clark Henderson, who from 1981 to 1983 headed New World's post-production team, has spoken to me wryly of Corman's penchant for investing in every possible educational device, "like somehow the kids wouldn't grow up smart if he didn't do that—or smart enough." But Corman, famous for being frugal both with his wealth and his emotions, was doubtless showing love (in his own fashion) by spending money.

Because the three children were frequent visitors over the years to the New World office on San Vicente Boulevard, their exploits assumed mythic proportions among Corman's staff. Though Catherine was widely considered angelic, and Brian, at this stage, remained a shadow of his slightly older brother, Roger Martin struck everyone from the start as a force to be reckoned with. For instance, Joe Dante was in the screening room watching dailies of *Grand Theft Auto* (1977) when the toddler, sitting on his daddy's lap, began to chant in a soft singsong, "Money-money-money-money. Money-money-money-money." "Apparently," says Dante, "they had either taught the child, or the child had figured out on his own, that a good word to say around Daddy was 'money.'"

While some of the legendary antics of Corman's brood over the years cannot be verified, many on the Corman payroll have experienced Roger Martin's penchant for mischief. He teased one screenwriter by announcing that his firing was imminent. Anna Roth, whose job as Roger's assistant included chauffeuring the Corman kids, remembers Roger Martin suddenly grabbing the wheel of the moving car and pretending to act out a battle scene. His fondness over the years for power plays has reminded more than one observer of his father. On November 12, 1998, writer-actor Daryl

Haney summed it up: "You feel that certain things that are half suppressed in Roger were fully bloomed in his offspring."

• • •

It's fair to wonder about Julie Corman's role, both in the rearing of the children and the running of New World Pictures. Old-timers who have known Roger since the 1950s tend to feel that in Julie he has found the perfect mate. Beach Dickerson said to me on October 2, 1998, "She is exactly what he wants. She is his own image, what he created." This perception of Julie as someone molded to Corman's specifications, like the proverbial Bride of Frankenstein, cannot be terribly comfortable for her; perhaps it has contributed to her sometimes prickly emotions around the office.

Those who have observed the couple over the decades have always felt some sympathy for Julie's delicate position. A capable, ambitious woman with a genuine love of good literature, she is torn between trying to fit into Corman's world, and working to maintain her own autonomy. In the early days, when Joe Dante used to spot her with Siegfried Kracauer's *Theory of Film* under her arm, she was clearly determined to absorb what her spouse had to teach about the art of filmmaking. In practical terms this meant trying to graft an ultrathrifty streak onto a basically generous nature.

Paul Bartel told me of one Christmas early in the marriage when Julie struggled to find the right gift for Corman's mother. Knowing that Anne Corman enjoyed walking, she decided to give her a pedometer. According to Bartel, "Mrs. Corman's reaction was that this was a foolish waste of money, and she gave it back." Such incidents obviously persuaded Julie that frugality was the highest of virtues. Bartel's description of Julie as a fledgling producer—"She kept trying to outcheap Roger, often without knowing what she was talking about"—is echoed by several crew members from her early productions, which include *Crazy Mama* (1975), *The Lady in Red* (1979), and *Saturday the 14th* (1981).

Julie Corman's love of babies and children is quite evident. Attorney Alida Camp, who produced films for Corman's Concorde–New Horizons Pictures in the early 1990s, remembers Julie's graciousness when Camp's son Seth was born. Camp often discussed child-rearing with Julie, who made it clear that Roger's style of tough talk and sky-high expectations was not hers. Camp notes a key distinction: that Julie was more naturally demonstrative with the children, while Roger tended to focus on their accomplishments.

But Julie was not about to forfeit her career goals for her children's sake. In 1983, when the youngsters were eight, seven, and six, she was interviewed by Gwen Jones of the *Los Angeles Herald Examiner*. To Jones she explained that whatever was most pressing got her immediate attention: "My family knows that when I'm in production I'm not available, but that I will return." When reporters asked about her ability to strike a balance, Julie was inclined to bristle. In the Jones interview, she anticipated the question of how she juggled career and family before it was even brought up. She made it quite clear that for her such inquiries were fundamentally sexist: "No one asks my husband how he does it."

Julie told Jones, "I think you should say that Roger takes care of the children." When Jones asked if that was true, Julie answered, "That's what he tells me. He says he does it all." The comment smacks of sarcasm, but she quickly made amends by noting that Roger really did spend a great deal of time with their offspring. Still, an undercurrent of frustration runs through this interview, as well as all the others from the 1980s that touch on Julie's complex home life.

Parenting, of course, can be an exasperating business. Spouses, especially those with strong personalities, are rarely in complete accord as to what their child needs to grow into a happy, healthy adult. No wonder, then, that the Corman children's formative years were a time of great tension for everyone concerned. But the marriage survived, as did the children. And so did the members of the office staff, though they frequently bore the brunt of what was going on in the Corman household.

Chapter 9

PIRANHAS AND OTHER FISH STORIES

You work for Roger [Corman] until he can't afford you anymore.

JOHN SAYLES, director-screenwriter, 1981

IN 1977 CHRISTIAN BLACKWOOD produced and directed *Roger Corman: Hollywood's Wild Angel,* a documentary so pleasing to its subject that Corman ended up distributing it. The 60-minute picture added mightily to the filmmaker's mystique by interviewing directors who had used their Corman experience as a stepping stone to fame and fortune. It also promoted the image of New World as "Hollywood's hottest studio," a place where the exploitation films of old were rapidly giving way to bigger, braver pictures. Though the documentary did not spotlight a single woman, and though it focused almost entirely on directors-in-the-making, it attracted young hopefuls of both genders and various backgrounds, all of whom sought at New World the chance to spread their creative wings.

Certainly, the late 1970s was a time when creativity flourished at the company, which was then promoting itself as "America's Biggest Independent." (The reasoning was that AIP had entered the ranks of the major Hollywood studios.) A tough little 1976 thriller called *Jackson County Jail,* starring Yvette Mimieux and newcomer Tommy Lee Jones, was hailed by Vincent Canby in the *New York Times* as "filmmaking of relentless energy and harrowing excitement that recall the agitprop melodramas of the thirties." Canby's high regard for the New World product line is evident in his comment that *Jackson County Jail* "has the drive, movement, and economy of narrative that are the marks of Corman films, good and bad."

Despite New World's growing credibility with the critics, moviemaking could still seem like a game. When Jon Davison, Allan Arkush, and Joe Dante approached Corman with the idea of making their own first film, they promised it would be New World's cheapest picture. The idea was to borrow footage from past New World releases, shoot some new material, and assemble it all into a wacky story about a bottom-of-the-barrel movie company named Miracle Pictures. ("If it's a good picture, it's a Miracle!") Davison produced, and Arkush and Dante were allowed out of the editing room long enough to take turns directing the satiric feature, which was dubbed *Hollywood Boulevard* (1976). The cast was populated with Corman regulars, including Candice Rialson, Mary Woronov, and Dick Miller. Director Jonathan Kaplan, writer Chuck Griffith, and journalists Todd McCarthy, and Joe McBride could be spotted in smaller roles. Paul Bartel stood out as a pompous Erich Von Stroheim–type who spoofs the Corman style by announcing that "in this film we are combining the myth of Romeo and Juliet with high-speed car action and a sincere plea for international atomic controls in our time."

Fortunately, Corman enjoyed the joke. He also enjoyed the fact that this 83-minute feature—made in ten days on a $70,000 budget—couldn't help but make money. Twenty-two years later, Arkush reminisced with me about the evening the movie premiered in a theater on the real Hollywood Boulevard: he and his two colleagues took turns photographing each other beneath the marquee. This seemed, at the time, all the reward they needed. Davison noted, "It wasn't like we were connected to any sort of larger movie business." Dante agreed, "It was a separate little enclave that we were happy to be part of." Amazingly, *Hollywood Boulevard* lives on, at least in the memory of some of its devoted fans. American Cinematheque's Sasha Alpert reports that when Quentin Tarantino was interviewed by her colleague Todd McCarthy, he named *Hollywood Boulevard* "one of my very favorite movies about the making of movies."

In Blackwood's 1977 Corman documentary, one upcoming co-production was used to symbolize the bright future of New World Pictures. This was *I*

Never Promised You a Rose Garden (1977), based on Joanne Greenberg's well-known 1964 novel about a young girl confined to a mental institution. The film was approached by Roger and company with the seriousness that befits a prestige project. Bibi Andersson—revered as a member of Ingmar Bergman's cinematic stock company—played the kindly psychiatrist, and a promising young actress, Kathleen Quinlan, was cast in the difficult central role. The drama was directed by Anthony Page, a veteran of the British stage, making his big-screen debut. Of the producers who shared credit on the film, Edgar J. Scherick has gone on to become a major player in the motion-picture industry, with his name on such admired small films as *Mrs. Soffel* (1984) and *Rambling Rose* (1991).

The finished product did gain a modicum of respect. At the Golden Globe Awards ceremony held in January 1978, *Rose Garden* vied for a Best Drama statuette, and Quinlan was a nominee for Best Actress. Later, Hollywood veterans Lewis John Carlino and Gavin Lambert garnered an Oscar nomination for their screenplay, but lost to Alvin Sargent, who wrote *Julia*. Although Corman partnered with Scherick and others to make *Rose Garden* on what, for him, was a grand scale, Joe Dante is convinced that "they just didn't have enough money to do the movie properly. It's a movie all about a fantasy world that they just couldn't afford to create." *Rose Garden*'s grosses were touted in a *Boxoffice* ad as $7,455,688, on a budget estimated by *Variety* as $3 million. *Variety*'s Joseph McBride figured Corman's financial contribution as under $750,000, so he surely made some money. The film, however, lacked the staying power that denotes a classic, and a discouraged Corman returned to doing what he did best.

Corman was far happier making *Eat My Dust!* (1976), an action comedy that featured a little romance and a *lot* of car crashes. The film had instant teen appeal, because it starred Ron Howard, then extremely popular from *American Graffiti* (1973) and the TV sitcom series *Happy Days* (1974–84). When we spoke in January 1999, Howard explained how he came to make a Corman movie. In 1976 he was twenty-two years old and was trying to launch a second show-business career as a director. He had studied at the USC Film School, but could not convince the studios to back a script he had co-written. In accepting the lead role in *Eat My Dust!*, Howard struck a deal with Roger that guaranteed him the chance to write and direct (as well as star in) a follow-up project. Corman eventually decided the follow-up would be another teen car-crash comedy in the spirit of *Eat My Dust!* It would be called *Grand Theft Auto* (1977), because this title had scored well in one of the infamous Corman polls.

Of course, working for Roger meant accepting Roger's standards. Though *Grand Theft Auto* had one of New World's higher budgets (about $750,000), conditions could still be grim. On location in the southern California desert town of Victorville, second-unit director Allan Arkush remembers that the catered meals were so dreadful that Ron Howard's wife Cheryl ended up cooking for everyone. And when Howard found himself short of extras for a climactic destruction-derby sequence, his appeals to the boss went unheeded. But Corman told the discouraged young director in fatherly fashion, "If you do a good job on this picture, you'll never have to work for me again." (His own riposte obviously pleased Corman, because he was to repeat it more than once. When Corman first heard Mark Governor's score for the 1989 remake of *The Masque of the Red Death,* he patted the young composer on the shoulder and said, "That was a good job. If you continue to do work like this, you'll never have to work for me again." Others have heard the line under similar conditions.)

Ron Howard soon learned to shoot in the Roger Corman style, achieving at least twenty camera setups a day. (Major Hollywood productions average between eight and twelve.) Corman crews were always vying for the record of most setups in a single day. *Weekly Variety*'s Charles Schreger reported that at one point during the four-week shoot, Howard got in ninety-one.

But the main lesson Howard learned from Corman involved tailoring the film in the editing room for maximum audience appeal. Roger was then using a testing service through which preview audiences could register their likes and dislikes by turning a dial near their seats. The fact that Corman didn't bother to check the demographics of his "guinea pigs" made the output highly unscientific: Howard recalls groups of grandmotherly ladies watching his slightly raunchy teen flick. Still, Corman took the results very seriously. Ron told me, "We'd look at those graphs, Roger would spread them out on the floor, and he just kept trying to cut out the stuff between the peaks. Which would be a little ludicrous at times, but I have used . . .

a similarly ruthless philosophy on every film I've done since then. It really taught me a lot—that as a result of that honing and shaping, there is no question that the movie was becoming more and more enjoyable to the audiences." Today, though his success with such projects as *Parenthood* (1989), *Backdraft* (1991), and *Apollo 13* (1995) has earned Howard the right of final cut, he still relies heavily on preview audiences to tell him where his films need work.

Grand Theft Auto was a big moneymaker, earning $2.5 million in rentals (according to *Weekly Variety* for January 4, 1978). Nor was its success confined to theatrical bookings. Once when Howard was visiting New World, Corman told him the picture had just been sold to CBS Television for $1.1 million on the strength of Howard's *Happy Days* connection. A clause in Howard's contract as the star of the film would give him a percentage of the sale. Roger acknowledged Howard's windfall with his trademark grin, saying, "That makes your 7½ percent look pretty good. . . . And it makes my 92½ percent look *goddamn* good." Though today Howard calls Corman "a bit of a character," he considers his membership in that unofficial alumni Corman group, "a real badge of honor." From the first, says Howard, "I was very proud of those roots, and I've always remained proud of them."

Howard had become a New World director because his film-school background and his box-office clout made him a potent combination in Hollywood. In the Concorde era, Corman has given directing opportunities to other name actors, among them Talia Shire *(One Night Stand)* and Andrew Stevens *(The Terror Within II)*. Stevens's deal, like Howard's, required him to both write and star in the sequel to a profitable Corman film in which he had played the central role. To land a Corman directing gig without the benefit of a film-school education, it clearly helps to be a notable movie or TV name.

But Corman has also allowed minor actors, writers, and office personnel to become directors, largely because of his quixotic faith in their abilities. Howard R. Cohen described for me his conversation with Julie Corman, just after her husband had agreed to let him direct *Saturday the 14th* (1981). Julie told Cohen in friendly fashion, "I know it's going to go to your head, now that Roger's going to let you be a big director. Here's the truth. Directing is very easy for Roger. He thinks anybody can do it. And if he likes you he'll let you do it." Julie's words certainly undercut the notion that Roger possesses a special ability to spot directors-in-the-making. His famous eye for talent is also disputed by skeptics who point to the law of averages: If you give enough people a start, some of them are bound to make it big. Certainly, several of his protégés have turned out to be dismal flops; others are no better than mediocre. Over the years, however, Corman has often been quick to recognize those with the brains and determination to succeed at any cost, and that can be considered a talent in itself.

•   •   •

In 1975 a blockbuster called *Jaws* changed Hollywood forever. The emergence of *Jaws* (which had a production budget of about $12 million and grossed some $470 million worldwide) marked the moment when, as director Adam Simon puts it, "A movies and B movies switched places." Simon explains that throughout Hollywood history, the studios' biggest budgets were traditionally devoted to emotional dramas, historical epics, and adaptations of novels. Action, science fiction, and other genre features were made on the cheap. Today, however, the reverse is true, with budgets at or near $100 million reserved for genre movies like *Armageddon* (1998) and *Wild Wild West* (1999). Other examples include *Godzilla* (1998) and *The Haunting* (1999), both of them remakes of films made four decades earlier, at one-tenth the cost. Personal stories and serious drama now survive mostly outside the studio system, on the indie circuit, and at film festivals. Simon credits Steven Spielberg and George Lucas with "making heaven and earth change places," because they were among the first to apply A-minus level skills and marketing to what had formerly been drive-in fare. As a result, the studios discovered "they could make money worldwide on a scale that Hollywood had never made before."

The rise of the B movie to respectability and big box office clearly owes something to Roger Corman. Bill Davidson's 1975 profile of the "King of Schlock" in the *New York Times Magazine* speaks of the "ultimate compliment" paid to Corman by an unnamed executive at Universal Studios, which had released *Jaws*. "What was *Jaws*," this executive asked rhetorically, "but an old Corman monster-from-the-deep flick—plus about $12 million more for production and advertising?" Roger was immensely pleased with this reference, and still mentions it frequently. Over the years, the attribution of the quote has changed. When he was interviewed by Jan Golab of *KCET Magazine* in November 1988, and by the *Hollywood Reporter*'s Kirk Honey-cutt on May 14, 1998, he proudly cited a nonexistent *New York Times* review in which Vincent Canby called *Jaws* "a big-budget Roger Corman film." Canby may not have written this, but the phrase still contains some truth. Former Concorde screenwriter Robert King points out that in today's Hollywood, dominated by action-oriented filmmakers like Michael Bay, Jan de Bont, Roland Emmerich, and John Woo, "there's nowhere you can go that *isn't* Corman."

When *Jaws* first made its big splash, however, Corman's chief thought was how quickly he could devise a low-budget rip-off. The major coup was snagging a young writer who had published fiction but never written a produced screenplay. John Sayles (b. 1950), who as a boy had been fond of monster and giant cockroach movies, attacked the assignment with zest. His first goal was to craft an effective genre piece, but (with Roger's blessing) his script evolved into what many call an ironic commentary on standard monster-from-the-deep fare. *Piranha* (1978) was praised by hip critics for its covert sociopolitical message; in *Take One* magazine, reviewer Bruce Kawin quipped that "Brecht would have loved it."

When we chatted in February 1999, Sayles told me he had learned storytelling structure from Corman and Frances Doel: "When do you need suspense rather than action? ... When do you need comedy to give people a break from the suspense? That's what I found that Roger and Frances were very good at." He also discovered how to write for a Corman budget, and how to approach a script in terms of its marketable elements. ("How could you advertise this film?") Such practical experience served him well in 1980, when he wrote and directed his own first feature. As a result of writing New World's *Piranha*, *The Lady in Red* (1979), and *Battle Beyond the Stars* (1980), Sayles had accumulated $40,000 to put toward *Return of the Secaucus Seven*, a film in which "I started with very little money, and said, 'What can I do well?'"

Secaucus Seven, which features a group of college activists who reunite ten years later, is often hailed as a forerunner to the major studio release *The Big Chill* (1983). It kicked off Sayles's long filmmaking career with a flourish: Since 1980 he has directed a dozen movies, most of which he has also written, edited, and had a hand in producing. Unique among Corman graduates,

Sayles has remained far removed from the studio system. Like Corman himself, he is a true independent, determined to be free of outside control. So it's not surprising that the two men respect one another.

But their standards are not the same. Though both admire quality, Corman never strays from the dictates of the bottom line. As Sayles told me, "The difference between [Corman] and popular filmmakers like George Lucas and Steven Spielberg is that they would go into debt, at least when they were younger and needed to, to make the picture better." Roger, of course, would never consider this option. It comes down to the principle on which virtually all Corman alumni agree—that Roger is a great businessman who once had the potential to make great art.

·   ·   ·

Piranha did well at the box office, thanks in part to the savvy work of director Joe Dante. Corman promptly rewarded Dante with another directing assignment, *Humanoids from the Deep* (1980). Unfortunately, in Joe's words, "it was the same movie I just did. I don't think that people usually turned down pictures that Roger offered them." Thus ended the formal association between Dante and Corman that had begun back in 1973. Joe clarified for me, "It wasn't a conscious decision to leave Roger. It was just that after a while people noticed you, and pretty soon they started offering you actual dollars to do actual projects that didn't have to be made in ten days." When we spoke in November 1998, former New World sales exec Frank Moreno proposed a theory that Corman's refusal to pay people what they're worth has the effect of pushing them out the door, thus freeing him up to bring in the next generation of young hopefuls who will work for nearly nothing.

Several former longtime employees have mentioned to me Roger's cordial send-off when they left to make films on their own. For instance, when assistant Anna Roth was hired by Francis Ford Coppola, Corman took her to lunch, obviously pleased to see two of his alumni connect. Yet, when I spoke to former business-affairs chief Paul Almond, he noted Corman's occasionally ambivalent behavior; if employees stick around too long, Roger becomes impatient for them to move on and better themselves. However, as in Almond's own case, when they unexpectedly announce their departure, the boss can feel slightly hurt. In my own experience as a member of the

Corman team, I have seen key employees who have indicated their plans to leave, being subjected to Roger's anger and suspicion. Never once, however, has Corman tried to retain a valued staffer by matching another company's offer. He'd far prefer that his graduates go shine elsewhere, trusting that their glory will reflect back on him.

• • •

When Joe Dante turned down *Humanoids from the Deep*, the directing job went to New World veteran Barbara Peters (sometimes billed as Barbara Peeters). Unfortunately, Corman decided the finished film needed more nudity. His solution was to dismiss Peters, much as he had done with Paul Bartel, and add footage hastily shot by others. John Sayles described this addition for me: "There's a blonde woman who's attacked in a tent, and there's a brunette woman with much larger breasts who runs out of the tent after she's attacked." As reported in the *Los Angeles Herald Examiner* for April 21, 1980, leading actress Ann Turkel unsuccessfully petitioned the Screen Actors Guild to halt the film's release, on the grounds that it bore no resemblance to the motion picture she was hired to make. The whole matter quickly blew over, but not before the *Los Angeles Times* had touched on the controversy as part of a long analysis of women's place in the film industry. At this point Roger wrote a letter to the editor, protesting the *Times*'s underlying implication that he was a male chauvinist. In his own defense, he pointed to his "record of employing more qualified women in responsible positions than any other producer in Hollywood."

It was typical of Corman to excuse himself based on his reputation as an equal-opportunity employer. While his strides in this area have always been impressive, it's also true that the T & A ("tits and ass") quotient of his films has continued to rise over the decades. The 1998 documentary *Some Nudity Required*, which casts a cold eye on the portrayal of women in today's B movies, has caused many alumni to ponder exactly why Corman gravitates to sexually suggestive screen material. When Roger penciled into scripts, "Breast nudity possible here?" or asked directors to reshoot sex scenes for maximum exposure, were his motives pragmatic or prurient? One alumna from the New World period, Gale Anne Hurd, expressed to me her firm conviction "that he saw it from purely an economic perspective—which is, nudity sells."

Laurette Hayden served as Corman's assistant at New World in the early 1980s. Hayden, whose desk sat directly outside Corman's office with its always-open double doors, assured me that her boss's conduct was blameless when scantily dressed actresses arrived for casting sessions. She admitted, however, that part of her own job was to help with "breast checks," in which leading ladies were asked to bare themselves above the waist to prove that their bosom was suitably photogenic. Director Jim Wynorski painted for me a remarkable picture of one Christmas Eve when he, Laurette, and Roger lounged in the office, sipping champagne. They were waiting for two Manila-bound cuties to show up and (in Wynorski's term) "pop their tops." At the time, the very ladylike Hayden did not question the propriety of what she was asked to do. Gradually, however, after working on Corman movies like *Slumber Party Massacre* (1982), she came to feel that the New World attitude toward women and sex was tougher to justify, and that it was "harder to keep a sense of humor."

A sense of humor and an ability to laugh off bad taste were prized commodities when it came to plugging New World films. The official *Piranha* press kit advised exhibitors to create "exciting pre-publicity" by leaving dead piranhas on the banks of local lakes and streams: "Promote community interest and fear by organizing groups (Boy Scouts, citizen volunteers, etc.) to guard against the 'coming onslaught.' Give enterprising kids in your area a few bucks to make themselves scarce for a few days. Watch your grosses soar!!" This tongue-in-cheek approach, which bears the personal stamp of Jon Davison, was later to be replaced in New World publicity materials by a more serious form of hype.

But even when the marketing strategies became more earnest, Corman employees continued to regard their product line with a kind of gallows humor. Most of them would agree that the only way to stay sane while working for Roger Corman was to feel you were putting something over on a rather gullible public. At the same time, women in the Corman organization occasionally wondered if the joke was on them.

(L-R) Director Roger Corman and wife Julia arrive at the Huston Gala Cocktail Reception for the announcement of The Huston School of Film and Digital Media held at Trader Vic's in Beverly Hills, Los Angeles, California on February 27, 2003. *(Photo by Fraser Harrison/Getty Images). Credit: Getty Images.*

Bruce Dern and Peter Fonda in *The Wild Angels*. © *John Springer Collection/CORBIS.*

Peter Fonda Playing Guitar in *The Wild Angels*. © *John Springer Collection/CORBIS.*

From 1960 to 1965, Corman made eight adaptations of stories by Edgar
A. Poe starring Vincent Price, including *The Raven, The Masque of the Red
Death,* and *The Fall of the House of Usher.* Above, Price and Elizabeth
Shepherd in *Tomb of Ligeia.* © *OHLINGER JERRY/CORBIS SYGMA.*

Retrospective: Actor Vincent Price. © *OHLINGER JERRY/CORBIS SYGMA*.

A portrait of the American director Roger Corman and the American producer Samuel Z Arkoff. They worked together on many Egar Allen Poe films and on *Attack Of The Crab Monsters* and *The Last Woman On Earth*. © *Rufus F. Folkks/CORBIS.*

Producer Roger Corman on set of *Little Shop of Horrors*. © *Shelley Gazin/CORBIS.*

Dennis Hopper (L) and Roger Corman answer questions at a screening of the documentary *Easy Riders, Raging Bulls* followed by a questions and answers session with the filmmakers at the Egyptian Theatre on January 30, 2003 in Hollywood, California. *(Photo by Kevin Winter/Getty Images). Credit: Getty Images.*

Roger Corman with his Lifetime Achievement Award during the award ceremony of the First Annual American Film Marketing Association Honors Event on February 22, 2001. The award honors independent film-making and success after a lifetime of work. © *Reuters NewMedia Inc./CORBIS.*

Chapter 10

TO THE STARS

We're at the real growing-pain stage, in between the shift
from a one-man operation to a major corporation.

ROGER CORMAN, 1980

FOR THOSE WHO worked at the San Vicente Boulevard
headquarters in the late 1970s, when its paint was still fresh and its carpets
still clean, New World Pictures was a place full of energy and excitement.
Members of Roger Corman's staff, all of them passionate cinema buffs,
helped each other learn the ropes of low-budget filmmaking. After hours,
when the latest crisis had been averted, they might gather at someone's
home for wine, bridge, and movie talk. At times the camaraderie extended
to weekend softball games at a local park.

But the family feeling that marked this era was to be put to the test by a
new development. The overwhelming success of *Star Wars* (1977) convinced
Roger that he, too, should try an outer space screen epic. Prior to 1980, Corman movies had always been shot on practical locations, rather than on
soundstages. It was with science fiction in mind that Corman set about pur-
chasing the property that became his Venice, California, studio facility. *Battle Beyond the Stars*, intended as a "*Magnificent Seven* in outer space," was
filmed there in 1980. For this co-production with Orion Pictures, Corman
claimed in his 1990 memoir, he invested a whopping $2 million. The total
budget was reputed to be $5 million (though staffers from the period contend

it was somewhat less), and *Variety's* Lane Maloney records that the film quickly racked up over $11 million. True, *Battle Beyond the Stars* hardly approached *Star Wars* in terms of technological innovation, but it was a huge risk on Roger's part to rely so heavily on special-effects wizardry. The first gamble, of course, was the creation of a full-time studio in which to house an effects stage.

Paul Almond, functioning as New World's attorney, negotiated the purchase of the Hammond Lumber Company's lot and buildings on Venice's Main Street, about four miles from the Brentwood headquarters. Almond explained to me that the site, located just three blocks from the Pacific Ocean, fell under the jurisdiction of the California Coastal Commission. This meant he was required to placate a local community group comprised of aging hippies who were deathly afraid of gentrification. After lengthy wrangling, the group issued an ultimatum—that New World pledge not to modernize the buildings' shabby exteriors, nor to improve their looks in any way. Almond, a savvy negotiator, looked grave, then promised to see what he could do, in exchange for major concessions on other points. As he tells it, "I went back to Roger and said, 'I can close the deal but there's one really onerous condition. We can't modernize the outside of the buildings.' Roger looked at me, I looked at him, and we just burst into laughter."

For nearly two decades after the deal went into effect, the Corman studio still looked from the outside like a decaying lumberyard. For years the Hammond Lumber sign remained in place because Corman balked at paying for its removal, and so the occasional visitor would wander through in search of a two-by-four. The property, perhaps 50,000 square feet, or about half a city block, boasted three rather makeshift soundstages, one of them housed in a tin shed. (When Concorde made *Carnosaur* in 1993, Roger insisted that his dinosaurs be taller than the seventeen-foot *Tyrannosaurus rex* designed for Spielberg's *Jurassic Park*. Staffers pointed out the problem: Concorde's biggest soundstage had ceilings only sixteen feet high.) There was also a ramshackle wooden post-production building that had been sinking steadily for years, and was regarded with suspicion by the fire marshals.

The establishment of a studio, and the hiring of personnel to staff it, meant the start of a caste system that still persists. The creative decision-makers who worked in New World's main office tended to be Ivy Leaguers or Stanford University graduates with little practical filmmaking experience. Many of the editors, effects specialists, and production people housed at the studio acquired their skills at leading film schools like UCLA or New York University (NYU). Despite their scholastic credentials, these film school grads felt Roger regarded them as blue-collar. Inevitably, tension grew between the two factions. Studio types rarely fraternized comfortably with the office staff, whom they considered potential Corman spies.

It did not help that Roger expected his new studio team to save money by doing more with less. Though the workload was huge, he would issue outrageous fiats limiting the number of crewmembers and the types of equipment that could be used on a given job. So whenever Corman set foot on the studio lot, a primitive early-warning system swung into effect, giving workers time to hide the extra employees and such banned necessities as a coding machine for the editing room. By the time Deborah Brock ran post-production, a clever production manager had worked out a scheme whereby the words "Jennifer is here," delivered over a walkie-talkie, would let everyone know of the boss's arrival. Despite the need for such subterfuge, and despite the fact that studio employees could be subject to mass firings when Corman felt his payroll was getting out of hand, Brock actually pitied the staffers at the San Vicente headquarters. She told me on October 14, 1998, that she felt they faced far more pressure because they worked directly under Corman's nose.

• • •

Although Corman's visits were infrequent, those who worked at the Venice studio dealt with other obstacles. Because the shooting stages were never properly soundproofed, and because the studio was located directly under a flight path for Los Angeles International Airport, making a film could be nightmarish. Director Larry Brand recalls that "you're trying to shoot a period piece, and you've got planes and motorcycles zipping by." Also, the exhaustion that comes from working long hours with makeshift equipment sometimes took its toll: crew members made errors that could have been costly, or even dangerous. Gale Anne Hurd served as assistant production manager on *Battle Beyond the Stars*. She vividly described to me how "half the time it would be raining, and the roof leaked, and there'd be four inches of water on the ground, and people were using power tools while standing in the water. Thank God OSHA never came by, and thank God nobody died."

During the frantic pre-production period for the sci-fi epic, work went on nearly around-the-clock. (The studio boasted an army cot or two, and workers caught whatever sleep they could.) One day Hurd was going over costs and schedules with James Cameron, the film's new art director, when they heard a piercing scream. It seems a crew member kneeling on the floor had stuck a matte knife in his pocket, its blade protruding. A second man had tried to step over him, but the unseen blade had caught his leg, severing his femoral artery. Blood spurted dramatically, and the cut man was convinced he was going to die. Hurd told me, "Jim had the presence of mind to take his shirt off, make a tourniquet, tie it, and we both drove him to the hospital." Within hours, the wounded man was back on the set.

Twenty-six years old and largely self-taught, Cameron had talked his way onto the crew for *Battle Beyond the Stars* by promising to build a front-projection camera rig for inexpensive special-effects shots. Corman was unimpressed with his results, but Cameron rebounded into the position of model-maker, and then art director, devising sets out of little more than foam core, hot glue, gaffer's tape, and spraypaint. He had everyone collecting Styrofoam containers from McDonald's hamburgers—when spraypainted silver, these looked impressive lining the walls of a spacecraft corridor. Corman assistant Laurette Hayden describes how "if the actors should turn around quickly and slam into the wall, the whole thing would crumble. Then you had to go back and get more [hamburger] boxes."

Jim Cameron eventually directed second unit (including a "maggot rape scene") for Corman's 1981 science-fiction follow-up, *Galaxy of Terror*, which according to *Weekly Variety* earned $4 million in North American rentals. Corman then recommended Cameron be hired as the director of *Piranha II* (1981), which, despite its title, was not made by New World. In 1984, the year before they became husband and wife, Cameron and Gale Anne Hurd collaborated on a futuristic film of their own, *The Terminator*. She produced and he directed; the film's enormous success would launch both of them on their major Hollywood careers.

When Cameron had first arrived at New World Pictures in 1980, he brought along a college friend named Randy Frakes. Frakes (now a screenwriter, but then an effects specialist) worked side by side with Cameron, and so he was able to observe the conjunction of two of Hollywood's most interesting mavericks. As Frakes saw it, Cameron lacked the temperament to fit in comfortably at New World. Cameron's ambitious sets for *Battle Beyond the Stars* nearly killed him, because he micromanaged every detail. Says Frakes, "He hardly ever slept for six weeks straight. It's amazing the guy is still alive today." Though Cameron and Frakes tried pitching script ideas to story editor Frances Doel, their concepts were always too grandiose for the low-budget Corman environment. But Cameron attracted favorable notice from Roger because, in Frakes's terms, Jim is the kind of man who can always come up with a quick solution to the problem at hand. Frakes assured me that if Cameron had not gotten his break from Corman, he surely would have found it elsewhere: his fierce determination made success inevitable. Frakes concedes, however, "it *was* Corman who opened the door."

When the *Hollywood Reporter* named Gale Anne Hurd among 1998's fifty most powerful women in entertainment, she told an interviewer that the New World job had been her career turning point. Although Hurd and Cameron now have been divorced for many years, they remain in frequent professional contact. Hurd disclosed to me that prior to the March 23, 1998, Academy Award ceremony at Los Angeles' Shrine Auditorium, she urged him to thank Corman from the stage when he received his inevitable slew of Oscars for *Titanic*. Jim's failure to acknowledge the man who started them both on their way has caused her genuine regret. The question still remains, whether a talent like Cameron would have succeeded regardless. In Gale Anne's view, he "wouldn't have gotten a foot in the door, I don't think. To go from being a guy building spaceship models to art director to second-unit director in those three steps, that doesn't happen anywhere else."

• • •

While Corman's interest in film production would wax and wane through the years, there's no question that he was excited about *Battle Beyond the Stars*. Much of the picture's budget went toward visual-effects equipment, including an optical printer and an early version of a motion-control camera. Curiously, he entrusted his biggest-ever project to a first-time director. Jimmy T. Murakami, whose background was in animation and art direction, soon found himself overwhelmed, especially when it came to working with actors. Those on the set, like Randy Frakes, report that star Richard Thomas often took charge. Behind the scenes, Corman himself was literally calling the shots. Post-production specialist Clark Henderson shared with me his memories of *Battle Beyond the Stars*. It was his first film, and his job was to keep the "craft service" table stocked with tasty treats for cast and crew. One Sunday, while preparing for the next week of shooting, he witnessed Corman blocking out whole scenes for Murakami's benefit. Though Roger's tone was gentle and he was clearly not trying to humiliate his director, Murakami never directed another live-action feature for Corman or for anyone else.

While it was Corman's emotional commitment to *Battle Beyond the Stars* that caused him to step in and prevent Murakami from possibly foundering, this move also made the filmmaker, by now in his fifties, more volatile than ever. Henderson discloses that when a clumsy-looking special effect was screened for him at a mixing stage, Roger burst into a furious tirade that revealed his own paranoia: "What kind of stupid idea is this? This is sabotage. They're trying to get me!" As Henderson remembers it, Roger then flung something across the room, denting a wall. Most Corman employees have seen tantrums of this sort from time to time. Laurette Hayden once faced the task of having the large window in his office repaired after he threw his marble pen set through a pane of glass in a fit of rage. As she details, "The whole thing shattered and spewed onto San Vicente Boulevard. And he just looked at me, and very calmly said, 'Go call the glass people.' We never spoke about it after that."

The most dramatic display of Corman's temper came at a sneak preview. After *Battle Beyond the Stars* and its slightly cheaper follow-up, *Galaxy of Terror* (1981), Roger was no longer committed to science fiction on an ambitious scale. But he continued to borrow visual effects from these films for low-budget knockoffs. One such film was *Mutant*, also known as *Forbidden World* (1982). Corman and Julie attended the movie's sneak preview at the Culver Theatre in Culver City, California, along with some of the production staff and a visiting German director. Unfortunately, *Mutant* struck many in the blue-collar audience as hilarious; one man in particular had a loud, braying laugh that Roger felt was encouraging others.

Here I'm presenting Clark Henderson's version, as he related it to me on October 15, 1998, because he was at Roger's side during virtually the entire episode. (Others, including the film's director, Allan Holzman, corroborate the essential details.) Corman's first plan was to slip Laughing Boy a twenty-dollar bill in exchange for keeping quiet. Yet when he located the man in the last row of the theater, Roger instinctively lashed out, apparently striking him on the side of the head; Corman then prudently moved away, but after the movie was over the victim had his revenge. Henderson describes what happened under the old-fashioned marquee in front of the theater: "Before [Corman] got past that little ticket booth, the guy ran out with a . . . big popcorn container full of Coke, and poured it on Corman's head and all over him. Just drenched him in Coca-Cola." Corman started to swing; Julie desperately grabbed his arm; a burly theater manager half-nelsoned the assailant to the ground; some of Corman's sturdier staffers hustled their boss away. It was an episode that would quickly become legend.

•   •   •

The Culver Theatre incident suggests how seriously Corman takes his reputation and his product. While he normally keeps his emotions tightly in check, he can flare dangerously when he feels he has been made to look foolish. Corman is hardly proud of these unfortunate outbursts, and it's fair to guess that he views his own histrionics with alarm. Certainly, he dislikes emotional neediness in those around him. Surprisingly, though, I know of several cases in which he served as a calming influence on a young employee who was losing control on the job.

As the editor of *Death Race 2000* (1975), Tina Hirsch found her own work grinding to a halt because a co-worker she had fought against hiring had a drinking problem. She remembers how Corman came upon her as she was pacing furiously around the editing room, so angry she was loudly muttering obscenities. Said Hirsch, the normally genteel Corman "was red as a beet. I have never seen anybody so red in my life. . . . He couldn't believe he was hearing this [language] coming out of this dainty little girl." After she had calmed down, Corman reassured her that the offending co-worker would be terminated. And then, said Hirsch, "he gave me a bonus—unheard-of in the annals of the Corman world. He gave me a bonus of $250, which was my salary."

Gale Anne Hurd had almost the same experience. When the twenty-five-year-old Hurd was co-producing New World's *Smokey Bites the Dust*

(1981), she became apoplectic about difficulties with the sound-effects track. "It's the worst day of my life," she wailed to Roger, horrified to have let him down. Said Corman, "Now, Gale, I want you to remember, it's only a movie." This was a far cry from the usual impression he gave—that every task was crucial, and the fate of the company was hanging in the balance. Hurd, too, was financially rewarded after her outburst: "He was paying me $4,000 to produce the entire movie, pre-production through post-production, but after that he gave me a $2,000 bonus."

Years later, under similar circumstances, Concorde post-production supervisor Deborah Brock was not given a bonus. She did, however, witness a unique side of Corman. They were meeting in his office; he was angry about some current problem at the studio. Overtired and frustrated, Brock suddenly burst into tears, blurting out, "Look, we're all doing the best we can." Roger begged her not to cry, saying, "I get so wound up in this stuff. I'm so sorry." He then called to his assistant, "Deb's upset. Bring some coffee or some tea, or—I don't know. . . ." But the assistant was not at her desk, and so Corman himself escorted Brock down the hall to the tiny office kitchenette, where he awkwardly prepared a cup of tea.

What these anecdotes have in common is a bright young female assistant, stressed to the breaking point, awakening Roger's feelings of paternal concern. Hirsch theorizes that she got her bonus "because he saw how much I cared. . . . And he loved that. Because he does, too." But though Corman respects all employees who have a passion for filmmaking, he seems more emotionally responsive to women.

Director Katt Shea brings up the flip side of the gender issue: "I think he feels more comfortable yelling at women, because they're not going to beat him up." Her words provide a telling counterpoint to a comment by Jonathan Winfrey, who spent several years running Corman's studio. Winfrey is one of many people who are convinced that Corman prefers female employees. He theorizes that he himself was handicapped not only by his gender but also by his height. A strapping young man well over six feet tall, Winfrey had "always noticed that I was one of the few people who could look [Corman] right in the eye." Winfrey speculates that Roger feels uneasy with anyone who might pose a physical threat to his authority.

•   •   •

In early 1983, rumors started to circulate in the trade press that Corman was selling New World Pictures. For years he had resisted Barbara Boyle's urging that he augment the company's capital by going public. As his 1990 memoir make clear, he had no desire to lose control of the operation he had built over the previous decade. But as the 1980s began, and Corman reached age fifty-five, his global enterprise was starting to feel cumbersome. He was ready for an offer he couldn't refuse.

The initial inquiry came from a trio of Hollywood attorneys: Harry Evans Sloan, Lawrence L. Kuppin, and Larry A. Thompson. Their aim was to buy the entire company, including its distribution network and its library of over one hundred films. By the time the dust had settled, Bob Rehme (who had moved on from New World to become the president of Universal Pictures) had joined the buyers' contingent, and the library remained in Corman's hands. When the sale went through, both BJ Franklin in *Screen International* and Richard Klein in *Variety* mentioned a sales figure of $16.5 million. Rehme, however, would not discuss this with me. When we met on December 3, 1998, at a deli in Westwood, California, he also shrugged off rumors that the loss of the Corman library was a serious blow to New World's new owners. They quickly took the company public, erected an impressive new building, got deeply involved in quality television shows like *The Wonder Years* (1988–93), and purchased Marvel Comics. Then, in 1989, they sold New World to Revlon's Ronald O. Perelman, who in 1996 dealt it to Twentieth Century–Fox. Today New World does not exist.

Most of the Corman veterans stayed with the revamped New World organization under its new owners. About a dozen employees joined Corman's own brand-new film production company, which at first was dubbed Millennium. After a few months, the Millennium team returned to the San Vicente headquarters, from rented space across the street. The plan was to continue making films both at the Venice studio and overseas, and to distribute them through what everyone called "the *new* New World." But things quickly changed. In October of 1983, Millennium was renamed New Horizons; shortly thereafter, Corman was suing his old company for monies owed. His timing was excellent: Producer Brad Krevoy, who was then Corman's head of business affairs, reveals that Roger—either luckily or craftily—had chosen to file suit at precisely the moment that New World was about to go public. There was a countersuit, and then a settlement. In 1985 Corman launched Concorde as a distribution company, and today his entire organization is formally known as Concorde–New Horizons Pictures.

Early assistant Kinta Haller sees it as Corman's pattern to keep building companies, sell them, and then start over again. In her mind, it's the process, not the accomplishment that really intrigues him. Corman probably hoped to re-create the spirit of New World at Concorde–New Horizons, but the industry was changing so dramatically that he was bound to be disappointed. One longtime Corman employee speculates that "from the time he sold off New World, he never truly did have something that he felt a great deal of satisfaction about." This was because, by the mid-1980s, making money had become a function of turning out movies in bulk. So the brave inventiveness of many New World pictures would soon become a thing of the past.

Laurette Hayden, who then headed the publicity department, was one New World employee who chose to stick with the company after it changed hands. She was exhausted from her Corman duties, and looked forward to making bigger, higher-profile, slightly less exploitative movies. It turned out to be a good experience. Still, she told me not long ago how much she missed both the low-budget Corman quickies and the art films: "I felt that I lost the magic of the extremes of Roger's company. The filmmaking aspect was not as much fun. I kept looking back and thinking what an incredible time that had been, and how much I learned."

Part Four

CONCORDE–NEW HORIZONS

(1983–2000)

Chapter 11

SEX, SURPRISE, AND VIDEOTAPE

If she doesn't strip, the audience will feel cheated.

ROGER CORMAN, regarding the casting of a leading lady, 1997

BACK IN 1976, in an interview connected with an ad for Eastman Kodak film stock, Roger Corman had said, "I like to give each picture personal attention, so New World will handle no more than ten to fifteen pictures" over a year's time. In 1983, when New World Pictures began outgrowing his concept of a boutique enterprise, the fifty-seven-year-old Corman sold out and started over with a smaller, more manageable operation. By the early 1980s, however, the drive-in theaters were gone, and the major Hollywood studios had learned how to make genre films on big budgets. Some prime examples of B-movie genres that were given the star treatment in this era include the $11 million monster–from–outer space flick *Alien* (starring Tom Skerritt and Sigourney Weaver, 1979) and the dressed-up film noir thriller, *Body Heat* (with William Hurt and Kathleen Turner, 1981). A classic 1956 black-and-white horror entry, *The Invasion of the Body Snatchers,* was remade by United Artist in 1978 in Technicolor and Dolby Stereo, with a stellar cast headed by Donald Sutherland and Jeff Goldblum (a Warner Bros. version, featuring Meg Tilly, was filmed in 1993).

In this atmosphere, with Corman's favorite genres being usurped by the major studios, he needed to find additional strategies for keeping revenue flowing. At Concorde-New Horizons in the mid-1980s, the key to profitability seemed to lie in volume: more movies meant more money. Corman, of course, was heartened when this theorem proved to be true. What he didn't foresee, however, is that he was creating his very own Frankenstein monster—a company that grew so large so fast that it threatened to overwhelm him.

In 1986 making ten films on budgets that were (or so he claimed) in the $2 million to $5 million range, Corman grossed a whopping $96.7 million, with profit earnings of $7.4 million. This figure, noted Wolf Schneider in the *Hollywood Reporter* for March 26, 1987, represented his highest proceeds since 1977, which was his best year ever. Corman's response was to increase production dramatically. Without adding to a staff that totaled perhaps seventy-five employees, he planned fifteen films in the same budget range for 1987, and over twenty for 1988. In 1989, as recorded by *Variety*'s Joseph McBride, he grossed $97.2 million and netted $8.6 million, at a time when other independent film companies (like the Cannon Group and De Laurentiis Entertainment) were dropping like flies.

One secret to Corman's remarkable success in this era came from a young attorney-to-be he had met in 1983 at a Stanford football game. Brad Krevoy was a Stanford University grad; Corman was impressed to hear he had also been student-body president at Beverly Hills High School. Though not really cut out to be a lawyer (as he himself would cheerfully admit), Krevoy was always alert to new business possibilities. For him, the wave of the future was video. He foresaw a day when every home would have a videocassette player, and he urged Corman to jump in early, while the ever-cautious Hollywood studio bosses were still dragging their heels. (A previous New World video deal with Warner Bros. had foundered, supposedly because some of the films offended one key executive's moral sensibilities.)

Almost immediately, Krevoy became Corman's head of business affairs, putting the new philosophy to work. When we spoke on September 25, 1998, Krevoy recalled for me that "as the video business grew, we were at one point the largest supplier. We had deals with every major video-distribution company in the world, to the point where we had orders in excess sometimes of thirty to forty films a year." Aggressive pre-sales thus led to the need to grind out ever more movies in order to satisfy contractual obligations.

With demand for the Concorde product soaring, Corman could no longer pay close attention to every film from start to finish. Director Steve Barnett, who worked at Corman's studio from 1985 through 1990, watched the company change. In the early days, when Concorde pictures were still given a limited theatrical release before being sent out on video, Roger chose each project and kept abreast of the development process. He also attended a rough-cut screening of every film and made invaluable notes. Unfortunately, says Barnett, "as we became more of a home-video company and we began to make so many movies, [Corman's] involvement with each show was less and less, and I think the movies suffered as a consequence. Because, as talented as these people might have been, Roger's guiding hand as a producer was really important."

In Barnett's eyes, Corman's increasing detachment changed the spirit of the place. "It's like going from a really nice university where you have this renowned professor who's got thirty guys in his class, to UCLA where there's three hundred guys, and now you're [being taught by] a grad-student section leader, as opposed to the guy you came to study under. That's what happened when he went to video, because there were too many projects, there were too many things to pay attention to."

No wonder, says Barnett, the quality of the features declined. It didn't help that, as time passed, Corman's tendency to economize by recycling sets and stories reached outrageous proportions. For example, *Deadly Desire,* released direct-to-video in 1994, was shot from a script virtually identical to that of *Kiss Me a Killer* (1991), but with the genders in the love triangle switched. There were instances, too, where only the characters' names were changed the second time around.

•   •   •

When Concorde–New Horizons was launched in 1983, Corman hadn't yet lost his infectious enthusiasm for the filmmaking process. But there were many distractions. For one thing, Krevoy was negotiating complex overseas production deals, notably in Argentina. And the company's legal minds soon became embroiled in the lawsuit against New World's new owners (over details of the purchase agreement), followed by other litigation. Though Roger has no great affection for lawyers, he sometimes enjoys the challenge of legal maneuvering. Former Concorde assistant Anna Roth remembers once picking him up at the airport: He greeted her with a cheerful, "Who are we suing today?"

Perhaps the most remarkable suit against Corman was that filed by the Hell's Angels. Former staff attorney Alida Camp has described for me how a Concorde action picture called *Nam Angels* (1989), shot in Manila, featured bikers who ride behind enemy lines to rescue captive American soldiers. Veteran Corman director Cirio Santiago, wanting his actors to wear matching emblems on their leather jackets, blithely copied the Angels' logo, which happens to be trademarked. Their lawyer duly claimed that the movie had sullied the Angels' sterling reputation. Corman settled amicably, but for a while, the bikers were a colorful presence in the office waiting area.

At first one promising new outlet for Corman's creative energies seemed to be television, a medium he had previously all but ignored. But the glacial pace of TV decision-making appalled him, and he was never fully comfortable in a roomful of men wearing business suits. In 1986 the NBC network showed interest in backing a series, and noted science-fiction writer Harlan Ellison was hired to create the pilot for *Cutter's World*, a father-son outer-space saga modeled on the old TV western *The Rifleman* (1958–63). Thanks at least in part to network bureaucracy, it didn't happen. Years later, in 1991, Krevoy launched a deal with an established cable network to turn *The Little Shop of Horrors* into a weekly live-action series. The writing team of Bill Rabkin and Lee Goldberg (now executive producers of the CBS-TV series *Martial Law*) developed a sample script, and Roger dutifully attended meetings at which well-dressed executives dithered, asking that all the jokes be underlined and black humor be marked with an asterisk. Rabkin informed me that Corman later remarked ruefully, "In the time it's taken these people to commission a second draft, I have commissioned, shot, and released five movies." Ultimately, the *Little Shop* project never moved beyond the talking stage.

Rabkin, a TV veteran, remembers his Corman period (circa 1991) with fond amusement. He recalls Corman telling him of a recurring nightmare—that a film he had completed was still sitting on a shelf somewhere because in the daily confusion at Concorde, no one had remembered to release it. Rabkin also treasures the conversation that occurred when they chanced to visit the Venice studio while an erotic thriller was being filmed. When Rabkin noted that he'd seen the same plot the previous night on television, Roger jauntily replied, "Oh, yes, we've made this movie before. I think we'll make it two or three more times before we're done with it."

. . .

Corman's home life was also busy. In November of 1983, he and Julie sold their Brentwood residence. To suit the needs of their growing family, they expended well over $1 million for a venerable 6,500-square-foot Georgian home with nine bedrooms, a guesthouse, and a swimming pool. The new house, about a mile from their San Vicente office, was located on La Mesa Drive, an elegant Santa Monica street boasting century-old magnolia trees. Actor-contractor Beach Dickerson spent most of 1984 on an extensive remodeling job, which included a circular loft (complete with observation window) in which the three children were to study, and a tubelike shower in the middle of the master suite. Dickerson describes the look as "*Architectural Digest* right down the line." He remembers Corman moving the family in early to hurry the builders along, effectively traumatizing everyone. He also recalls his surprise when Julie brought little Mary Corman to the new house in an infant carrier.

Mary Tessa Corman was born in late 1984, when the family's other children were nine, eight, and seven years old. Julie chose the baby's name, telling *Drama-Logue*'s Joan Crosby that her husband at first protested that it was overly common. Earlier, Dickerson was hardly the only one to be surprised when Mary made her presence felt. Former sales executive Frank Moreno, who loves teasing, accidentally learned of the impending arrival when he walked into Corman's office and quipped, "When's the next one due?" Corman turned crimson, and Moreno guessed the secret.

Ginny Nugent, Corman's assistant at the time, discloses that both Cormans were deeply embarrassed by this unexpected baby. Because of their advanced ages (she was forty-two, and he, nearly sixty), they were also deeply concerned that something might be wrong with the child. Much medical testing was done out of town, and for a while Corman was rarely at his desk. Fortunately, all went well, though when I congratulated Roger, he admitted he'd always believed that a logical number of children to have was two, one to hold with each hand.

Mary's presence may have slowed Julie's budding career as a producer, but not for long. Julie prides herself on producing movies and children almost simultaneously. An interview in *L.A. Weekly* notes that Catherine was born after Julie had spent a full day on the set of *Crazy Mama* (1975), and she made *Moving Violation* (1976) while seven months pregnant with Roger Martin. When Mary was five months old, Julie told *Drama-Logue* about the new baby's smooth integration into her professional routine: "She is our love child, Roger's and mine. I take her everywhere with me." As an infant, Mary accompanied Julie to meetings, movie sets, and charity functions. She soon became a familiar fixture at the Concorde office; as a small girl she liked to hang out in the accounting department, where there were always kindly souls ready to mother her.

While Corman's creative staff was largely made up of whiz kids just out of college and ready to devote their lives to moviemaking, Concorde was a surprisingly good place for women with families of their own. Roger theorized that mothers of school-aged children were a valuable source of labor because they were committed, intelligent, and unlikely to make demands. For years his foreign-sales department was composed of two women, Pamela Abraham and Pamm Vlastas, who tailored their hours to their children's school schedules. Because my son was in preschool when Corman persuaded me to return to work for him in 1986, I was able to keep limited hours—come in only four days a week, and tackle the rest of my workload at home. Roger was proud of our arrangement, feeling it put him in the vanguard of progressive employers, and I have always been grateful that his flexibility allowed me to spend time with my growing youngsters.

•   •   •

Corman's personal assistants, culled from America's leading universities, were expected to perform a wide range of services. This was certainly true for Ginny Nugent (from Stanford University) and Anna Roth (from Columbia University), whose tenures span the period 1983 to 1988. The three of us had a lively conversation on October 6, 1998. I learned that, in addition to paying Roger's bills and screening his telephone calls, Nugent was asked to come in one weekend to help paint the office. She also supervised the remodeling of his La Mesa Drive home: Corman assured her that "building a house is just like making a film." Roth remembers her very first day on the job, when Corman ran out of gas in Beverly Hills' Benedict Canyon and she (then a newcomer to Los Angeles) had to quickly track him down. Remarkably, he had called her at the office because he didn't know his own home telephone number. Roth finds it disconcerting that "he wasn't aware of his gas gauge or his home number or even his home address. At the same time, he was very detail-oriented and very precise." Once, writing with a pencil stub on a tiny scrap of paper, he showed her the formula by which he worked out his video contracts, using presales to guarantee $250,000 in profit before each film was even in the can.

Though Corman was becoming less hands-on with his film editors and directors, he enjoyed teaching these young women the secrets of movie production. They took charge of overseas filmmaking in Argentina and the Philippines, learned marketing and casting, and worked to add plot logic to botched acquisitions like *White Star* (1985), featuring Dennis Hopper at his most incomprehensible. They served as talent scouts—at the American Film Institute, Roth spotted the work of both director Carl Franklin and cinematographer Janusz Kaminski, and brought them to Corman's attention. They also met important filmmakers like Martin Scorsese, who came to urge his old boss to invest in *The Last Temptation of Christ* (1988), but was turned away when Corman decided that religious movies just don't sell. All of this was excellent preparation for their future careers. Nugent left Corman to work for Gale Anne Hurd, and is now a producer in her own right (her latest is *Anywhere But Here,* 1999). Roth detoured into multimedia, but is currently writing a television series for Warner Bros.

Having been with Corman since 1982, the tail-end of the New World period, Nugent chose to leave in 1986 partly because she saw the company turning into a video factory. Movies were being ground out on twelve-day schedules, and Corman had become more unreasonable about decent equipment and fair treatment of his crews. (Given that Corman crews were always nonunion, he could easily withhold from them such expected niceties as on-set meals during long shooting days.) By mid-1986, Nugent had also started to dislike the increasing competitiveness among some of her Concorde co-workers. As Corman's reputation for launching filmmakers continued to grow, he attracted those who were perhaps less interested in collaborating on movies than in furthering their own careers at any cost.

Anna Roth, who stayed on through 1988, also noticed some staffers becoming secretive and controlling. In part this was a function of Corman's new need to delegate authority: those put in charge were bound and determined to make sure their contributions got recognized. Roth surmises that Corman was aware of this new divisive spirit, but that he found it beneficial to have staff members (and the unpaid interns who hoped to replace them) all vying to impress the boss. Roth has seen, and respects, the filmmaker side of Corman. "But when he becomes a movie mini-mogul, then he doesn't care—he almost lets people fight it out, like survival of the fittest."

The other reason Nugent and Roth chose to leave involved their growing discomfort with the flagrantly sexual nature of much Concorde product. They had to check the bare breasts of Corman's leading ladies, and outline for Corman specific nude scenes to be included in each film. They worked on spicing up French imports, like *Emmanuelle 5* (1987), that were basically soft-core pornography. Anna recalls with disgust writing the contract of a young actress bound for Manila: "I actually had to negotiate, inch by inch, how much pubic hair would show." For Ginny, the last straw came when director Jim Wynorski told her of his casting plans for *Big Bad Mama II* (1987). When he announced that "we've got to get some girls in here who'll take 'em out and let 'em breathe," she knew it was time to find another line of work.

* * *

Jim Wynorski, a large teddy bear of a man with the tastes of a perennial adolescent, told *Time* magazine in 1997 that "breasts are the cheapest special effect in our business." Wynorski ought to know. By now he has directed some forty direct-to-video features, all on rock-bottom budgets, and has branched into producing as well. (When we spoke, he was working on *Final Voyage*—featuring Erika Eleiniak and Ice-T—a film that meshes *Die Hard* with *Titanic*. It's tempting to imagine the violinists fiddling topless as the ship goes down.)

Wynorski was born to thrive in the giddy Corman environment. Corman was already a hero to him back in 1980 when, as a young man with an advertising background, he came to Julie Corman's office to pitch story ideas. He walked out that day with a job as New World's head of marketing, and from then on he was a Corman regular. During our long conversation in the fall of 1998, he told me that "I got caught up in it so fast, it was like a twister coming by. . . . That's the world an impatient person like me loves to work in. Because it's instant gratification."

Wynorski's first big success came when, on a $40 budget, he recut the trailer for an unsuccessful Italian-made New World horror film called *Something Waits in the Dark* (1979). Wynorski's "Coming Attractions" reel, which lured potential ticket-buyers with the promise of seeing "a man turned inside out," incorporated new footage of "this guy running around, covered with slime . . . all his veins hanging out, chasing a girl in a bikini." The film, retitled *Screamers* (1979), opened in Atlanta, Georgia, on a Friday. Early Saturday morning Corman phoned Wynorski and demanded that his new material be edited into the film itself, to appease the disappointed audiences who "rioted in the drive-ins last night, tore out the speakers, tried to lynch the manager."

After Corman spotted Jim Wynorski's gift for tapping in to the male subconscious, Jim was put to work concocting scripts *(Mutant, Sorceress,* and *Screwballs)* that featured action, comedy, and women without clothing. Before long, he was also a director. Wynorski's exuberant, "Let's put on a show" approach is especially evident in the making of *Sorority House Massacre II* (1990), also fondly known as *Nighty Nightmare*. It seems that the house sets from *Slumber Party Massacre III* (1990) had been left standing at the Concorde studio. On a Friday afternoon in late May 1990, Wynorski secretly got Julie Corman to stake him $150,000. He spent three days writing a quickie slasher flick, and two more days casting actresses who were game, well endowed, and not members of the Screen Actors Guild. By Friday, with the Cormans out of town for Memorial Day weekend, Wynorski was shooting. The following Wednesday, Corman finally discovered what was going on. He saw the finished product, recognized its commercial potential, and said, "Jim, I want you to make this film again. . . . Use the same script, use the same cast."

Because the original sets were now gone, this follow-up took place in an office tower, fictional home of the Acme Lingerie Company. It was called *Hard to Die* (1990), and fans like critic Joe Bob Briggs, editor of the popular *We Are the Weird* newsletter, celebrated its excesses: "Sixteen breasts. Twelve dead bodies. Hot pants. Tube tops. Denim cutoffs. Camisoles. Bustiers. . . . Bimbos drenched by fire sprinkler system for an extremely apparent reason. Neck-cracking. Multiple splatter. Gratuitous flashback footage from *Slumber Party Massacre* [1982]." Corman was delighted by this seat-of-the-pants style of moviemaking, which reminded him of his own early days. Wynorski insists, "He loved me for trying to do these things." Jim also maintains that he and Corman share the same film aesthetic: "Big chase and a big chest. That's the formula. If you put those two ingredients in a movie, you're going to have a good time."

In appearance and in personal style, however, Roger Corman and Jim Wynorski are nothing alike. Roger resembles a minister or a college professor; Jim projects the air of something akin to a satyr, though one equipped with a heart the size of New Jersey. Though they make an unlikely duo, there's a cordial relationship between them. As director Mark Griffiths has observed, Corman suspends his normal restlessness when he and Wynorski shoot the breeze.

Certainly, Roger appreciates roguish behavior and the chutzpah involved in getting something for nothing. Former post-production head Steve Barnett cited Corman's glee in sneaking forbidden material past the Motion Picture Association of America ratings board. When Steve was a newly hired film editor, Roger asked him to "add six frames to the shot of the girl taking off her top. I think we'll just be able to see her nipple, but it will be so subliminal I don't think anybody will really notice, including the MPAA." Such adolescent naughtiness supports producer Thom Mount's contention that Roger, for all the dignity he projects, is really a boy at heart. Director Joe Dante is not alone in theorizing, as he did on November 5, 1998, that "Jim Wynorski is the side of Roger that he may have inside, but he never lets anybody see."

• • •

When actress Katt Shea brought Corman the idea for a film about murders in a strip club, complete with a female detective who goes undercover as a stripper to solve the mystery, he instantly gave the project a green light. At least, that's what he later told an interviewer from the syndicated TV show *PM Magazine*. The truth is that despite his enthusiasm for the unclad female form, Corman at first strongly resisted Shea's 1986 pitch. *Stripped to Kill* finally got made in 1987. Looking back, Katt expresses her amazement at the stripper trend she's helped launch. "Little did I know that it would affect Roger for the next ten years."

Shea, who played a featured role in Concorde's *Barbarian Queen* (1985), found unexpected inspiration when her then husband Andy Ruben persuaded her to visit a Los Angeles strip joint. For her, *Stripped to Kill* was less an opportunity to launch a directing career than a chance to prove "that strippers were artists . . . and this was their only outlet." Roger's yearlong delay in approving the project stemmed partly from Shea's inexperience; he also doubtless recoiled from the fact that the narrative she wanted to tell contained a key transvestite element. But ultimately Corman was swayed by a strong woman who believed in something with all her heart. "From the very start," says Katt, "I was so passionate about this thing, and it was such an artistic perspective that I was taking—I think that impressed Roger from the beginning: that I was a serious filmmaker, and a force to be reckoned with."

Once Shea had completed a UCLA Extension directing class, Corman gave her a $700,000 budget, far bigger than what was available to later Concorde filmmakers. She hired real strippers for the featured roles, contracted Kay Lenz to play the female lead, and had no trouble with Corman until she made the mistake of showing him a rough cut that was over two hours long. (Roger requires that all his features come in well under ninety minutes, in order to fit into no more than four standard shipping cartons.) Furious, he stormed into the cutting room and began ruthlessly hacking away.

Shea is one director with no respect for Corman's editing skills: "He left in all the stripping, and he took out all the story." That would have ended their relationship, but *Stripped to Kill* became something of a phenomenon, especially on video and in overseas markets. Shea told me, "It was the biggest movie in France for the year. And I got invited back to make another movie."

Shea made a total of four films for Corman, all of them produced and co-written by Andy Ruben. Three of the four focus on strippers and their world. The thoroughly offbeat *Dance of the Damned* (1988), which was designed to take advantage of existing house-interior and nightclub sets, imaginatively sets up an all-night encounter between a stripper and a vampire. Shea's down-and-dirty style was distinctive enough to gain critical respect: In 1992 she and Ruben were honored at New York's Museum of Modern Art with a retrospective that featured their Corman films as well as their later New Line Cinema hit, *Poison Ivy* (1992), starring Drew Barrymore. In recent years Corman has happily imitated the "Katt and Andy" scripts for nonSAG quickies with titles like *Midnight Tease* (1994). And, of course, the strip-club milieu briefly became trendy even in major-studio films, with *Showgirls* (1995) and *Striptease* (1996) the obvious high-priced examples. Says Katt, "I didn't know it was going to lead to this, and I apologize to the entire world for it."

Out of Katt Shea's pictures emerged a young woman who was to be one of Concorde's quintessential stars for the next decade. Maria Ford was discovered by Anna Roth and Andy Ruben, dancing nude in a seedy joint in the San Fernando Valley, over the Hollywood hills from Los Angeles. She had the angelic face of a young Marilyn Monroe, a lithe body, and all the right moves. She made her film debut in *Dance of the Damned*, after which Shea's *Stripped to Kill II* (1989) was built around her talents.

With Roger's blessing, Ford went on to appear in nearly twenty Concorde movies. Though she specialized in sweet but sexy victims like the one she played in *Naked Obsession* (1991), she also portrayed seductresses and tough lady cops with increasing histrionic skill. Because Maria was bent on a serious acting career, she was sometimes personally ambivalent about the flagrant nudity that was always built into her screen roles. But her presence on-screen in various stages of undress was to set the tone for much of Corman's output for years to come.

Chapter 12

GOING PLACES

He's the best friend that a new filmmaker in this town has.

CARL FRANKLIN, director, 1997

TO TALK ABOUT Concorde–New Horizon films in terms of sequels, knockoffs, and tawdry skin flicks is not to tell the whole story. In fact, many Concorde veterans remember the late 1980s as the company's golden age, in which there was plenty of room for new ideas and new talent. This was a time when exciting young directors put their personal stamp on conventional genre-film assignments. And Roger Corman, always on the lookout for exotic locales that would accommodate American filmmakers, discovered Peru.

As he had done years before in the Philippines, Roger took the initiative. He was flying to Buenos Aires, Argentina, to check on a co-production when his plane was forced down in Lima, Peru, by bad weather. Screenwriter Fred Bailey told me the story of how Corman "got off the plane, took a taxi into town, opened up the yellow pages, and got somebody to find motion-picture production listings. Made a few calls asking who was the best filmmaker in Lima. . . . They all said, 'Luis Llosa.' Called him up, made a deal, and was back on the airplane to Argentina within a couple of hours." Llosa (who in 1997 directed the Columbia Pictures hit *Anaconda*) proved to have genuine filmmaking skills. And Peru as a nation boasted a wealth of scenic possibilities: towering mountains, grasslands, jungle, the Amazon River, and picturesquely crumbling South American colonial cities. With Llosa acting as local producer and sometime director, Roger was to use Peru as a backdrop for several upcoming urban thrillers, Vietnam battle dramas, tales of futuristic squalor, and even a Jules Verne adventure saga.

One of Llosa's Concorde films was designed to capitalize on the story of a Brazilian environmental activist named Chico Mendes, whose murder in 1988 made headlines worldwide. The film *Fire on the Amazon* (on which I share a writing credit) was shot in 1990, completed in 1991, and surfaced briefly on video in 1993. Today it is notable chiefly because of its torrid jungle love scene between star Craig Sheffer and actress Sandra Bullock, who was then wholly unknown. When her roles in *Speed* (1994) and *While You Were Sleeping* (1995) turned Bullock into America's Sweetheart, Corman pondered how best to maximize the potential of the film, which at one point was retitled *Lost Paradise*. On August 16, 1996, Roger claimed to Jeffrey Jolson-Colburn of the *Hollywood Reporter* that holding the picture back while waiting for Bullock's star to rise had been part of his plan all along. His editors subsequently expanded the love scene slightly, in order to show more of Bullock in the altogether. In February 2000, Concorde's sales staff at the American Film Market was hawking two separate versions of *Fire on the Amazon*, one R-rated and the other a brand-new unrated cut featuring one single additional shot that Bullock's fans will presumably not want to miss.

Filming in Peru could be hazardous, especially because great stretches of terrain were then controlled by the anti-government guerrilla faction known as the Shining Path. Director Mark Griffiths remembers that when he was scouting locations for his Vietnam action feature, *Heroes Stand Alone* (1989), he and colleagues were detained at gunpoint by the Peruvian military, who accused them of representing Amnesty International. Former assistant Sally Mattison recalls that on another occasion several Corman people, including actor Michael Moriarty, were hassled by gun-toting revolutionaries. Moreover, in light of Peru's limited technical resources, Corman made some serious miscalculations. A nuclear-submarine drama called *Full Fathom Five* (1990) turned out to be a lamentable mess, even though the talented Carl Franklin was its director.

Still, good screen work got done. Roger's favorite Peruvian film was probably *Crime Zone* (1988), because he had supplied its key concept: "Bonnie and Clyde in the future." This audacious love story, starring David Carradine and Sherilyn Fenn, was written by Daryl Haney, who described for me how Corman himself came up with the film's central vision of a world in which crime is obsolete, and so the police department must reinvent it. Because at this time it was rare for the boss to meet with writers in story conferences, Haney cherishes his recollection: "At moments like that, you could see the spark in Roger." But Haney also made clear that Corman, for all of his outwardly gracious manner, often seemed distracted. "He wasn't altogether there, in the seat across from me. A little bit of him was out the window, was up in the clouds someplace, or on the freeway."

Haney first came to Concorde for *Daddy's Boys*, a project with a unique history. One day in 1987, when Jim Wynorski was about to shoot *Big Bad Mama II* on rather handsome Depression-era sets, Corman became particularly morose. He stormed out of the office, and—as was his custom—crossed San Vicente Boulevard to pace the parklike grounds of the Veterans Administration medical complex. Brad Krevoy (who told me the story on September 25, 1998) saw him at a distance, talking earnestly with men who looked like strung-out disabled veterans. Before long, Corman was back, reenergized, telling the amused Krevoy about a new, outlandish scheme. The idea was to make a second film at night while *Big Bad Mama II* shot during the day, thus allowing those fancy sets to do double duty. *Daddy's Boys* (1988) was the end result of Roger's brainstorm.

For the next several weeks, Corman and his staff were wholly caught up in this odd little movie. Roger exercised his engineer's passion for logistics, planning out a schedule through which each *Daddy's Boys* sequence could piggyback on the sets and lighting already in place. Joe Minion, a young NYU graduate who had written Martin Scorsese's offbeat film *After Hours* (1985), was recruited by Anna Roth to direct his first (and only) released film. Minion pressed Daryl Haney into service as his leading actor. On a Tuesday, Haney borrowed the cash to fly from New York to California; by Wednesday he was trying on his wardrobe and also writing scenes for the picture, which went before the cameras on Thursday. Since there was certainly no money for hotel rooms, both Minion and Haney wound up camping on Roth's living-room floor.

Because of the preexisting sets and costumes, Roger stipulated that *Daddy's Boys* had to revolve around rural bank robbers, circa 1933. Haney concocted a black comedy with an oedipal twist: A family of lawless hillbillies sets out to recruit a new mother. But the script was understandably ragged, and the production team faced crises aplenty. Minion gave up in midshoot, and others—even Roger himself—pitched in to help direct. The movie, shot in a mere eight days, proved to be strange and funny. It would ultimately play (to a tiny crowd) at the American Film Institute Film Festival, but commercial theater chains wanted no part of it. Still, it got some attention in Europe and on video, and Corman mentions it fondly in his memoir. It has remained close to his heart because, as Haney remembers Anna Roth telling him at the time, "it makes him feel like he's young again. . . . It's the kind of thing he used to do with Jack Nicholson and all those guys, on a wing and a prayer."

• • •

Most Concorde projects were generated in-house, based on Corman's readings of current social, political, cultural, and filmic trends. Larry Brand was the rare writer whose unsolicited script, *The Drifter* (1988), so impressed Roger that Brand was hired to make his directing debut as well. As a member of the Writers Guild, Brand was far more costly than most Concorde screenwriters, though Roger offset this expense by skimping on his director fees. Brand ended up writing and directing three Concorde features, played co-starring roles, and even earned residuals. As he told me, "I may be in the *Guinness Book of World Records* as the highest-paid Corman guy."

Corman clearly respected Brand, though Larry's determination to make art was not always in sync with Roger's own interests. (When asked by Brand if he would back an art film, Corman replied, "Well, if it was an art film with a lot of sex . . . ") In 1989 Corman asked Brand to remake one of his own most celebrated films, *The Masque of the Red Death* (1964). It may seem surprising that Corman chose to redo a picture that had helped form the basis for his personal reputation as a director. Brand insists, however, that Corman is far too pragmatic to be sentimental, especially when the sets are already built: "Remakes were free, he didn't have to pay anybody for the rights . . . he had a castle lying around." Aside from matters of budget, Corman never interfered with Brand's stark vision of guilt and redemption, sin and power. Corman even permitted a final credit sequence that, while somewhat costly, ended the film on a dramatic note. This helped convince Brand "that unlike many other notoriously cheap producers, he's a filmmaker at heart. He looked at that shot, and he understood it was right for the film. It added production value that transcended the couple thousand dollars it was going to cost him. And I've always appreciated him for that."

Brand had found it embarrassing to shoot the obligatory sex scene for *The Drifter*. On *The Masque of the Red Death*, however, which starred Adrian Paul and Clare Hoak, he and Corman agreed on a plot element that required full frontal nudity. It was meant to be thematic, not gratuitous: During a major crowd scene staged in a medieval banquet hall, arrogant noblemen force peasant girls to perform a kind of sad striptease for their amusement. The scene took on added drama when Maria Ford, hired as one of the peasants, suddenly balked at removing her clothing. Her revolt spread among the other on-screen peasants. Shooting ground to a halt as an earnest young head of production, Rodman Flender, raced to the set and gently talked Ford into fulfilling the terms of her contract.

Mark Governor, who composed the score for the updated *Masque of the Red Death*, played a musician in this tense scene. He remembers being cued by Brand to stop the music as the young women slowly began to strip, some of them weeping, covering themselves with their hands as best they could. When the music stopped, said Governor, "it was the most horrible feeling you could have. Everyone was ashamed and embarrassed, just like they were supposed to be in the film. No one wanted to be there. So that got captured on film. And then later, when I did the score, on top of that we added all these dissonant strings, so it's probably the most depressing nude scene in a movie."

On his final Concorde picture, *Overexposed* (1990), Larry Brand had the unique experience of talking Corman out of using nude footage. The film contains one erotic coupling between star Catherine Oxenberg and William Bumiller. (As sometimes happened when Concorde used name actors, a body double was hired for Oxenberg's on-screen nude shots.) But an additional sex scene was also filmed, with a different double standing in for

Oxenberg. Aside from the fact that the breasts in the two scenes didn't match, Brand objected to the fact that the earlier scene "was so patently just to show tits." Nevertheless, "the real reason I hated the scene was that it sucked all the energy out of the later scene, which should be sexy." Brand made this speech to Corman, who—to both their surprise—accepted Larry's logic. Brand speculates that Roger prefers to avoid confrontation: "If you make an impassioned case for something, I don't think he wants to be the bad guy and say no to you. But for whatever reason, he let me cut the nudity out of that scene."

Brand, who never formally studied filmmaking, agrees with the notion that Roger operates the ultimate film school. He shared with me his belief that those who've made movies under Corman conditions will thereafter never be intimidated on the job: "I think you really have to develop a style, and that comes out of having very limited resources and limited options. . . . When you're told you only have time to cover a scene with one angle instead of three—or two instead of five—you have to make those angles count. And it becomes a film that is really *your* film." Says Brand, "The trick with Roger for me was always trying to sneak one by him. Trying to do a film that on the one hand gave him just enough sex that he felt he wasn't being cheated, just enough violence or threat of violence that he felt it was commercially viable, and at the same time trying to make a film that was about something. It was kind of a ballet. It was this intricate dance that you had to do to appease the gods, the god of your artistic intent and the mercantile god of the Corman School."

· · ·

One reason Corman could be tolerant of Larry Brand's artistic scruples was that in this era—the late 1980s and early 1990s—virtually every Concorde film released on video made money. In 1989 Corman hit on a formula that ensured his financial success for years to come. When martial artist Jean-Claude Van Damme was riding high with *Bloodsport* (1988), Don "The Dragon" Wilson got a message on his home answering machine: "Hi, my name is Roger Corman. If you're the Don Wilson that's the kickboxing champ, I'd like you to come in and read for my film." Wilson, a longtime world light-heavyweight kickboxing champion, duly auditioned, and was told by Roger, "You're going to become a big motion-picture star." They shook on a deal that gave Wilson $1,000 a week for his first film and a flat $25,000 for his second.

Corman's faith in Wilson was fully justified. *Bloodfist* (1989) took in $1.7 million in limited theatrical release, and sold 80,000 cassettes for MGM, which then handled Corman's domestic video output. *Bloodfist II* (1990), a hastily made follow-up, sold 50,000 cassettes. (These figures appear in Joseph McBride's *Variety* piece for May 30, 1990.) Before long, Wilson was being paid a year-round salary of $4,000 a week to appear in six more *Bloodfist* films, and Corman was launching his own video distribution company.

As Wilson makes clear, Corman "manufactured an action star." Once Wilson had signed on, Corman built his career by enrolling him in acting classes and hooking him up with publicist Milt Kahn. Wilson is impressed that Corman was color-blind enough to choose an Asian for his leading man. Though he considers his physique "American," Don—whose mother is Japanese—has an undeniably Asian face. Having gone on to earn top billing in action flicks for other low-budget companies, he now claims to having played the hero in "more Hollywood films than any Asian in the history of film. Twenty-three starring roles." (An interesting contrast is Sessue Hayakawa [1889–1973], a Japanese actor remembered by movie buffs for his leading roles in silent films and for his Oscar-nominated performance as the prison-camp commandant in 1957's *The Bridge on the River Kwai*. In a Hollywood career that stretched from 1914 to 1962, Hayakawa specialized in playing honorable bad guys and exotic lovers who generally lost the girl in the last reel.)

Wilson also appreciates Corman's shrewdness in seeking out a true kickboxing champion, because serious fans of martial arts know the difference between a genuine athlete and a wannabe. Yet Corman himself was hardly a purist; before the martial-arts craze largely played itself out, he was promoting sexy Catya Sassoon (star of several Concorde action flicks) as a female world champion, until Wilson advised him to desist.

As Concorde's former story editor, I can speak to Roger's determination to exploit the martial-arts genre for all it was worth. *Bloodfist*, written by Robert King in 1989, was a conventional but effective narrative about a martial artist who seeks revenge in the ring for his brother's death. Three years later, I was asked to move the script's locale from Manila to Los Angeles, and to change the inscrutable old Chinese mentor into a black street bum. The rest of the story remained virtually unaltered. The project came together in two weeks, to fill a Christmastime production gap at the studio: *Full Contact* (starring martial artist Jerry Trimble) was released on video in early 1993. Three months later, I helped transport the same script into outer space; this time it was called *Dragon Fire*. A female variation, *Angelfist*, with Catya Sassoon in Wilson's original role, appeared later in 1993, and at one point a medieval sword-and-sandal version was on tap.

Wilson's own offscreen love interest of many years, Kathleen Karridene, owes her career as a makeup artist to Concorde. After making her first Concorde feature, *The Terror Within* (1988), Karridene did makeup on seventeen Concorde productions in two years, quickly becoming what she now calls "a pro at naked people." She also learned how to live without sleep, working thirty-six straight hours on *Nowhere to Run* (1989) rather than turn the job over to a stranger who might botch the film's continuity by leaving some makeup detail overlooked.

Karridene's dedication exemplifies the spirit that pervaded Concorde crews in this era. She insists that "everyone loved what they were doing, and we were so proud of what we were doing." When she returned years later, however, "it was so different. They were just there to make their money." Today, as a busy union makeup artist for major studios and television networks, Karridene appreciates having learned her craft at Concorde: "We work now, and we make lots of money, and everybody complains. And nobody knows what it's really like. . . . I'm so glad that I did it, that I did it for so long, because I never complain about anything."

• • •

After the birth of her fourth child in late 1984, Julie Corman plunged back into filmmaking. Many agree that she felt herself to be in professional competition with her much older, much more celebrated, husband. Certainly, she was determined not to languish in his shadow. She made sure interviewers realized that her money, too, was invested in the family business, and that she was an integral part of the decision-making team. When Gwen Jones of the *Los Angeles Herald Examiner* asked whether Corman and Julie shared similar producing styles, Julie was quick to claim that she hadn't really been around when her husband was producing, and that they operated wholly independent of one another.

While the Cormans were supportive of each other's work, and stepped in to lend a hand when needed, Julie sometimes chose to go her own way. At times this meant finding outside financing for her pet screen projects. After the sale of New World in 1983, she formed her own small company, Trinity Pictures, through which she produced the made-for-television children's film *The Westing Game* (1997), among others. But for all Julie's autonomy, the fact remains that she was occasionally insecure in her office role. One old-timer remembers watching her pace at the door of Roger's office, hugging her arms to her chest "like a junior-high-school girl going into the principal's office, terrified of whatever she had to tell him."

Julie Corman has real strengths as a producer, among them, taste and fierce determination. The late writer-director Howard R. Cohen described her as "the toughest negotiator I've ever seen." Yet Cohen quickly added that those who call her a "dragon lady" haven't seen "the sweet and tender side that gets involved in social causes and cares deeply about people." Over the years, she took a personal interest in Cohen's career in a way that her husband did not. Cohen also appreciated her lighthearted moods: Once, in the studio's mixing room, some dance music was playing, and he and she spontaneously launched into a Fred Astaire and Ginger Rogers routine, to the astonishment of everyone present. Cohen insisted to me that "she likes to be silly, except nobody knows that, nobody ever gives her a chance to be silly."

Julie once told me how she persuaded her spouse to join her in a ballroom dance class at a nearby community college. (It didn't work out, for a rather remarkable reason: Roger refused to lead.) We also chatted familiarly about how, inspired by a mutual acquaintance who was a professional flutist, she had taken up flute lessons, with the goal of marching in the local Independence Day parade. I feel lucky to have known Julie's gracious and generous side: she bought a lovely gift when there was a special event in my family, and she introduced me to some outstanding literature. But her moods were unpredictable. At times I felt I had a friend; on other days she barely deigned to know my name.

Concorde's production people tend to remember Julie Corman for her arbitrary cost-cutting measures. For a battle scene in *Last Resort* (1988), a crew member recalls how "Julie became obsessed with the cost of [bullet] blanks, because they cost fifty cents apiece. So she gave the director one box, saying, 'This is your war scene.' " As time passed, however, Julie became more sophisticated about filmmaking, as well as more selective about her subject matter. While some of Julie's efforts were typical Corman fare, such as *Chopping Mall* (1986), by the late 1980s she was branching out into more unusual movie projects.

She went to Ireland for the filming of *Da* (1988), an adaptation of a popular Broadway play about a writer (Martin Sheen) haunted by the ghost of his dearly departed father (Barnard Hughes, repeating his Tony Award–winning performance). The drama's Irish setting strongly appealed to her sense of family heritage, and her handling of the movie won her serious industry respect. She also tried adapting a famous science-fiction story, Isaac Asimov's "Nightfall." Sadly her 1988 screen version, *Nightfall*, written and directed by Paul Mayersberg, succumbed to the weight of its own ambitions, and was lambasted by critics and audiences alike.

Also in 1988, Julie released *The Nest,* a rather mundane horror film about killer cockroaches that marked the screenwriting debut of Robert King. King, who has since gone on to become a well-paid Hollywood screenwriter *(Speechless, Red Corner),* was hired for $3,000 to turn out a script in three weeks. A version by another writer had been scrapped, they were six weeks away from shooting, and Julie was in a frenzy. King remembers how he first arrived at the Concorde office, thinking he was going to pitch his concept. Instead he was hired on the spot, and hustled into a room where he was asked to crank out a story outline. In that same room, someone was casting body doubles for *Big Bad Mama II* (1987), and another staffer was on the phone trying to round up a flock of chickens. For King, this first day epitomized Concorde—"an insane place where no one paid attention to you. . . . Everybody did their own thing and it was a creative hotbed, but no one took it very seriously."

King subsequently wrote two films for Roger Corman, *Bloodfist* and *Silk 2* (both 1989). He firmly believes the Concorde experience was formative for him as a writer. Today, "I procrastinate right up to a deadline, and then force the deadline to keep me creative. That's a very big Corman technique, which is: 'We need it now! Go do it!' " King is convinced that he does his best work with his back against the wall, relying on raw panic to free him of rules and expectations. Still, though Concorde taught him practical filmmaking, he admitted he has never been able to use his Concorde features as industry calling cards: "You don't show the cockroach script; you don't show the cockroach movie. You take what you learned, and go on from there."

Another successful graduate of this period is equally vehement about not letting his Concorde efforts represent him in mainstream Hollywood. Carl Franklin (b. 1949) directed his first feature, *Nowhere to Run* (1989), for Julie Corman. He then went overseas to make two other vehicles, *Eye of the Eagle 2* (1989) for Julie, and *Full Fathom Five* (1990) for Roger, before moving on to major studio projects, including 1998's *One True Thing*. Franklin is grateful to the Cormans for giving him a start: "Thank God for Roger Corman! I wish that there were more." Still, he pointedly avoids naming his Concorde films during media interviews. When I mentioned to filmmaker Ron Howard that Franklin, too, had a Corman connection, Howard was openly surprised. But he quickly grasped Franklin's logic in keeping his Corman output buried: "Everybody thinks that *One False Move* [1991] was his first film, and he probably likes to just leave it at that." Writer-director Adam Simon, whose stint at Concorde coincided with Franklin's, shared with me Franklin's advice that he never show his Corman pictures—as samples of his work: "Not because they're bad movies, but because maybe people don't know how to watch those movies."

Julie Corman's projects have proven to be a launch pad for other promising filmmakers. One movie was unique, however, because it introduced a whole new Concorde genre: the PG-rated teen wilderness adventure. Julie had optioned *Hatchet* (1987), a young-adult novel by Gary Paulsen. This is the uplifting story of a boy's fight for survival after his plane crashes in the Canadian woods. Though *Hatchet* is well known in middle-school circles, prudence dictated that it be renamed: If a movie of that title were released by Concorde, it would be taken for a slasher film. And so *A Cry in the Wild* (1990) was born. In the summer of 1989, the script was coming together, a director had been hired, and logistical matters were being ironed out. Naturally, there were last-minute crises, and at one point things seemed to be at an impasse. That's when Julie abruptly departed for Europe, leaving the fate of the film in the hands of her hard-pressed assistant, Byrdie Lifson Pompan.

Lifson Pompan, at twenty-two, had already worked for Julie for two years. So it did not surprise her to be stuck with such headaches as tracking down a trained bear. (The novel called for a moose, but a movie-savvy moose proved unattainable.) Lifson Pompan confirmed for me Julie's familiar pattern: " 'Fix it!' That's how everything was. . . . She would come into my office with this kind of impossible-to-define piece of metal, and say, 'This came from my garbage disposal. Fix it!' " Fortunately, the story of *A Cry in the Wild* has a happy ending. Julie returned one week before filming began, the production ran smoothly, and the finished work did so well—the Internet's MovieBuff database records that it grossed $1.5 million in domestic theatrical release alone—that it spawned several more Concorde family-adventure entries. For her pains, Byrdie Lifson Pompan was deservedly rewarded with an "associate producer" credit on the movie.

Of course, any assistant of Julie's ended up dealing with her husband, whose snap judgments were one of the most trying parts of Lifson Pompan's job at Concorde. If there was bad news that Roger needed to know, Julie would send her to deliver it. One day she was asked to book a last-minute family trip to Hawaii. The company travel agent had recently died, and so Lifson Pompan quickly made the arrangements herself, paying full retail. The Cormans were to leave in the morning; suitcases were packed, and a car was ready to drive them to the airport. When Byrdie arrived at the office that day, she was startled to see Corman and Julie waiting for her. Julie announced, "Return the tickets. He saw the price of the tickets. We're not going to Hawaii."

Nor was dealing with Julie's own caprices much easier. When thwarted, Julie made those around her fully appreciate her displeasure. More than once, she brought Lifson Pompan to the point of tears. After a good-hearted co-worker protested on the young woman's behalf, Julie took Byrdie to lunch and announced, "I want to make one thing very clear. You're not here to cry. You're here to make other people cry." By the same token, says Lifson Pompan, "when she [Julie] was in a good mood, she was great to be with. And to this day she's always been incredibly thoughtful, and invites me to her Christmas parties, and always makes me feel special when I'm there." Lifson Pompan, who is now a wife, a mother, and a successful talent agent with Creative Artists, acknowledges that Julie has been, "in a weird way, an important role model in my life."

•　　•　　•

Julie's departure for Europe on the eve of the filming of *A Cry in the Wild* was not quite as capricious as it may have seemed. Corman had accepted a major studio deal to write and direct *Roger Corman's Frankenstein Unbound* (1990). Production, which had begun in May of 1989, was continuing in Italy, and she needed to be with Roger at this stressful time. The sixty-three-year-old Corman had confided to former assistant Ginny Nugent that, although he missed directing, he probably no longer had the patience to make a go of it. After two decades on the sidelines, he certainly also feared risking his reputation by getting back into the game. But a man like Corman doesn't easily turn down money. Nugent relayed to me that Roger had told her, "They're going to pay me a million dollars. . . . How can I say no?"

Frankenstein Unbound was the brainchild of producer Thom Mount, who had worked for Corman in the mid-1960s when Peter Bogdanovich was shooting *Targets* (1968). Mount's admiration for the Edgar Allan Poe films and his sense of Corman as a great contributor to the Hollywood scene prompted him to seek a major new showcase for Corman's talents. Mount explains that "the reason I went after *Frankenstein,* frankly, is that I thought this was relatively unexploited at that time, [that it was] classic material that would fit Roger's directorial style and allow him to make something that was interesting and odd." Mount's hope was that, on the strength of this film, Roger would set aside his obligations as a company head and continue directing movies. Beyond the lucrative studio deal (Warner Bros. took the international rights, and Twentieth Century–Fox handled domestic), Mount promised Corman "the best script we can get, the best cast we can get, the best music we can get, and the best advertising campaign we can get." The budget allotted was in the vicinity of $11.5 million, a fortune by Corman's own production standards.

The first order of business was to arrive at a strong script. Roger initially handed the writing chores over to an office intern, but he soon graduated to a series of well-known writers, among them Wes Craven and Floyd Mutrux. At length he turned to a novel, *Frankenstein Unbound* (1973), by Brian Aldiss, which added a time-travel element and some hazy metaphysical musings to Mary Shelley's familiar story from the nineteenth century. A film critic named F. X. Feeney was largely responsible for the adaptation, but Roger himself was heavily involved with the script development process. The fact that two studios had a say in both story and casting decisions was something Corman clearly found disconcerting. He was happy, however, with the stellar cast that featured John Hurt, Raul Julia (as Dr. Victor Frankenstein), Bridget Fonda (as a sensuous Mary Shelley), Jason Patric, and rock star Michael Hutchence.

In Italy, says Mount, "I think Roger had a lot of fun. I think he was also at least partially terrified. . . . He seemed throughout the experience to be less at ease directing than I had hoped. On the other hand, there were times when it was worth everything, because you could just see Roger having a great time on the set. Certain sequences, certain actors, certain situations— Roger was just flying. He would actually smile." Mount noted that Corman was happiest when dealing with action scenes, or with mechanical gadgets like a futuristic automobile. "He loved playing with the toys. The closer we got to the toys, the more fun he was having."

At Mount's insistence, the entire Corman family came to Italy for much of the ten-week shoot. Fourteen-year-old Catherine, in fact, did a commendable job in a featured role, that of a hapless servant girl who is accused of witchcraft and dies on the gallows. Mount found Julie's presence particularly helpful: "She really was an ally in holding out for quality. . . . I think she's honest, and I think she encourages Roger's better instincts."

The relationship between Corman and Mount turned out to be the reverse of the usual one, in which the director has a huge vision and the producer must fight to keep him within bounds. In studio terms, the film's $11.5 million budget was rather modest—a typical picture of that era might cost $17 million, and most big films came in at $25 million. Still, Corman persisted in cutting corners. Both cost-conscious and impatient, he tried to get away with fewer takes than Mount thought necessary for an A-level production. And Corman was shocked to hear that Mount's classy poster for the movie cost $100,000. Mount surmises that "part of him really loved working on a movie where the financial problems were simply somebody else's. At the same time, he couldn't quite separate himself—there was a real knee-jerk tendency to just rebel against the spending of money."

Aside from money matters, Corman was most bothered by the need to shoot a sex scene for *Frankenstein Unbound*. When last directing films in the 1960s, he had had little occasion to film on-screen lovemaking between his leading characters. Although, at both New World and Concorde, Corman the producer encouraged frank sexuality in his erotic thrillers and stripper movies, as a director he seemed unable to adjust to the new standards. Mount told me, "What little sex or semi-sexual material existed in the script, Roger effectively cut out before he had to shoot it. Roger just wouldn't cross that bridge." Though some Corman staffers maintain that part of the problem was the casting of a very young Bridget Fonda opposite a very middle-aged John Hurt, Mount believes that Corman's personal discomfort made a convincingly erotic scene impossible. In Mount's words, Corman "faded completely" in the face of this challenge.

When *Roger Corman's Frankenstein Unbound* was announced, post-production specialist Clark Henderson was one of several former employees who worried about the wisdom of the project. Henderson confesses to having agonized over the fact that "I'm too much of a coward and he's too much—even now—of an odd, misplaced father figure. I can't tell him what I should tell him. If I were a good friend of this man, who's been good to me, I would tell him that this is a stupid idea. . . . It will ruin his whole directing reputation." Henderson's initial fear was that audiences would decide belatedly that Corman had never had much talent. Fortunately, this didn't happen, said Henderson, "because people just assumed he'd gotten older and wasn't any good anymore."

Upon the release of *Frankenstein Unbound* in autumn 1990, critical reaction was not entirely negative. Though Mount admits that the film hardly measured up to his own expectations, he claims that those reviewers who didn't trash the movie were quite enthusiastic. In England, Richard Combs penned a long, respectful analysis for *Sight and Sound,* and throughout Europe interest in the release ran high. But Vincent Canby in the *New York Times* was dismissive, and Gary Giddins in the *Village Voice* typified many American critics in carping, "The science is potty, the fantasy mundane, the horror muted, the humor regrettable." Longtime Corman fans may not have been deterred by comments like these, but it's hardly surprising that most audiences stayed away. In its first year, the film only grossed $37,000 in domestic theatrical release, according to Art Murphy's *Boxoffice Register,* though foreign and video sales helped offset these grim numbers. No wonder Corman shows no sign of directing another feature anytime soon.

Actor David Carradine maintains that he found *Frankenstein Unbound* "intensely original, a very unusual and absorbing picture." Though aware of the movie's flaws, he insists that "[Corman's] treatment of the monster was completely without parallel. Nobody had ever done the Frankenstein monster that way." Because he himself had played a character named Frankenstein in *Death Race 2000* back in 1975, it's not surprising that Carradine would focus on the film's monster, who is a uniquely soulful and articulate version of the creature that movie audiences know and love. Perhaps Roger lavished special care on his monster because he understood something about creations that get out of hand.

By 1990 Corman was back from Europe to take full charge of Concorde–New Horizons Pictures. Despite his best efforts, the seven-year-old company kept threatening to grow beyond his control.

Chapter 13

FAST-FORWARD

*These are not B or B-plus pictures. These are A-minus
pictures. It's a subtle differentiation.*

ROGER CORMAN, 1994

THE YEAR 1990 brought a resurgence of interest in the
lengthy filmmaking career of Roger Corman. In the mainstream media, the
sixty-four-year-old "King of the Bs" was suddenly big news. His name and face
were everywhere. One example: An intriguing spread in *GQ* featured a dignified Corman sitting behind his desk, on top of which perched ballerinas in
full *Swan Lake* regalia. A headline screamed, "Shocker! Horror-Meister
Roger Corman's Favorite 'B' Work is Ballet." Encouraged by *GQ*'s Marion
Long, Roger pondered the notion of futuristic choreography, adding that "a
ballet about the Hell's Angels isn't a bad idea at all." (This odd journalistic coup
occurred when *GQ* asked Corman to name an interest that readers might find
surprising. He vaguely recalled that circa 1950, as a young man in Paris
without much command of the language, he'd taken his dates to the ballet.)

In the summer of 1990, as horror buffs awaited *Roger Corman's
Frankenstein Unbound,* Corman's memoir appeared in bookstores. *How I
Made a Hundred Movies in Hollywood and Never Lost a Dime,* published by
Random House, made a small splash worldwide and remained in print
until 1998. The slim but cheeky 237-page volume is full of lively anecdotes
and laudatory quotes by Corman alumni, who presented their former boss

in the best possible light. Reviewers found the work amusing, and took the opportunity to hail Roger anew for his career achievements.

The evolution of the book project reflects once again the contradictions of a man whom former Corman sales exec Frank Moreno described to me as "a very private person, who also has a tremendous ego, and loves publicity." At first, Corman stayed aloof. When he needed to pick a co-writer, he asked Anna Roth to read three showbiz biographies and choose among their authors. She settled on Jim Jerome, a veteran interviewer for *People* magazine. Roth remembers, "[Corman] didn't really care."

Once the book was finished, however, he was concerned enough about its contents to ask me to pore over the page proofs, not once but twice, in search of anything that might tarnish his image. On my first read-through, I was bothered by the fact that, in naming then current members of his creative staff, he grouped them in terms of their university affiliations. Those with degrees from Harvard and Stanford got included, those from Yale and Cornell were overlooked. I diplomatically argued that, for purposes of office morale, it was wise to mention everyone, or no one. Corman duly incorporated the extra names I had suggested. But he never thought to include me in his text until I finally pointed out that my ego, too, deserved a boost. Still, my duties on the memoir were simple compared to those of the staffer to whom Corman entrusted the most delicate job of all: drafting his very touching dedication, namely, "to my wife, Julie—my best friend, strongest supporter, and most valued critic. I love you."

* * *

In 1991 the disappointment of *Frankenstein Unbound* notwithstanding, Corman's own morale was still high. His cameo role as FBI director Hayden Burke in *The Silence of the Lambs* was widely noted. In the wake of the film's huge success, director Jonathan Demme told interviewers how much he owed to his old mentor. Corman's greatest moment, however, came on June 12, 1991, when his star was unveiled on Hollywood Boulevard, between Sycamore Avenue and North Orange Drive.

The effort to get Corman a Walk of Fame star was spearheaded by producer Brad Krevoy, who told me that years earlier he had spotted in Corman's memorandum book his wistful notation that there were only forty-two stars left on Hollywood Boulevard. (Recently, the number of remaining blank stars has been expanded.) Once Krevoy became an industry player, he started networking on Corman's behalf. Meanwhile actress-writer-director Linda Shayne, who had whimsically promised Corman a star for his birthday, rounded up glowing letters of recommendation from thirteen celebrities, including Ron Howard, Jack Nicholson, and Martin Scorsese. It took two years for Shayne and Krevoy to gain the approval of the Hollywood Chamber of Commerce and raise the mandatory $15,000 fee, thus ensuring that Roger Corman would join the ranks of showbiz immortals.

When the big day arrived, grateful alumni pulled out all the stops. At the unveiling ceremony, Talia Shire spoke graciously on behalf of her brother Francis Ford Coppola. Among the well-known faces in the crowd were David Carradine, Diane Ladd, Nancy Sinatra, and Shelley Winters. Afterwards, hundreds of guests adjourned to the Hollywood Roosevelt Hotel for a formal luncheon sponsored by a long list of corporate donors, including cable networks and home-video companies. Also involved were such major individual sponsors as Peter Bogdanovich, Jim Cameron, Gale Anne Hurd, and John Sayles. The fact that Concorde's entire office staff was invited—and that we could officially shut down the office for one afternoon—made the event very special indeed.

The mood was one of affectionate good humor, as reflected in Andrea King's account for the *Hollywood Reporter*. Director Joe Dante, the jovial master of ceremonies, reminisced about how his New World duties in the 1970s included cleaning out Corman's garage. Writer-director Howard R. Cohen confided that when he asked for a helicopter to film a dramatic finale, Corman responded, "I'll get you a ladder." Former AIP chief Sam Arkoff, celebrating his seventy-third birthday, told the crowd that "Corman does not march to a different drummer—he *is* a different drummer." This quip made a good cue for the zany Stanford University band, which had traveled down from Palo Alto as a raucous surprise.

Moviemaker Jim Wynorski, introduced as the man most likely to be the next Roger Corman, delighted the crowd with a short tribute film he and Shayne had compiled, containing clips from Corman interviews and features. When Roger himself mounted the rostrum, he observed that giving opportunities to untried young talent had turned out to be "a fair trade" all around. He was roundly applauded when he summed up his future with

Jack Nicholson's line from *The Little Shop of Horrors,* "Don't stop now!" Press reports of the luncheon mentioned that proceeds would be used to establish the Roger Corman Film Awards at Stanford University, helping to fund two student films a year. But no one seems to have followed through on setting up an endowment. Professor Henry S. Breitrose of Stanford's Department of Communication (there is no formal film department at Stanford) recalls that, following the tribute luncheon, a gift was made in Corman's name to the student film production fund. Although Corman still regards Stanford as a prime source for bright young assistants, an ongoing monetary connection has not been established to date.

· · ·

At the Walk of Fame ceremony and luncheon, Corman was aglow with happiness. But as the 1990s progressed and the business climate turned less hospitable toward low-budget films, he became increasingly moody. His first assistant, Kinta Haller, insisted to me that back in her day, when Corman was young and low-budget filmmaking was a daily adventure, she had never regarded him as depressed or truly temperamental. For more recent staffers, however, Corman's rages and dark moods are all too familiar. Producer Michael Amato, who started at Concorde in 1993, evoked for me the image of Corman that is remembered by most of his recent employees: "You walk in his office, and he's just staring out the window."

The problem was partly fatigue. Rodman Flender, a Concorde head of production who aspired to direct, used to envy all those who passed his desk on their way to hear Corman give his director's speech: "I'd hear bits and pieces of it, I'd see him animatedly jump around the room. I remember thinking, 'I can't wait until it's my turn.'" The day finally came, just prior to the filming of *The Unborn* (1989). But when Flender eagerly sat down to receive the word of the master, Corman turned to him and said, "Rodman, you know most of this stuff. And, frankly, I'm just tired of the sound of my own voice."

Physical problems didn't help matters. Laura Schiff, yet another Concorde assistant, recalls that Roger threw out his back on the eve of a fourteen-hour flight to Manila. The staff begged him to buy a first-class ticket, for maximum comfort on the trek, but he staunchly refused. Schiff explains that Concorde actors who went overseas were always required to fly coach, and "the thing about Roger is, he wouldn't let you go first-class, but he wouldn't turn around and go first-class himself, either. He definitely did not spend money on himself." He did, however, gladly accept the airline's offer of a free upgrade for the Manila trip. And he was always happy to attend film festivals, anywhere in the world, that provided cushy travel arrangements for himself and his family.

Corman's truly serious back problems began in the summer of 1993, when he was sixty-seven years old. He had taken the family to Europe. The official story is that he was annoyed by all the dawdling at a train station, and so picked up everyone's luggage and tried to carry it himself. He came home in need of surgery, but had a bad reaction to the post-operative medication. Corman returned to the office a stooped old man, skinny and frail, with a stubble of white beard and pants held up with suspenders; it would be several months before he returned to his normal appearance. More recently, there has been a stomach ulcer, and other ailments also have plagued him, contributing to dramatic mood swings.

When we talked in late 1998, actor-filmmaker Andrew Stevens said of Corman, "I think his company ebbs and flows on his moods." That's why, when Stevens has financial matters to discuss, he checks out Roger's current frame of mind with an assistant before venturing into the office. Though the film business has its share of genuine frustrations, Corman is more and more prone to reach his boiling point about matters that most would regard as trivial. One notorious story concerns an office thermostat. It was Roger's habit to regulate the temperature himself to save energy costs. On hot days, staff members kept turning up the air-conditioning to cool the stuffy building. When Corman saw one thermostat readjusted for the third time that afternoon, he reportedly let out a cry of rage, grabbed a stapler, and smashed it against the thermostat unit until it broke. Then he ducked into his wife's darkened office and sat staring into space.

· · ·

Director Joe Dante has his own theory about Corman's increasing volatility: "He's making a widget, and he used to make movies. And I think that can't be anything but depressing for him." In the early 1990s, however, Corman sporadically tried to break the mold with screen projects that were more than safe investments. On October 26, 1989, one week after the Loma Prieta earthquake struck northern California, Corman told Andrea King of the *Hollywood Reporter* that a $12 million feature called *Quake* would go before the cameras in March of 1990. He claimed this would be a "very serious film intended to take a look at California politics, the reluctance of the state government to fully fund the highway renovation and maintenance programs, and the reluctance of Americans to pay higher taxes to fund such things." Corman had every intention of making *Quake* (though not, of course, on a $12 million budget), and hired award-winning novelist Madison Smartt Bell to write its screenplay. But, several writers later, the movie that emerged (in 1993) was not a serious social indictment at all, but rather a low-budget thriller about a psycho who takes a woman hostage in the post-quake rubble.

The civil disturbances that paralyzed Los Angeles in May of 1992 also prompted Corman to swing into action. *People* magazine for June 1, 1992, quotes him as saying, "I've had an idea for years to do a picture about the dichotomy between the rich and the poor. The riots provided me with an opportunity to get master shots that otherwise I would not have been able to get." To achieve a broad perspective, he hired a trio of writers, led by George Hickenlooper *(Hearts of Darkness)*. On November 9, 1998, I spoke to one of the three, Matt Greenberg—he vividly described how Corman summoned the team into his office and grandly announced, "I think it's going to be a very important film; with you, George, I think it's going to be a very fine film; and I think it's going to make a statement. Now if you don't mind, I've got to go somewhere. . . ." Corman's detachment from the project came to symptomize what was wrong with it from the outset. Its script, entitled *Night of a Thousand Fires,* was never completed, but Roger seemed too preoccupied to care. At a time of economic difficulties, he was busy downsizing his product line, and reserving his attention for *Carnosaur* (1993).

• • •

Carnosaur began with Corman's shrewd realization that Steven Spielberg's upcoming *Jurassic Park* (1993) would cause dinosaur mania to sweep the land. Roger bought the screen rights to a clumsy British novel, scrapped all but the title, then hired Adam Simon to write and direct something more visceral and audacious than Spielberg could muster. Diane Ladd, coming off her Best Supporting Actress nomination for *Rambling Rose* (1991), signed on to play the mad scientist, Dr. Tiptree. Her flamboyant performance helped earn the picture one upturned thumb on Gene Siskel and Roger Ebert's TV program devoted to film reviews. Nonetheless, thanks to the budget paring, the dinosaurs were awkward and unconvincing (which didn't stop them from being reused in three more Corman movie epics). But Roger achieved his goal: getting *Carnosaur* into theaters in May of 1993, a full month before *Jurassic Park,* to capitalize on the public's impatience to see dinosaurs run amok on-screen.

Corman infuriated Adam Simon not only by abruptly slashing the budget of *Carnosaur* from $3 million to $850,000, but also by bragging to the media about how much money he had spent on the project. On December 2, 1993, Roger recapped the film's first six months for Kathleen O'Steen of *Variety.* He recounted how (following a brief but successful release in theaters) 85,000 videocassettes were sold, adding up to $4.1 million in video revenue, which made *Carnosaur* Concorde's top grosser ever. Corman informed O'Steen he had made the film for $5 million. This was deeply humiliating to Simon, who told me he felt *Carnosaur* looked particularly shoddy if judged by the industry's expectations of what $5 million could buy.

Simon, a promising graduate of the USC Film School, had first come to Concorde to make *Brain Dead* (1990) for Julie Corman. One of Concorde's truly ambitious projects, this offbeat psychological thriller derived from *Paranoia,* an unfinished script that Charles Beaumont had written in the 1960s, just prior to his untimely death. *Brain Dead* encompassed multiple layers of reality, and Roger was so unsure of the results that he asked directors Carl Franklin and Katt Shea to watch the film and pass judgment. Although it was released virtually intact after Franklin praised it, *Brain Dead* never had huge appeal for mass audiences. (Years after the fact, Simon discovered that his cinematic idol, director Sam Fuller, had sought to give *Brain Dead* a prize when it screened at a French film festival. The only hitch: The movie was being shown out of competition, because Corman had declined to pay the entrance fee. Simon smiles ruefully over this bittersweet moment, one of many that have come out of his Concorde experience. As he told me on October 8, 1998, he finds it both thrilling and painful that "my greatest childhood hero had in fact seen that film and thought it should get an award, and because of Roger's cheapness, it hadn't.")

Nonetheless, Corman took a personal interest in *Brain Dead* because of its connection with his old friend Beaumont, author of *The Intruder* (1962) and *The Masque of the Red Death* (1964). But the two assignments he gave Simon after *Brain Dead* were standard genre fare: an erotic thriller (1992's *Body Chemistry II*) and a monster movie *(Carnosaur)*. Simon, who boasts a truly quirky sensibility, worked hard to make these conventional movies in unconventional ways. Yet he admits his Concorde output consists of "movies that are made to be seen two or three times, but . . . that most people never see once." Simon's Concorde efforts have gotten him some big studio writing assignments, as well as a small cult following. Still, he told me, "they were not exactly giant career-builders."

Adam Simon's experience helps explain why, in the 1990s, Concorde has stopped being the destination of choice for many film-school graduates. What has made the key difference is the emergence of the Sundance Film Festival as the place where a talented young filmmaker can become an overnight star. In 1989, the year Simon made *Brain Dead,* Steven Soderbergh debuted at Sundance with *sex, lies, & videotape.* This independent feature, made for $1.2 million, won critical acclaim and went on to be a huge commercial hit. Its $24 million take at the domestic box office (the figures come from showbiz statistician Art Murphy) instantly propelled Soderbergh into the Hollywood mainstream. Since the experience of Soderbergh, studio executives have been on the lookout for the next big thing to emerge from the festival circuit. This was Quentin Tarantino's route to fame and fortune, and though it may not work for everyone, it has the virtue of allowing young moviemakers the freedom to pursue their personal visions. (*The Blair Witch Project,* the cheaply made 1999 horror film that raked in $28 million domestically in its first weekend of wide release, is a prime example of what can be done today with an inventive idea, a $40,000 production budget, and the use of the Internet as a clever advertising tool. The movie was snapped up at Sundance by Artisan Entertainment after its popular Web site helped trigger a bidding war.)

Most recent Concorde directors agree that Sundance changed the basic formula for success. If you can finance your own movie (with help from your relatives and your credit cards) and then get it into a prestigious festival, there's far less need to jump through Roger Corman's flaming hoops.

. . .

During the 1990s, Corman was more wedded than ever to straight-ahead genre movies, and to sequels that largely repeated what had worked before. Erotic thrillers and martial-arts pictures were still very much part of the mix. Corman tried to spice up formulaic scripts with gimmicks, like giving a cameo role to star running back Roger Craig in *Naked Obsession* (1991), and incorporating baseball veteran Steve Garvey into the cast of *Bloodfist VI* (1994). In this era, an array of Third World countries provided attractive backdrops for the Corman product line. Concorde action films (1992's *The Berlin Conspiracy*) and horror movies (1993's *Dracula Rising*) took advantage of Eastern European locales that were newly available after the disbanding of the Soviet Union. Later in the decade, a deal with Mosfilm gave Corman folk the dubious benefit of shooting on a vast, though dilapidated, Moscow soundstage.

Always one to seize on a trend, Corman found unexpected success with family features for a while. Julie Corman's *A Cry in the Wild* (1990), mentioned earlier, spawned her *White Wolves* (1993) and a sequel, *White Wolves II* (1995), prompting Roger to tell *Variety*'s Kathleen O'Steen that he planned to devote one-third of his own output to films that were rated PG. Julie had long had a personal affinity for family projects, but for Corman this new interest was out-of-character, to say the least. At one point, even director Jim Wynorski was pressed into service making movies that were endearing rather than erotic. For *Munchies* (1992), Wynorski cast an adorable preteen named Jennifer Love Hewitt in a featured role; the following year, he teamed her with Howard Hesseman in *Little Miss Millions,* which gave a family-friendly spin to the Clark Gable–Claudette Colbert romantic comedy *It Happened One Night* (1934). In the early 1990s, before the enthusiasm for wholesome movies inevitably ran its course, the same Corman team that was usually knee-deep in scripts about strippers and nuclear terrorists, found itself happily pondering magic skateboards.

. . .

Curiously, the era of wholesome family films coincided with the period when Corman's own family demanded serious attention. The three eldest Corman children were then in their mid-teens. There was a time when Corman had demonstrated his parental involvement by coaching his sons' basketball teams to league championships, but those days were long over. (In

Corman's memoir, Julie described him as being so intense that these teams "had no alternative but to win." She also noted that Roger worked tirelessly on a play that would allow a team member with a physical disability to score.) In 1991, the same year that his brother Gene's second son was married, Catherine started applying to colleges. Characteristically, Roger was soon caught up in the whole lengthy process. As for the two boys, they found their own ways to remind Dad of their existence.

Catherine had so excelled at her prestigious girls' school that she graduated at age seventeen, one year early. Julie openly campaigned for her eldest child to take time off—perhaps work on a film or explore other creative outlets—but she was overruled. Catherine's college applications quickly became a project for the entire office staff. I for one read countless drafts of her application essays; at one point, Corman even asked me, "as a friend," to offer tips for improving one of her classroom assignments, in hopes that it would earn her the best possible grade in a difficult course. Catherine, a gifted and diligent student, hardly needed my help. But Roger was prepared to do whatever it took to smooth her pathway into a distinguished university.

When it boiled down to a choice between Stanford and Harvard, school alumni on the Corman staff were recruited to discuss with Catherine the relative merits of these two lofty institutions. Corman himself went back and forth about which option his firstborn should pursue. Laura Schiff, a Stanford graduate, told me that "whatever he wanted at the moment, that's what he wanted, and there was a lot of pressure to do that." Ultimately, Catherine ended up at Harvard, where she won grants toward combining creative writing and the fine arts. After graduating in 1996, she worked on poetry and on an opera, and tried adapting a virtually unfilmable novel, Herman Melville's *The Confidence Man* (1857), for the screen.

Meanwhile, Roger Martin and Brian were proving to be far more of a challenge than their high-achieving older sister. The two boys—both tall, lean, and athletic like their father—were like him, too, in being absolutely determined to have their own way. There was no question that the boys were bright, but in classic teenage fashion they resisted authority for all they were worth. So Roger and Julie, like so many parents, often found themselves called into meetings with school administrators to discuss their sons' latest shenanigans.

A clue to the boys' antics comes from a former Corman employee who spoke to Roger Martin just before his departure for a well-known East Coast prep school. When the employee enthused, "You're so lucky to be going to a great school like that," Roger Martin replied sardonically, "Yeah, the luckiest kid in the world." It appeared that the Corman sons' rebelliousness was a natural outgrowth of life with a famous and very busy father, who seemed at times to alternate between obsessing over their achievements and ignoring their existence. The common view is that Roger Martin and his brother were searching for dramatic ways to question their roles within the Corman universe. Says one ex-staffer, "I think the boys were desperate for attention." It's tempting to say that Corman, who once solemnly advised me that the key to good parenting is making time to talk to your children, occasionally forgot to take his own advice.

Today, happily, the brothers seem to be thriving at their respective colleges. At the University of California at Berkeley, Roger Martin has learned to apply his formidable brainpower to the study of computers. Brian started out at the idyllic mountaintop campus of the University of California at Santa Cruz, then switched to Duke University in Durham, North Carolina. In his junior year, he upheld family tradition by transferring to Stanford University, his father's alma mater. Onetime head of production Michael Amato told me that when he recently encountered Roger and Julie Corman at a wedding reception, he inquired about the boys. Julie smiled with relief, saying, "They're doing well, and Roger Martin is working on the Web site for Concorde."

Corman clearly would like nothing better than to welcome all four of his children into the family business. I've heard rumors that when Catherine graduated from Harvard, Roger offered to let her run his company but she declined. At any rate, after stays in Santa Barbara and New York City, she has returned to Los Angeles. Increasingly, Catherine (a tall, slender brunette with her mother's good looks) has been working on Concorde productions, including a fledgling film venture in India that started up in 1998. In 1999, she served as producer on a rock-climbing movie, *Don't Let Go,* that was shot on location in Northern California. There's no telling whether the boys too will gravitate back into the fold.

Mary, now in her mid-teens, is a student at an exclusive Los Angeles prep school. She is interested in art, and has tried hard (with Julie's encouragement) to turn her father into a Sunday painter. Remarkably, this prospect seems to appeal to Roger, but his natural impatience adds tension to what's supposed to be a relaxing hobby. I'm told he got very nervous when trying watercolors for the first time, and Mary was forced to calm him down. Those who have observed the family over time are convinced that Corman's style with his sons and with his daughters has been very different. Like many a father, he has doted on the girls, but made tough demands on the boys, while also shrugging off their misbehavior as somehow being manly. This may explain why the girls have given him (and his staff) a much easier time.

The extended Corman family still continues to be part of the scene. Anne Corman, the family matriarch who outlasted her husband by sixteen years, died at the age of ninety-two on April 2, 1994. But Corman remains connected to brother Gene, his wife Nan, and their two grown sons. (Craig is an attorney, educated at Stanford and the University of Michigan. His wife is also an attorney, with a Harvard law degree. Todd, married to actress Jennifer Runyon since 1991, is an assistant director on major studio films like *D3: The Mighty Ducks* [1996]. There are now several grandchildren.)

An item in the *Hollywood Reporter* for April 12, 1994, claiming that Roger would join forces with Gene and his Chateau Productions to co-produce a $20 million film about the fugitive financier Robert Vesco, was pure hype. Roger, however, is currently playing a part in the Hollywood dream of one of Gene's children. Gene has said that his son Craig resembles the young Roger, in not being satisfied with the profession for which all his schooling has prepared him. Now, thanks to his uncle, Craig Corman is making his debut as the writer-director of *Vital Parts* (1999), a Concorde film shot in Manila. The word is that he's got talent. Nothing would please Roger more than seeing the start of his own creative dynasty.

Chapter 14

FUTURE TENSE

*I want to ease back and have a boutique company
that I can manage myself.*

ROGER CORMAN, 1996

MOST CONCORDE–NEW HORIZONS employees wear more than one hat. Sometimes they have little choice in the matter. For example, though he had no plumbing experience, a legal intern named Ted Schipper was once summoned to fix the Jacuzzi upstairs at the Corman home. He did his best, but suddenly water was dripping through the ceiling in the living room. And Julie was having a party that weekend.

This story came to me courtesy of Michael Amato, who began as an unpaid intern at Concorde and within two years moved up the ladder into the post of "production chief." Now he and Schipper run their own small company, Mount Royal Entertainment, with *Dead Man's Curve* (1998) as their first completed project. Like most Corman graduates, Amato and Schipper want to emulate their mentor's success in the motion-picture field. But, as Amato makes clear, they hardly hope to be Roger Corman clones. Says Amato of his former boss, "I guess it's the game that he likes, and that's what he's so involved in. There doesn't seem to be anything else in his life beside that game." For Amato himself, "It's more than a game. I want to make something that I'm proud of, that my heart and soul are into."

Amato became Concorde's head of marketing in 1993, at a time when the company's direct-to-video sales were in decline. In an era marked by a glut of video product, the major studios dominated the marketplace by forcing retailers to buy multiple copies of their titles and by attracting consumers' attention to their releases through strategic merchandising tie-ins. The result was that small independents were effectively shut out.

Corman's solution was to make even more films on even slimmer budgets. With only one assistant, Amato cranked out ad campaigns for thirty-six movies a year, while also handling promotional materials for the major film markets. (By contrast, Concorde's main competitor at the time, Trimark Pictures, released twenty-two in a year, and its marketing staff numbered eleven.) Initially, each of Michael's campaigns cost about $4,000, mostly for the hiring of freelance graphic designers. Then Corman decided to slash costs by using cut-and-paste methods. When told that modern advertising required computer technology, Corman sent Amato to the Corman house to tackle ad campaigns by using the home computer owned by his son, Roger Martin.

Amato invested in a scanner, and began working from 9:00 A.M. to 6:00 P.M. at the office, then from 6:00 P.M. to 1:00 A.M. at the Corman home. He recalls that "the longest week I ever worked was 102 hours." Did he get paid extra? "No, of course not." At times, when a cocktail party was in progress, Corman would bring guests upstairs to have Amato demonstrate his product line via the computer screen. Occasionally, Michael felt awkward, as when he chanced upon Roger reading the newspaper in his pajamas. But there were nights when Corman, home late from a meeting or social event, would suggest, "Let's go downstairs and have some drinks." Said Amato, remembering one such evening, "It was one of the closest moments I've ever had with Roger, in his living room downstairs, where we were both drinking scotches and just talking—not really about work, but about where I was from and where I grew up, and the artwork that he had on the living-room wall, talking about his sons and which colleges they were going to go to."

Reflecting back on those rare private interludes, Amato notes that "it feels good to sit down with Roger and see him happy. For some reason you always want to please the guy." Michael's experience parallels that of generations of employees who have regarded Roger Corman as a benevolent but distant father figure. Many alumni have spoken to me of their strong compulsion to gain Corman's approval, even if this meant habitually deferring to his opinions on filmmaking matters. Whenever marketing-related problems arose, Amato would march into Corman's office, intent on expressing his views. But, given his admiration and respect for the man, he would always be won over to Corman's own outlook. So the meeting would end with his complete capitulation: "Whatever you say. I'll work all night on this, get it done for tomorrow."

• • •

When he was at Concorde–New Horizons, Michael Amato sensed in Corman a strong dissatisfaction with the ongoing state of the company. This was not entirely new; Roger has always been restless when faced with the status quo. Occasionally he was to pour his excess energy into money-making projects, few of which proved financially rewarding. There were real-estate investments, a winery, even an organic farm on which he lost huge sums of money. ("It was like *Monopoly*," says a former staff attorney.) Closer to home, Corman entered into secret negotiations to sell or redevelop the Venice, California, studio property. He dabbled in animation— the idea was to build an animation studio in Manila—and for a few years in the mid-1990s tried launching a comicbook division. In 1994 Corman put his 250-title film library on the block, for a figure that Alan Citron of the *Los Angeles Times* reported as $18 million. None of these schemes came to fruition, but ultimately he would get even more creative in launching new business ventures.

The year 1995 was marked by big changes at Concorde. A pact with the Showtime cable-TV network led to the first of three seasons of *Roger Corman Presents,* a series of made-for-television science-fiction and horror flicks. Concorde churned out thirteen of these quickies between January and June 1995, for airing beginning in July. Most were original stories, but several (including *Wasp Woman, Not of This Earth,* and *A Bucket of Blood*) were remakes of Corman movie classics. Roger claimed the idea was to find a new take on old material, but many would disagree. Joe Dante, who is admittedly biased, told me that, from a creative point of view, he was appalled by what was done to his 1978 feature, *Piranha:* "[Roger] simply took the exact same script, word for word, hired a kid to shoot it, used all the special effects from the old movie, and the only thing he didn't do is he didn't remind them it was supposed to be funny. And so it's a totally straight version of a movie that was done tongue-in-cheek originally. And it's unwatchable."

(Amazingly, the chance to remake *Piranha* yet again recently sparked a bidding war among major Hollywood studios. The fact that former Concorde writer-director Adam Simon has written a new *Piranha* script for Twentieth Century-Fox is highly ironic, given that the original got its start as a low-budget parody of a big-studio film.)

By 1996 the second year of the Showtime cable series, Michael Amato had been elevated to handling Concorde's production chores. One of his assignments was to oversee a remake of the 1980 New World entry, *Humanoids from the Deep*. At one special-effects house, he found a group of Corman enthusiasts prepared to design fantastic new monster suits for the project at a bargain price. Roger, though, insisted on carbon copies of the odd, campy costumes from the original release. His rationale soon dawned on Amato—Corman planned to recycle stock footage from the first film and incorporate it into the update.

While the demands of the Showtime cable-TV project were keeping the wheels of production humming, Corman turned his attention to Ireland. In response to threats of new European quotas on American-made films, he purchased property in Galway, on Ireland's unspoiled western coast, for the building of a new studio. *Variety*'s Andrew Hindes reports that half the studio's $3.4 million cost was financed through subsidies from the Irish Ministry of Culture. By November 1995, Corman had formed an Irish company, Concorde Anois, through which to produce movies, and in 1996 the first feature was shot at the facility. Curiously, it was *Bloodfist VIII*, because Corman wanted Don "The Dragon" Wilson to help in training stuntmen who were brand-new to moviemaking. Though some stage-trained actors lived in the vicinity, Concorde staffers had to start from scratch in teaching basic skills to locals eager to hire onto the film crew.

Those who have seen the completed studio complex say it is surprisingly state-of-the-art. It boasts two soundstages and post-production facilities, but its most remarkable feature is the Manor House, built both for filming and for lodging visitors in oversized bedrooms that can easily be converted into sets. One challenge faced by Corman's office staff has been coming up with appropriate scripts. Though the Galway locales have been used as rather unconvincing stand-ins for contemporary New England, they are actually best suited to period pieces. So Concorde's story people have had the rare pleasure of mining classic authors now in the public domain—Henry James and Robert Louis Stevenson, among others—for plot ideas. Filmmaking in Ireland generally precludes nudity, though not violence. David Carradine, one of many name performers who have been happy to visit Galway on Corman's dime, described to me his role in *Stray Bullet II* (1999): "I think we kill every cop in Ireland."

Such enterprises do not always sit well with the Irish people. In 1997 the *Hollywood Reporter*'s Martina Devlin covered a flap between Concorde and two Irish newspapers, the *Sunday Times* and the *Irish Independent,* which charged that Roger's company was receiving substantial government tax breaks to promote violence and lewd sex on-screen. The fact that the studio sits in a Gaelic-speaking region devoted to the preservation of native culture has also prompted local criticism. A former Concorde director noted with amusement that since Corman became a presence in Ireland, divorce has been legalized, *Playboy* magazine has appeared on newsstands, and at least two local actresses have willingly taken their clothes off for Concorde's cameras.

But the Irish government, grateful for Corman's part in bringing new jobs to an economically depressed region, has offered him honorary citizenship. Both Roger and Julie love the Irish countryside (Julie's grandparents on both sides are Irish-born), and many surmise that the Cormans will one day retire to Ireland, perhaps as soon as a suitable castle can be found. Still, those who know Corman well can't imagine him enjoying a quiet retirement. According to former sales executive Frank Moreno, "He will never retire." Producer Michael Amato agrees: "I can't see him golfing; I can't see him playing bingo. . . . He's the kind of guy that will probably die on the job."

•   •   •

Roger Corman may not want to retire, but he has definitely considered ridding himself of the juggernaut that is Concorde–New Horizons. In late 1996, NASA's discovery of possible life on Mars elicited the usual Corman announcement: he was planning a $20 million outer-space feature, *Mars Lives.* While discussing this project with Benedict Carver of the publication

Screen International, he also revealed that he was in serious talks with producer Elliott Kastner (1987's *Angel Heart,* 1994's *Frank and Jesse*) concerning
the sale of the company. Carver's story, published on December 13, 1996,
mentioned a selling price of $70 million; this sum was said to cover, in
addition to the company itself, a library of 340 movies, plus twenty-three
more in production, and twelve in development. (The studio in Ireland was
specifically excluded from the discussions.) Corman's reason for selling
must have sounded familiar to those who remembered the fate of New
World Pictures. As Corman informed the *Hollywood Reporter*'s Jeffrey Jolson-
Colburn on December 9, 1996, his goal was to scale back his operation so
that he could once again be personally involved with every new project.

Mars Lives* was never made, and despite months of negotiations, Concorde–New Horizons ultimately never changed hands. In early 1997, however, articles in such reputable publications as the *New York Times* and the
Wall Street Journal reported that the sale was imminent. Both papers quoted
the selling price as $100 million, mentioned a 378-film library, and noted that
Corman planned to continue producing independently under the Concorde name. On September 3, 1997, Scott Hettrick of the *Hollywood Reporter*
was still speaking of the Kastner sale as nearly final.

Insiders agree that Corman truly wanted the deal to go through, that he
welcomed the chance to reassert control by starting over on a much smaller
scale. During fourteen months of protracted haggling, his employees were
faced with uncertainty about their own careers. Concorde at its best could be
a happy, friendly place. (When times were good, I remember Halloween costumes, a brownie bake-off, and even a bikini contest at the studio.) But the
tensions of the negotiation period encouraged the spread of the "cliques and
clubs" mentioned by Michael Amato, as everyone tried to keep up with the
latest scuttlebutt.

· · ·

Corman's failure to close the sale left him very downhearted. He was not
wholly cheered by the accolades that continued to mount. There had been
a time when Roger was far more esteemed in Europe than at home. As
early as 1967, he was honored by the Cinémathèque Française, and he had
become a sought-after guest at the world's major film festivals. In the
1990s, however, Hollywood finally revised its thinking, coming to view the

erstwhile schlockmeister as an elder statesman. True, some of his new honors were somewhat lacking in dignity: At USA Cable's "Up-All-Night First Annual B-Minus Movie Awards" ceremony, he accepted the Golden Crab Award. But in September 1996, he was voted the recipient of the Career Achievement Award given annually by the Los Angeles Film Critics Association. Leonard Maltin, the association's president, told *Variety*'s Leonard Klady that "it's a well-deserved honor. I don't think anyone can claim to have gone their own way as successfully as Roger. He's made pictures that ascend [sic] what we think of as limitations of genre, provided the launch pad for some of our best filmmakers, and distributed great films by the world's top filmmakers."

The selection of Corman was not without controversy. Todd McCarthy, film critic and columnist for *Variety*, was present when the vote was cast. In his column for January 10, 1997, he revealed that Roger was chosen as a palatable substitute for director Elia Kazan (b. 1909), whose naming of names in 1952 before the House Un-American Activities Committee still makes him anathema to many in the film industry. In the March 1997 issue of *Los Angeles* magazine, McCarthy insisted that the choice of Corman "wasn't for artistic reasons." Said McCarthy, who had himself been Roger's head of publicity from 1975 through 1977, "[Corman] wasn't willing to do quality work. He had Peter Bogdanovich, so why didn't he produce *The Last Picture Show* [1971]? He worked with Jack Nicholson, so why didn't he produce *Easy Rider* [1969]?"

Despite McCarthy's carping, more recognition was to follow. In early 1997, Corman was named the winner of the Golden Eddie Filmmaker of the Year Award, given by the American Cinema Editors. That February, the Los Angeles County Museum of Art booked a series of Corman features, culminating in a tribute evening at which Peter Bogdanovich served as master of ceremonies, with other speakers such as American International Pictures co-founder Sam Arkoff, director Carl Franklin, and producer/production designer Polly Platt. After the speechifying, *The Intruder* (1962) was screened for the star-studded audience.

In November 1997, Corman received the Lifetime Achievement Award of the Casting Society of America. At the CSA banquet in Los Angeles, Corman stunned his casting director, Jan Glaser, by warmly praising her before her peers. As screenwriter Fred Bailey has noted, "You don't get too many compliments from Roger. One compliment becomes a jewel that you keep." When we spoke on February 5, 1999, Glaser told me she saw Corman's praise as "a very precious jewel in front of a lot of important people." But the kind words did not, regrettably, guarantee job security. In November 1998, one year after the CSA banquet (and six months after Corman was honored among a group of distinguished producers at the Cannes Film Festival), Roger told Glaser that her services were no longer needed. He explained apologetically, "I'm in my seventies, too old for the hassles of production." He then took over the casting chores for an upcoming film himself. But in trying to schedule auditions on Christmas Eve, he betrayed the fact that he was sorely out-of-touch.

• • •

The reason Corman felt he could do without a casting director was that, as of late 1998, his staff had just completed its most massive undertaking ever. This was the *Black Scorpion* television series, intended by Corman as a way of countering the near collapse of the direct-to-video market. *Black Scorpion* had been introduced in 1995 as a TV movie for Showtime's *Roger Corman Presents*. A sequel appeared the following year. Both featured actress Joan Severance as Darcy Walker—lady cop by day, superhero by night—who uses brains, brawn, and a really cool car to defeat villains with funny names like Gangster Prankster and Aftershock. The films captured the pop-art flavor of the old *Batman* TV series (1966–68). On June 10, 1995, Corman told Glenn Kenny of *TV Guide,* tongue firmly in cheek, "Where we economized was on the Scorpion's costume—it doesn't cover up a lot of her."

Both films did well, especially overseas. Aware of the success of the long-running *Hercules* (1995–2000) and *Xena* (1995–present) syndicated TV franchises, Corman dedicated the Venice studio solely to the production of his new *Black Scorpion* series. It was, in a sense, a daring venture—not because of its bold subject matter or innovative stylistics, but rather because Roger was taking a huge financial risk. When he and I spoke briefly on August 7, 1998, he called this "the biggest gamble of my life." Having churned out twenty-two one-hour episodes with "no financing, no outside deals," he now faces tremendous pressure to sell the series in markets both in the U.S. and overseas.

Colleagues like Frank Moreno worry that Corman has acted out-of-character by financing the massive project completely out of his own pocket, with no guarantees of recouping his expenditures. According to Moreno, "He's not a gambler on this level. . . . That's not the Roger I've known for years." Others, however, feel that TV syndication is a smart move for Corman at this stage of his career. So far, there have been some nibbles in Europe, but as of early 2000, still no firm commitments. It remains to be seen whether Corman, in betting on the worldwide television market, will hit the jackpot or roll snake-eyes.

Production on the *Black Scorpion* series started in spring of 1998, and continued to the end of the year. A mere five or six days were allotted per episode. So Corman, who had once told journalist Digby Diehl that he missed making five-day movies, was now turning them out on a conveyor belt. The fact that the overworked crew got only a few days off between episodes meant that morale inevitably sagged. Roger's mood was particularly volatile: one office employee told me he ranged from upbeat in the morning to "raging inferno in the afternoon. . . ." In late 1998, things became so tense that Corman swore off local production for the near future. Said a disheartened staffer, "He's convinced we can't do anything anymore—that we can't actually get actors, a director, props, and so on to the same place at the same time. It got as bad as that by the end—it really did."

At the beginning of 1999, when local production had ground to a halt, Corman rented out his studio to other film companies, and seriously considered selling the property. But in Ireland, after a few quiet months, some screen projects continued to move forward. And Corman became truly excited about plans to film at an elaborate new studio facility in Hyderabad, India. For a debut project, he chose to revisit the Isaac Asimov science-fiction story, "Nightfall," filmed by Julie in 1988. With his usual fondness for hype, he touted his new *Nightfall* as the first Hollywood picture to be made entirely on location in India (although that is not really the case). And he spread the word that the Science Fiction Writers of America once named Asimov's short work "the best science-fiction story of all time." (Science-fiction author Gregory Feeley insists that Roger was exaggerating the results of a poll taken to compile an anthology of stories written before 1965.) In light of the 1988 film's reception—Richard Harrington in the *Washington Post* had called it "rock bottom cinema"—Corman's decision to try again can be seen as either foolhardy or courageous. But it's vintage Corman to start a new venture by recycling an old idea.

As the last year of the twentieth century wore down, Roger seemed to find a new lease on life through a project spearheaded by his latest studio chief, Marta Mobley-Anderson. This enthusiastic young woman, a veteran of fifty-three Concorde films as well as the *Black Scorpion* series, forged a relationship with the American Movie Classics (AMC) cable channel, which had signed Corman to host the 1999 edition of its annual Monster-Fest. In the two months leading up to Halloween, Corman appeared on AMC weekly, introducing his classic horror films. Then as Halloween night approached, he starred in what Mobley-Anderson calls an "interstitial movie," a clever series of thirty-seven brief episodes that, when joined together, make up an hour-long thriller known as *The Phantom Eye*. The plot features Roger as the sinister Dr. Gorman, head of AMC's horror library, who sends two innocent film students down into the vaults, where they find themselves enmeshed in actual vintage monster flicks. *The Phantom Eye* was designed both to be integrated into AMC's Halloween-weekend movie marathon and to stand alone as a witty re-cap of horror genre conventions.

Corman clearly relished his role as what AMC has dubbed its "master of scare-monies." Such perks as his name on a huge billboard towering over the Sunset Strip surely appealed to his ego. And his involvement with *The Phantom Eye* has helped keep him connected to the filmmaking process. Vlad Wolynetz, producer of *The Phantom Eye* for AMC, remembers Roger as "a trooper": after a shaky start he knocked off fifty-two script pages in one day, an impressive feat even for an actor half his age. Both Wolynetz and Mobley-Anderson (who earned a co-producer credit) spoke to me optimistically in October 1999 about plans for future Concorde-AMC collaborations. But it's instructive that Corman, who once took his work and himself quite seriously, is becoming known among younger viewers largely as a screen personality with a deft comic touch.

The word went out on January 19, 2000, that Corman's Venice studio had been sold to a developer planning to build shops and condominiums. After a production lull, Corman's stated intent is to focus on Ireland and then establish a smaller studio in downtown Los Angeles. Meanwhile, he has retooled his staff to concentrate exclusively on completing and marketing existing product. Marta Mobley-Anderson has been asked to give up her studio responsibilities to become Vice-President of Worldwide Distribution. Frances Doel, who after years of service was rewarded with a vice-presidency and the title "Head of Development," now finds herself back where she started, as Corman's assistant. (Corman has assured her that this is not a demotion, but at the moment she remains, as she puts it, "a VP of nothing.") So for now, at least, the high intensity of the *Black Scorpion* period seems a thing of the past.

· · ·

Jonathan Winfrey, the director entrusted with the two *Black Scorpion* television movies, had what might be called the quintessential Concorde career. A UC Berkeley graduate who never bothered to get a film-school degree, Winfrey (b. 1963) first signed on as a Concorde set painter in 1987. He quickly progressed through the ranks, working as an assistant director and production manager, before taking over as studio head in 1990. This was a job with more than its share of frustrations. Still, there were moments of fun: "We all worked long hours; we'd all go out afterwards and either be sleeping with each other or be partying with each other, and it was a great group of people." Unfortunately, this couldn't last. In the fluid world of low-budget filmmaking, the ambitious were always moving on to better things. However, Jonathan stayed, waiting for his chance to be a director.

It came four years after he first stepped onto the Venice, California, lot. In short order, Corman sent him to Bulgaria, then Peru, to direct action features. (To this day, Winfrey's action footage continues to be spliced into other Concorde product.) Jonathan enjoyed making his two *Black Scorpion* flicks, but he hardly confuses them with art: "To me it's like a fraternity movie you watch on a Friday night when everybody's sitting around drinking beer. You get kind of bleary-eyed and numbed-out, but you're having a good laugh at the expense of this trash." After the second *Black Scorpion*, Jonathan heeded the adage that Concorde is a great place to start and an even better place to leave. Because he has a new family to support, saying no to recent Corman offers has not always been easy. But Winfrey reminds himself that "the way the industry works now, you've got to have something you can really show. I cannot show one Corman movie to anybody." Take his *Crisis in the Kremlin* (1992), made for a mere $250,000 in Bulgarian currency: "For what it was, it was really big. But the acting is mediocre, the script's mediocre—as a director you're the one who's responsible for all those performances, that writing."

Winfrey advises today's would-be directors that, rather than knocking on Roger Corman's door, they try going the film-festival route. As for himself, after several years of steady employment on TV "reality shows" like the Fox Network's *America's Most Wanted,* he's ready to call in some favors in order to make his own small film. He had hoped to find financing and distribution through Concorde, in exchange for a back-end piece of the action, but so far Corman has not been responsive. Which leaves Winfrey more than a little bitter; from Jonathan's perspective, "I made him enough money to put all his kids through college, and yet he can't return my phone calls."

Unlike many earlier staffers, Winfrey feels no nostalgia for Concorde. He's amazed by the fact that Corman chose to wear shabby clothing and to work in a run-down office with filthy carpets. Unfortunately, Roger "lives in this state of mind where he's always [thinking] 'I'm going to lose everything,' or 'I'm going to sell everything,' so there's no point in redoing anything." Jonathan connects Corman's bleak moods with the dark and dingy Venice studio. Its interior reminded Winfrey of "looking down the throat of a rhinoceros. It's kind of a symbol of where he really is."

Still, though Winfrey lacks affection for Corman, he acknowledges his debt to the Roger Corman School of Film. A friend insists that his Concorde connections mean he has an angel on his shoulder. Jonathan himself prefers a different metaphor to describe Corman's role in his industry career: "He was a vehicle, and I could drive it."

•   •   •

Winfrey claims, "When I first got in the business, I wasn't interested in making movies that were exploitative or derogatory towards women." But when you work for Corman, your standards change. As director of *Carnosaur 3* (1996), Winfrey shot a scene in which a giant dinosaur, surrounded by gunmen, attacks a female victim. Roger specified that the raptor undress her, revealing her breasts for the cameras. Though to Jonathan, the notion was ludicrous, he played along with the boss's orders. Winfrey told me, "He wanted that nudity quotient in there. . . . He definitely wanted to see all that stuff."

Regarding the superabundance of sex and nudity in Corman films since the 1970s, a debate has always raged about Roger's personal motives. As screenwriter Daryl Haney observed, the B movie is the place to see the male subconscious at work. If that is so, to what extent is Corman going beyond the demands of the marketplace and tapping into his own preoccupation with the undraped female form? Those who believe Corman finds a degree of personal gratification in his films cite examples like *Naked Obsession* (1991), for which he somehow just happened to visit the set while Maria Ford was filming a highly erotic striptease. (When I spoke to actor Rick Dean on November 6, 1998, he recalled Corman making a rare joke when the scene was over. Corman told Dean, "My glasses steamed up earlier." After a pause, he deadpanned, "I realized that I was holding a cup of hot coffee.")

To many, Corman is simply a red-blooded American male committed to satisfying both himself and his audience. However, Concorde sales executive Pamm Vlastas's dealings with foreign buyers taught her that, in later years, Roger did not always keep up with the fluctuations of public taste. She is convinced that "Roger would make those films with the strippers in them just so he could watch them." Some alumni even argue that, for the aging filmmaker, getting young women to remove their clothes on cue became a kind of power issue. Jon Winfrey cites Corman's indignation when star Joan Severance refused to do nudity of any sort on *Black Scorpion II*. Said Corman to Winfrey, "I can't believe this woman. I'm paying her a quarter of a million dollars and she won't take her clothes off for me." Still, when casting director Jan Glaser argued in 1997 that she could hire better actresses if they stayed dressed, Roger decided that "we'll take some of that nudity out. It's not selling."

Corman's predilections are relevant here, because of a documentary feature that debuted at the Sundance Film Festival in 1998. *Some Nudity Required* was made by Odette Springer, a former Concorde music supervisor taking an "up-close and personal" look at the making of exploitation films. Springer's fascination with the women-in-peril flicks made by Concorde and other low-budget companies led her to explore B-movie sex and violence in relation to her memories of her own traumatic childhood. To Springer, the documentary is ultimately about herself. But Corman is interviewed on-camera, as are Maria Ford, Jim Wynorski, and other Concorde regulars. When Springer, who still considers Corman a father figure, screened the 82-minute *Some Nudity Required* for her ex-boss, he stormed out of the room after only a few minutes, and then looked (in vain) for ways to prevent the film's release.

Corman's outrage is explained partly by the reviews the film generated. Although he was on-screen for less than three minutes, he was mentioned by every critic, and not always favorably. One of the more thoughtful pieces was written by the *L.A. Weekly*'s John Patterson, who noted that "Springer reveres the patrician, fatherly Corman in spite of her distaste for his movies, and this attraction/revulsion marks every level of her relations with her job and co-workers." But Corman was much more apt to fixate on *Variety*'s review, in which Glenn Lovell remarked that he "comes off as something of a dirty old man." Needless to say, the "dirty old man" label is one that Corman finds appalling. Filmmaker Joe Dante summed up for me Corman's own view of his subject matter: "He never thought of those pictures as seamy or seedy. He always thought of them as healthily dirty. . . . I don't think he ever thought of himself as a bad influence. With all the violence and all the sex, I think he always had a sort of happy attitude about it."

Corman alumni are split down the middle over the merits of *Some Nudity Required*. Some feel it contains more than a kernel of truth about sexist attitudes within the film industry. Others, citing key omissions, believe the picture is misleading in regard to Corman and Concorde–New Horizons. Certainly, this insightful but flawed documentary does not tell the whole story. But most agree that Corman has little reason to feel personally injured by his role in it. He comes across as charmingly self-deprecating, calling himself merely "a minor entry in the history of twentieth-century filmmaking." In respect to his focus on heroines who wear little or nothing, he mildly explains that "we're trying to, to a certain extent, exploit the women's beauty, yet at the same time portray them in a positive way."

Of course, the clips in Springer's screen study, many of them culled from Concorde slasher-type films, don't always show women at their best, which makes Roger's words seem either hypocritical or naive. But most viewers I know have found the on-screen Corman highly likable. I asked actor-filmmaker Andrew Stevens about rumors that suggested Corman deliberately left the country when *Some Nudity Required* opened for a brief Los Angeles run. His response was to shrug, "Frankly, I can't imagine anybody caring one way or the other." Yet Corman was obviously still smarting when he told me in August of 1998 that he had been "burned by a small matter." This concern with his public image may seem surprising in a man who has built his career on exploitation pictures. Nonetheless, Corman has always put great stock in his veneer of genial respectability, and he is morose indeed when it is threatened.

•   •   •

For Corman, contentment apparently does not come easily. One longtime employee, citing the internal struggle between Corman the artist and Corman the businessman, predicts, "He'll never be happy." Part of the problem is that Roger, for all his worldly success, has never lived up to his professional potential. He could have been a great filmmaker; he could have been Rupert Murdoch. Instead, he has settled for small achievements. Though Corman does not seem to envy others (such as Miramax Films' Harvey and Bob Weinstein) who have found fame and fortune by choosing a riskier path, his own determination to play it safe has hardly brought true satisfaction.

Frank Moreno, who considers himself a close friend, worries about his onetime employer. Said Moreno in the course of our long conversation, "I don't understand his fighting the trends in the last five, six years. I think that he's still trying to make the small exploitation films. I would love to see Roger working with a couple of talented people and producing two good films a year, rather than seeing him doing what he's doing right now. Because it's not for money anymore." To Moreno, Roger has reached a stage of life when he should be gambling on quality, not on a cut-rate television series. "Roger is a very wealthy man, and it's not going to change his lifestyle whether he makes another $20 million or not. Even if he lost $20 million, it's not going to change his lifestyle."

Frank Moreno is one of many who wish Corman would team with some of his protégés, past and present, to do something special. But, admits Moreno, "I don't know if he could stand the waste that's involved in big filmmaking today." Spending money to assure excellence has become so foreign to his nature that when a production supervisor recently suggested spending $2,000 to improve a film, Corman angrily snapped, "You are taking food out of the mouths of my children." So Corman seems psychologically incapable of risking any part of his fortune to achieve greatness. This goes beyond being cheap: Those who perceive Corman as hamstrung by his fundamental insecurity may well be right.

If Corman cannot step up to better things, and if his current efforts give him little pleasure, retirement might be the sanest option. Andrew Stevens, who, with an assist from Corman, has evolved from a popular television actor into a rising film tycoon, hardly blames Roger for no longer enjoying the moviemaking process. As he told me, "There was a time when the business was easier and more forgiving and more naive, but it was more fun. And I mean only five years ago. . . . It's not fun anymore." In Corman's case, said Stevens, "I'm not sure why—if at seventy-three years old, he doesn't absolutely love what he does every day, which right now he doesn't appear to—why he would do it at all. He's left his mark forever." Stevens feels that, given the fact that Corman is "revered and respected the world over," this might be a good time for him to rest on his laurels.

It rarely has been Roger's custom to indulge in nostalgia. Director Joe Dante comments, "I don't think he thinks backward at all. I think he thinks forward." This helps explain why Corman has always been so quick to discard relics of his past, even to the point of wanting to record over the soundtracks of his classic films. An assistant who was charged with cleaning the Corman garage, unearthed, along with other priceless memorabilia, *Variety*'s 1960 rave review of *House of Usher*. He presented it to Roger, who read it with a smile, then crumpled it and tossed it toward the trashcan. But Corman is not wholly unwilling to be sentimental about bygone days. He has been observed thoughtfully contemplating his old movie posters. He enjoys TV appearances, such as his recent AMC stint, that capitalize on past glories. And perhaps his greatest pleasure comes from attending film festivals and other gatherings where he's hailed for his movies of long ago. Actor Mel Welles, a veteran of the nostalgia convention circuit, reports how much Roger likes these encounters with his loyal fans: "When he's conducting a forum, he's a happy guy."

Corman's memoir ended with one of his favorite images, that of the Creature from the Haunted Sea sitting triumphantly on a chest of gold. If Roger identifies with this self-satisfied monster, it is because he, too, has managed, against all odds, to hang on to his treasure trove. But his "one for the money" approach has not brought him contentment. Maybe that's because he's really not the monster at all. Instead, he's the maker of the monster, which has been growing far too big for him to control. The monster is his money, his company, his reputation. Trapped in the shadow of what he has created, but armed with brains, ingenuity, and strength of will, he's struggling to break free before the final fadeout.

Epilogue:

WINDING DOWN

(2000–)

WINDING DOWN

"I deliberately leave the office around 4 o'clock every afternoon. I feel enough is enough."

ROGER CORMAN (2001)

THE DAWN OF a new millennium prompted Corman to update the name of his company. He had already tried out "Millennium" back in 1983, while starting afresh after the sale of New World Pictures, only to discover that no one could spell it correctly. This time, he settled on something far more user-friendly. On May 15, 2000 he told the *Hollywood Reporter* that Concorde-New Horizons—a cumbersome moniker for his increasingly cumbersome company—was no more. Henceforth, his smaller, leaner production empire would be dubbed New Concorde.

Partly the name-change was his response to the rising power of the Internet as a medium through which movies could be promoted and DVDs sold. As he explained to journalists, "Concorde-New Horizons.com" was much too long to make a good domain name. So the christening of New Concorde signified that Roger had officially entered the computer age. But in other respects, the new company was not much different from the old one. A recent office visitor marveled at the gloom and the bad carpeting. Trying to keep an appointment with a staffer, she found herself threading her way through teetering piles of scripts and cassette tapes. As she told me, "You know how they have these corn mazes? This was a cassette maze."

The Brentwood office may seem particularly cluttered these days because, following the dismantling of the Venice studio, it has absorbed what's left of Corman's production and post-production teams. Before the one-time lumber yard was turned over to real estate developers for $4.3 million, it went out in a blaze of cinematic glory. It was Roger's idea to immortalize the Main Street property in *Slaughter Studios*, in which young filmmakers break into a deserted soundstage, only to discover that it's haunted by a B-movie actor bent on revenge. For the climax of the film, which was shot in 2000 but not released until 2002, the decrepit old buildings went up in flames, and an era came to a dramatic end. As Corman himself described it on one of his recent DVD commentaries, "[The bankers] called and said: 'Roger, it's okay, we've got the money. So blow up your studio.'"

When the sale was first announced in January 2000, Roger told reporters he was on the lookout for a new site in downtown Los Angeles: "I want to build another studio, but not as big. We made money off of the real estate, and I'll use that to build something smaller, hold that for ten or twenty years, [and] we'll use the same real estate ploy." So far, a downtown L.A. studio hasn't materialized. But the fact that a man approaching his seventy-fifth year could make such long-range business plans suggests he is confident that his health and vigor will hold up for many years to come.

Certainly, there's no sense of him retiring anytime soon. He comes into the office daily, and has in the last few years returned to being an active participant, especially in the area of script development. Corman of course knows full well that the film industry is not what it used to be. He's talked to other producers, all of whom are finding it maddeningly difficult to come out ahead on low-budget independent commercial features. He's even said aloud that it might make economic sense for him to simply acquire completed pictures for distribution. Still, according to a longtime staffer, "making movies is what he does, and obviously he seems to have every intention of staying in the game."

•　•　•

For Corman, staying in the game means searching out new ways to sell old genres. The *Black Scorpion* fantasy-action series, which had caused so many Corman mood swings as the twentieth century waned, was Roger's valiant attempt to move into television while retaining his creative independence. By financing twenty-two episodes out of his own pocket, he hoped to interest a U.S. cable network in the entire package. Writer Craig Nevius, who had initially developed Black Scorpion's "lady cop by day/superhero by night" concept for one of Corman's 1995 Showtime movies, was on board as supervising producer. Nevius describes the year 2000, with its protracted negotiations involving the Sci Fi Channel and TNN, as "draining, debilitating" for all concerned.

Ultimately, Corman settled on the Sci Fi Channel, which began airing the series in January 2001. At first, the outlook was good. A tidbit in Variety on January 11, 2001, one week after the show's premiere, divulged that thanks to strong initial ratings, "Roger Corman now plans to produce—and finance—44 additional one-hour segs on a budget of $44 million." But the network, which takes science fiction seriously, did not prove to be a good fit for Black Scorpion's tongue-in-cheek approach. After the first five weeks, executives moved the series from its prime Friday night lineup to a less-attractive Saturday evening slot. As the remaining episodes aired, audiences gradually dropped away.

The generally-upbeat Nevius sees Black Scorpion's failure as simply a matter of bad timing. If it had appeared a few years later, when Spiderman and other superheroes were dominating movie screens, he feels its fate would have been far different. Though by now Nevius has segued into other projects, including his own small TV production company, he remains involved with Black Scorpion business. Roger dreamed up a quickie New Concorde film, The Sting of the Black Scorpion (2002), based on cobbled-together TV episodes, and he also set in motion a plan for a collectors' edition DVD. In November 2002, Nevius was asked to gather the cast (among them pop culture icons like Frank Gorshin, Adam West, and the late Lana Clarkson) for a well-publicized reunion at a comic book convention. Though Corman did not make a cent on his twenty-two episodes, he has not given up hope. He recently told Nevius, "I don't think Black Scorpion is done. I think Black Scorpion can go on forever."

While waiting to recoup what he spent on Black Scorpion, Roger has not been idle. Currently he's producing between five and eight pictures per year, and acquiring others to fill out his home video slate. The romance with Ireland has cooled: no New Concorde film has been shot at the Galway studio since *The Suicide Club* and *The Doorway* (both 2000), and the facilities are being rented out to other companies. But Corman's crews are still taking advantage of cheap production values overseas. One of Roger's inevitable "ripped from the headlines" movies, *Fire Over Afghanistan* (2003), was filmed in Bulgaria. And the upcoming *When Eagles Strike*, about a U.S. military mission to foil a Southeast Asian band of Islamic terrorists, was directed by the unsinkable Cirio Santiago in the Philippines.

Though the erotic thriller genre, once so dear to Roger's heart, has faded from view, Corman-style disaster movies are alive and well. Recent releases include *Avalanche Alley* (2001), which incorporates some rather dazzling stock footage left over from a big-studio mountain-climbing saga. There's also *Shakedown* (2002), described by head of development Frances Doel as "one of our hybrid disaster pictures," the story of "a group of terrorists with a bio-weapon who strike at the same time as a group of bank robbers at a downtown L.A. office building as a huge earthquake takes place." Upholding the monster movie tradition is *Raptor* (2001), yet another attempt to recycle old *Carnosaur* clips. *Raptor* also boasts a musical score composed by James Horner (of *Titanic* fame) back in his *Battle Beyond the Stars* days and borrowed for countless Corman epics ever since. Still to come is *DinoCroc*, about a town ravaged by a prehistoric crocodile, which Corman has called "the biggest special effects picture we've ever done." He has promised that the monster will be computer-generated, and suitable for sequels.

Always interested in technical innovation when it can help save him money, Corman has dropped his budgets even lower than usual to green-light a series of movies on digital video. These cut-rate films range from a spoof of reality TV called *Pleasure Island* to a children's story, *Flyin' Ryan*, about a boy with magic sneakers. As usual, the Corman publicity machine has been pumping out copy about much bigger projects, including a $20 million venture based on the life of Ho Chi Minh. Frances Doel confirms that Corman did indeed commission a script on this topic from an established screenwriter, though the project has long since been shelved. But she was thoroughly amused by Roger's announcement in the August 8, 2002 issue of *Variety* that he's planning *The Return of the Animator*, about "the head of an animation company who comes back to life in 2066, one hundred years after having been cryogenically frozen." Part of the joke, of course, lies in the cheeky reference to rumors surrounding the late Walt Disney. Doel was also tickled to learn that she herself is supposedly writing the script.

.   .   .

On the poster for New Concorde's recent thriller, *Avalanche Alley*, skiers swoosh through deep powder as a mountain of ice tumbles behind them. The caption screams, "FAST, FURIOUS, AND OUT OF CONTROL!" The obvious goal here is to capitalize on the hype surrounding *The Fast and the Furious*, the Vin Diesel street-racing movie, budgeted at $38 million, that had been summer 2001's surprise hit. Neal Moritz, who produced *The Fast and the Furious*, has explained to the press that he found his title while viewing a documentary about American International Pictures, where his father had spent twenty-three years in charge of advertising and publicity. The black-and-white 1954 version of *The Fast and the Furious*, shot for a slim $50,000, had been the very first film released by the company that would become AIP. It marked Corman's second outing as a producer, and he also took a story credit. So it's no surprise that the 2001 film's success made people with long memories think of him.

The references to Corman became even more frequent in 2003, with the release of *2 Fast 2 Furious*, whose budget had swollen to a reported $76 million. More than a few critics, in slamming this convoluted sequel, favorably cited Corman's stripped-down brand of filmmaking. For Manohla Dargis of the *Los Angeles Times*, the 2001 movie had proved far superior to its follow-up because it was simply "an easy guilty pleasure with little more than fast cars, young flesh, and lean-to-the bone story-telling, a formula that Roger Corman has banked on for half a century." In reading such reviews, which seemed to prefer Corman's own gritty style to big-budget Hollywood gloss, Roger was deeply pleased. He told an assistant with a smile, "They still remember me."

In fact, Roger Corman is in no danger of being forgotten. He continues to collect accolades from film enthusiasts the world over. In February

2001, he accepted the American Film Market's lifetime achievement award, leading the irrepressible Lloyd Kaufman of Troma Entertainment to hail him as "the Mozart of the independent film." In June of that same year, he was an honored guest at the Moscow International Film Festival, and two years later he headed for England to address the legendary Oxford Union debating society. Corman has enjoyed traveling to meet his fans ever since he was discovered by European cinéastes back in the 1970s. Cult favorite Jack Hill, who directed Corman's *The Big Doll House* in 1971, remembers that, when festivals sent Roger a first-class airline ticket, he would cash it in, buy a coach ticket, and pocket the difference. The consensus around the office is that he has not changed his ways.

As Corman's seventy-fifth birthday approached in spring 2001, the *Hollywood Reporter* slated a special issue in his honor. I was asked to question some of the industry's brightest luminaries about Roger's contribution to their careers. Francis Coppola faxed me his earliest recollection of Corman the businessman: "He offered me $90 per week to be his assistant, reminding me first that at RKO he got $45 per week for a similar job." Jack Nicholson's tribute to his old boss noted that "my first meeting with Roger Corman was in Jeff Corey's acting class, in which we were both very shy and stumbling neophytes. He was serious, I was serious, and we survived." Nicholson added that "with Roger you learn the basics, good basics and tough basics; you never really forget it. My feeling is that everyone whose career passed through Roger's office holds the same kind of unending affection and appreciation for his patience with us all."

Director Joe Dante, who has given his mentor a cameo role in *Looney Tunes: Back in Action* (2003), happily described for me his first boyhood encounter with Corman movies, a double bill of Roger's *The Day the World Ended* and *Not of This Earth*. In Dante's words, "[*The Day the World Ended*] was great, are you kidding? It was seminal! It was cool! It had radiation; it had monsters. The other one had a guy from outer space who fried people with his eyes. What more could you want?" Alas, none of these terrific quotes ended up in the pages of the *Hollywood Reporter*. Tribute issues depend heavily on advertising revenue, and the *Reporter* could not sell enough full-page congratulatory ads to make the Corman issue worthwhile. So perhaps Corman's many admirers within Hollywood, heeding their hero's mantra of frugality above all, were reluctant to part with their money.

That *Hollywood Reporter* special issue would have meant a lot to Corman. In many ways, he has never stopped looking for critical respect. It's rumored he had high hopes that 2000's *The Suicide Club*, based on a story by Robert Louis Stevenson and featuring a classy British cast, would be accepted for the prestigious Sundance Film Festival. But when speaking to the press, he modestly downplays his contribution to the independent film movement. Interviewed in November 2000 for the *Hollywood Reporter*'s own 70th Anniversary Special Issue, he insisted that "motion pictures are only a part of my life. I'm married. I have four children. My home life is more important to me. Possibly, I could've done more, but that's okay."

• • •

In painting himself as a family man first and foremost, Corman was deliberately understating his powerful drive to succeed. But it's true that family matters shaped his life considerably in the early part of the new millennium. In June 2000, the dean of New York University's Tisch School of the Arts announced that Julie Corman had been named the chair of its prestigious graduate film and television department. (Alumni include directors Ang Lee, Spike Lee, and Corman protégé Martin Scorsese.) Julie was introduced to the NYU film community in glowing terms: "Her track record as a successful producer combined with her outstanding reputation for nurturing talent makes her the ideal individual to lead our program." Many Corman observers hoped this would prove to be Julie's chance to shine on her own, without being eclipsed by her legendary husband.

Of course, the job necessitated a move to Manhattan. The plan was for teen-aged Mary to live with her mother and attend the exclusive Dalton School on the Upper East Side. Corman would become bicoastal, but would spend much of his time in New York. (Longtime Corman associate Frank Moreno predicted that Roger would be back in California at the first sign of winter, because he detests cold weather.) On November 30, 2000, the *Los Angeles Times* real estate section reported that the Cormans had bought a 5th Avenue apartment, with three bedrooms and 3200 square feet of living space, for $3.5 million. At first the new arrangement went well. In early 2001, producer Barbara Boyle (*Phenomenon*) told me that Julie was thriving in her new post: "She is loving it!" But by 2002 the experiment was over. Julie returned to her producing career and her office in the shabby building on San Vicente Blvd. She announced her frustration with NYU faculty politics, and explained that her children preferred having her in California.

As for the Corman children themselves, they are gradually making their way into the adult world. Mary graduated with flying colors from a California prep school, and warmed her father's heart by deciding to go to Stanford. (Unlike her older sister, she vehemently refused to let Roger circulate her application essays at the office.) Catherine, passionate about literature and the fine arts, pursues her own projects, including documentaries on the lives of painters. But she also holds the title of development associate in her mother's Trinity Pictures, and has overseen production on several New Concorde films, though her name appears nowhere in the credits. For *Nightfall* (2000), shot in India, she handled foreign bureaucracy and complex financial negotiations while still in her early twenties. The film's director, Gwyneth Gibby, marvels that she was able to show "so much aplomb for such a young person." Gibby also remembers Catherine's unfailing honesty and terrific sense of humor. Her insatiably curious mind leads her to seek out challenges, as when she came back from India bent on learning Sanskrit. Gibby is convinced that Catherine can succeed anywhere within the film industry, if she so chooses. Yet she keeps her distance from the day-to-day hubbub at New Concorde, apparently determined to forge her own path.

The overloaded office computer system has been the special province of the Corman sons, both of whom have tried giving it massive overhauls. But Brian, following his graduation from Stanford, enrolled in Columbia University School of Law, where he's reportedly doing well. Observers wonder whether someday he'll be drafted by Corman to run New Concorde's business affairs. The major surprise, though, has been Roger Martin Corman. Once the family's biggest hellraiser, he has been winning rave reviews from New Concorde regulars who contend he has outlived his bad-boy reputation.

Lenny Juliano, a veteran actor and screenwriter, first met Roger Martin on the set of one of Jim Wynorski's outrageous B-movies. Juliano insisted to me that "he's very shy, and I had no clue who he was." Within a short time Roger Martin had evolved from an extra into Wynorski's right-hand man and Juliano's pal. Roger Martin shares with Wynorski an encyclopedic knowledge of movies. He loves to laugh, but Juliano notes that his business acumen is reminiscent of his father: "All of a sudden he transforms before your eyes, because he's a really fun guy, and then when it comes to business . . . you almost want to snap to attention." Whereas Wynorski, in the time-honored tradition of Hollywood directors, is liable to blow his top when problems arise, Roger Martin knows how to stay cool. Juliano marvels, "I've never even seen him lose his temper. He's the most composed guy I've ever met." Given his leadership qualities and family connections, Roger Martin has naturally gravitated into the role of producer, but chose to remove his name from Wynorski's *Cheerleader Massacre*.

This decision should not imply, says Juliano, that the son is ashamed of his father's business. He may introduce himself simply as "Roger Martin," leaving off the famous surname, but he gladly acknowledges his family ties. Remarkably, the once-wild kid seems to have evolved into a sensitive and caring friend. When Juliano faced a career crisis, "he called me up totally unexpectedly, and he was as comforting as can be." Juliano is aware of Roger Martin's checkered past, but insists, "I'm sure he's come to terms with it. He's a grown-up. He's a man now, but he's still got the heart of a good boy."

Corman is proud of his children, but at times his fear that none of them will be willing to take over the company leaves him profoundly depressed. During some of these low periods, Julie has phoned Frank Moreno in San Diego, asking if Roger can come visit. The ebullient Moreno has a talent for teasing Corman into good humor. Frank and his wife Susan, another former Corman staffer, agree that Roger makes a charming and thoughtful houseguest. It's striking that Corman now feels such concern about the long-range fate of the business he built. Years ago, when he was a New World executive, Moreno came up with a plan for the company to take out "key man" insurance, in case something happened to the boss. Roger became furious at the notion that the insurance would pay off only if he died. As Moreno remembers it, he seemed to regard himself as invincible. When Moreno explained that the idea was to provide for the future, Corman snapped, "Fuck the future!"

• • •

For Corman, there may have been a time when the future didn't matter. But lately, as he contends with festival invitations and interview requests, posterity is certainly on his mind. It's also a hot topic among the many graduates of the Roger Corman School of Film. Corman alumni from every era ponder whether their mentor has true artistic sensibilities, or whether it all boils down to money. Writer/director Jack Hill, who won notoriety among cult movie fans for such durable genre flicks as *Coffy* (1973) and *Switchblade Sisters* (1975), thinks back to the 1960s in saying, "He had real talent, and you can see it in certain movies. [But] in a way, he was his own worst enemy." In 2000, Hill spoke to me admiringly of Corman-directed films like *The Wild Angels*, in which a biker funeral was illuminated by motorcycle headlamps both to add atmosphere and to save on the electrical bill. Hill sees Roger as almost afraid of admitting to his own artistic impulses: "He would like to brag about doing things just to save money, but some of those things that he says he did just to save money were actually clever, brilliant things. And it's questionable whether they really saved money or not. But he was really inconsistent about it."

Director Jon Purdy sees little reason to give Roger the benefit of the doubt. Purdy who shot three Concorde films in the 1990s, claims that "Corman has evolved into someone who is essentially manufacturing toilet seats. He has no interest in style or transcendent quality because there are only limited profits to be made on each release." For Purdy, Corman's chief goal is to fabricate his product line efficiently, leading to lower costs overall.

But sometimes, even now, Corman will take a calculated gamble in the name of art. Back in 1994, when Concorde-New Horizons was riding high, he had produced Purdy's own aesthetically-demanding first film, *Reflections in the Dark*. That occasional impulse to support creative movie-making (though only when it stands a chance of being commercially viable) continues to this day. During his recent New York sojourn, Corman was impressed with a short film by a recent NYU grad named Brian Sechler, who had grown up with a first-hand knowledge of the city's mean streets. Saying "this guy is a real talent," Roger promptly signed Sechler to write and direct a digital video project, which is currently titled *Rage and*

Discipline. The story centers on a Harlem gym, home to a group of amateur boxers who run afoul of a gang of drug-dealers. The actors are all non-professionals, the locations are the real thing, and Sechler's work has a raw authenticity that speaks well for his future prospects. So Corman, famous as the godfather of eager young filmmakers, has once again opened the door for a talented newcomer.

Throughout Hollywood, those who've never worked for Roger tend to buttonhole Corman graduates, trying to find out what he's really like. Craig Nevius explains, "He's the Wizard of Oz. And they want to know if he's really Oz the Great and Terrible or if there's some kinder, gentler man behind a curtain somewhere pulling the strings." In Nevius's eyes, Corman can fairly be called "a little bit of both." Nevius, creator of *Black Scorpion*, is well-versed in comic book superhero lore. Which is why he adds, "Like superheroes, like Black Scorpion, everybody has two sides. They have their alter egos and their real selves, and you bring out whoever serves you."

But it's hard to figure which is the *real* Roger Corman: the flamboyant showman or the man behind the curtain, the artist or the businessman, the generous father-figure or the miser counting his gold. In truth, he's all of these, and more. That is to say, he contains a multitude of possibilities. Corman himself has described the motion picture as "*the* true twentieth-century art form, because it's a corrupted form—part business and part art." Movies are unwieldy hybrids. So it's fitting that Corman, a hybrid himself, is still making movies after fifty years, ushering in the twenty-first century with his own extraordinary blend of sanity and madness.

FILMOGRAPHY

ROGER CORMAN'S FILMS are listed chronologically by release date. With a few major exceptions, I've included *only* those films on which Corman himself received screen credit. In the early days, he took no credit on some of the revamped Soviet science-fiction films for which protégés like Francis Ford Coppola shot additional footage. In both the New World and the Concorde–New Horizons periods, he chose to omit his name from a number of movies made under his auspices.

All films were shot in color, unless otherwise noted. I include Motion Picture Association of America (MPAA) ratings where appropriate. Because most Corman pictures exist in several print versions, the running times presented here may vary slightly from those listed in other publications. The abbreviation AIP stands for American International Pictures, the company through which many early Corman films were released.

• • •

Key to Roger Corman screen credits:

D	= director	Co-EP	= co-executive producer
P	= producer	AP	= associate producer
Co-P	= co-producer	SC	= screenplay
EP	= executive producer	A	= actor

THE EARLY FILMS (1954–70)

This list reflects features made by Corman prior to the founding of New World Pictures in 1970. It includes *Von Richtofen and Brown,* which was shot in 1970 but not released by United Artists until 1971.

Highway Dragnet (Allied Artists, 1954), 71 minutes, b&w; story, AP.

The Monster from the Ocean Floor (Lippert, 1954), 64 minutes, b&w; P.

The Fast and the Furious (American Releasing Corp., 1954), 73 minutes, b&w; story, P.

Five Guns West (American Releasing Corp., 1955), 78 minutes; P, D.

Apache Woman (American Releasing Corp., 1955), 83 minutes; P, D.

Swamp Women (Woolner Brothers, 1955), 73 minutes; D.

The Beast with 1,000,000 Eyes (American Releasing Corp., 1955), 78 minutes, b&w; EP (and uncredited D).

The Day the World Ended (American Releasing Corp., 1956), 82 minutes, b&w; P, D.

The Oklahoma Woman (American Releasing Corp., 1956), 72 minutes, b&w; P, D.

Gunslinger (American Releasing Corp., 1956), 83 minutes; P, D.

It Conquered the World (AIP, 1956), 68 minutes, b&w; P, D.

Attack of the Crab Monsters (Allied Artists, 1957), 68 minutes, b&w; P, D.

Not of This Earth (Allied Artists, 1957), 67 minutes, b&w; P, D.

The Undead (AIP, 1957), 75 minutes, b&w; P, D.

Rock All Night (AIP, 1957), 63 minutes, b&w; P, D.

Teenage Doll (Allied Artists, 1957), 68 minutes, b&w; P, D.

Carnival Rock (Howco International, 1957), 75 minutes, b&w; P, D.

Sorority Girl (AIP, 1957), 60 minutes, b&w; P, D.

Naked Paradise, aka *Thunder Over Hawaii* (AIP, 1957), 68 minutes; P, D, A.

The Viking Women and the Sea Serpent (AIP, 1957), 66 minutes, b&w; P, D.

War of the Satellites (Allied Artists, 1958), 66 minutes, b&w; P, D, A.

The Cry Baby Killer (Allied Artists, 1958), 62 minutes, b&w; P, A (uncredited cameo).

Machine Gun Kelly (AIP, 1958), 80 minutes, b&w; P, D.

I, Mobster (Twentieth Century–Fox, 1958), 80 minutes, b&w; Co-P, D.

Night of the Blood Beast (AIP, 1958), 65 minutes, b&w; EP.

She Gods of Shark Reef (AIP, 1958), 63 minutes; D.

Stakeout on Dope Street (Warner Bros., 1958), 83 minutes, b&w; P.

T-Bird Gang (AIP, 1958), 75 minutes, b&w; P.

Teenage Caveman, aka *Prehistoric World* (AIP, 1958), 66 minutes, b&w; P, D.

High School Big Shot (AIP, 1959), 70 minutes, b&w; EP.

A Bucket of Blood (AIP, 1959), 66 minutes, b&w; P, D.

Attack of the Giant Leeches (AIP, 1959), 62 minutes, b&w; EP.

Ski Troop Attack (Filmgroup, 1960), 63 minutes, b&w; P, D, A (uncredited cameo).

The Wasp Woman (Filmgroup, 1960), 66 minutes, b&w; P, D, A (uncredited cameo).

The Little Shop of Horrors (Filmgroup, 1960), 70 minutes, b&w; P, D.

The Last Woman on Earth (Filmgroup, 1960), 71 minutes; P, D.

House of Usher (AIP, 1960), 85 minutes; P, D.

Atlas (Filmgroup, 1961), 80 minutes; P, D.

The Creature from the Haunted Sea (Filmgroup, 1961), 74 minutes, b&w; P, D.

The Battle of Blood Island (AIP, 1961), 64 minutes, b&w; EP.

The Pit and the Pendulum (AIP, 1961), 80 minutes; P, D.

The Intruder, aka *I Hate Your Guts*; also *Shame* (Pathé American, 1962), 80 minutes, b&w; P, D.

The Premature Burial (AIP, 1962), 81 minutes; P, D.

Tales of Terror (AIP, 1962), 90 minutes; P, D.

Tower of London (United Artists, 1962), 79 minutes, b&w; D.

The Haunted Palace (AIP, 1963), 85 minutes; P, D.

The Raven (AIP, 1963), 86 minutes; P, D.

The Terror (AIP, 1963), 81 minutes; P, D.

Battle Beyond the Sun (Filmgroup, 1963), 75 minutes; P.

The Young Racers (AIP, 1963), 87 minutes; P, D.

Dementia 13 (Filmgroup/AIP, 1963), 81 minutes, b&w; P.

X—the Man with X-Ray Eyes (AIP, 1963), 80 minutes; P, D.

The Secret Invasion (United Artists, 1964), 95 minutes; D.

The Masque of the Red Death (AIP, 1964), 86 minutes; P, D.

The Tomb of Ligeia (AIP, 1964), 81 minutes; Co-P, D.

Blood Bath (AIP, 1966), 80 minutes, b&w; EP.

Planet of Blood, aka *Queen of Blood* (Filmgroup/AIP, 1966), 81 minutes; EP.

The Wild Angels (AIP, 1966), 93 minutes; P, D.

The St. Valentine's Day Massacre (Twentieth Century–Fox, 1967), 100 minutes; P, D.

The Trip (AIP, 1967), 85 minutes; P, D.

Voyage to the Planet of Prehistoric Women, aka *Gill Women of Venus* (AIP, 1968), 80 minutes; Co-P.

The Wild Racers (AIP, 1968), 79 minutes; EP.

Targets (Paramount/AIP, 1968), 90 minutes, PG-rated [originally R-rated]; EP.

De Sade (AIP, 1969), 92 minutes, R-rated; (uncredited D).

The Dunwich Horror (AIP, 1970), 90 minutes, unrated; EP.

Bloody Mama (AIP, 1970), 90 minutes, R-rated; P, D.

Gas-s-s-s! Or It Became Necessary to Destroy the World in Order to Save It (AIP, 1970), 79 minutes, PG-rated; P, D.

Von Richthofen and Brown (United Artists, 1971), 97 minutes, PG-rated; D.

THE NEW WORLD PICTURES ERA (1970–83)

All films were released through New World Pictures unless otherwise noted.

The Student Nurses (1970), 89 minutes, R-rated; EP.

Ivanna, aka *Altar of Blood*, also *Blood Castle*, also *Killers of the Castle of Blood* (1970), 94 minutes, unrated; P.

Angels Die Hard (1970), 86 minutes, R-rated; EP.

Angels Hard as They Come (1971), 90 minutes, R-rated; EP.

The Big Doll House, aka *Women's Penitentiary* (1971), 93 minutes, R-rated; EP.

Private Duty Nurses (1971), 80 minutes, R-rated; EP.

Unholy Rollers (AIP, 1972), 88 minutes, R-rated; EP.

The Big Bird Cage (1972), 88 minutes, R-rated; EP.

Women in Cages (1972), 78 minutes, R-rated; P.

Boxcar Bertha (AIP, 1972), 88 minutes, R-rated; P.

The Cremators (1972), 75 minutes, R-rated; P.

Final Comedown, aka *Blast!* (1972), 83 minutes, R-rated; P.

The Hot Box (1972), 85 minutes, R-rated; EP.

Night of the Cobra Woman (1972), 85 minutes, R-rated; P.

The Arousers, aka *Sweet Kill* (1972), 90 minutes, R-rated; EP.

Twilight People, aka *Beasts* (Dimension, 1972), 84 minutes, PG-rated; EP.

I Escaped from Devil's Island (United Artists, 1973), 89 minutes, R-rated; P.

Big Bad Mama (1974), 83 minutes, R-rated; P.

Cockfighter, aka *Born to Kill*, also *Wild Drifter*, also *Gamblin' Man* (1974), 83 minutes, R-rated; P.

Candy Stripe Nurses, aka *Sweet Candy* (1974), 80 minutes, R-rated; P.

Tender Loving Care (1974), 72 minutes, R-rated; P.

TNT Jackson (1974), 73 minutes, R-rated; EP.

Caged Heat (1974), 84 minutes, R-rated (uncredited P).

The Godfather Part II (Paramount, 1974), 200 minutes, R-rated; A.

Capone (Twentieth Century–Fox, 1975), 101 minutes, R-rated; P.

Death Race 2000 (1975), 78 minutes, R-rated; P.

Cannonball (1976), 93 minutes, PG-rated; A.

Eat My Dust! (1976), 90 minutes, PG-rated; P.

Fighting Mad (Twentieth Century–Fox, 1976), 90 minutes, R-rated; P.

Jackson County Jail, aka *Outside Chance* (1976), 89 minutes, R-rated; EP.

Moving Violation (Twentieth Century–Fox, 1976), 91 minutes, PG-rated; EP.

Grand Theft Auto (1977), 85 minutes, PG-rated; EP.

I Never Promised You a Rose Garden (1977), 96 minutes, R-rated; Co-EP.

Thunder and Lightning (Twentieth Century–Fox, 1977), 95 minutes, PG-rated; P.

Tigress, aka *Ilsa, the Tigress of Siberia* (1977), 88 minutes, R-rated; P.

Deathsport (1978), 82 minutes, R-rated; P.

Piranha (1978), 92 minutes, R-rated; Co-EP.

Avalanche (1978), 91 minutes, PG-rated; P.

Fast Charlie, the Moonbeam Rider, aka *Fast Charlie and the Moonbeam* (Universal, 1979), 99 minutes, PG-rated; Co-P.

Rock 'n' Roll High School (1979), 93 minutes, PG-rated; EP.

Galaxy Express (1979), 128 minutes, PG-rated; EP.

Saint Jack (1979), 112 minutes, R-rated; P.

Up from the Depths (1979), 85 minutes, R-rated; EP.

Humanoids from the Deep (1980), 80 minutes, R-rated; P.

Battle Beyond the Stars (1980), 104 minutes, PG-rated; P.

The Howling (Columbia, 1980), 91 minutes, R-rated; A.

Galaxy of Terror, aka *Mindwarp* (1981), 80 minutes, R-rated; P.

Smokey Bites the Dust (1981), 85 minutes, PG-rated; P.

The Territory (1981), 100 minutes, rating unavailable, P.

Forbidden World, aka *Mutant* (1982), 86 minutes, R-rated; P.

Der Stand der Dinge, aka *The State of Things* (Wim Wenders Productions, et al., 1982), 121 minutes, b&w; unrated; A.

Hell's Angels Forever (1983), 92 minutes, R-rated; Co-P.

Love Letters, aka *My Love Letters*, also *Passion Play* (1983), 98 minutes, R-rated; P.

THE CONCORDE–NEW HORIZONS ERA (1983–PRESENT)

All films were released through Concorde–New Horizons Pictures except where otherwise noted.

Space Raiders (a New World release of a Millennium Production, 1983), 82 minutes, PG-rated; P.

The Wild Side, aka *Suburbia* (New World, 1984), 96 minutes, R-rated; P.

Oddballs (1984), 91 minutes, PG-rated; EP.

Swing Shift (Warner Bros., 1984), 100 minutes, PG-rated; A.

Streetwalkin' (1985), 85 minutes, R-rated; EP.

Amazons (1986), 76 minutes, R-rated; EP.

Cocaine Wars (1986), 82 minutes, R-rated; P.

Big Bad Mama II (1987), 83 minutes, R-rated; P.

Hour of the Assassin (1987), 93 minutes, R-rated; EP.

Munchies (1987), 83 minutes, PG-rated; P.

Stripped to Kill (1987), 88 minutes, R-rated; EP.

Summer Camp Nightmare (1987), 87 minutes, PG-13-rated; EP.

Beach Balls (1988), 79 minutes, R-rated; EP.

Daddy's Boys (1988), 90 minutes, R-rated; P.

The Drifter (1988), 90 minutes, R-rated; EP.

Emmanuelle VI (1988), 80 minutes, R-rated; EP.

The Lawless Land (1988), 81 minutes, R-rated; Co-EP.

The New Gladiators (1988), 90 minutes, R-rated; EP.

Two to Tango (1988), 87 minutes, R-rated; P.

Watchers (Universal, 1988), 92 minutes, R-rated; EP.

Crime Zone (1988), 93 minutes, R-rated; EP.

Bloodfist (1989), 85 minutes, R-rated; P.

Heroes Stand Alone (1989), 83 minutes, R-rated; EP.

Hollywood Boulevard II (1989), 82 minutes, R-rated; EP, A.

Lords of the Deep (1989), 79 minutes, PG-13–rated; P, A (uncredited cameo).

Primary Target (1989), 85 minutes, R-rated; EP.

Silk 2 (1989), 85 minutes, R-rated; EP.

Stripped to Kill II (1989), 83 minutes, R-rated; P.

The Terror Within (1989), 88 minutes, R-rated; P.

Time Trackers (1989), 87 minutes, PG-rated; EP.

Transylvania Twist (1989), 90 minutes, PG-13-rated; EP.

Andy Colby's Incredible Adventure (1990), 75 minutes, PG-rated; EP.

Back to Back (1990), 95 minutes, R-rated; EP.

Bloodfist II (1990), 85 minutes, R-rated; P.

Deathstalker IV: Match of Titans (1990), 85 minutes, R-rated; EP.

Dune Warriors (1990), 80 minutes, R-rated; P.

Sorority House Massacre II, aka *Nighty Nightmare* (1990), 77 minutes, R-rated; EP.

Frankenstein Unbound, aka *Roger Corman's Frankenstein Unbound* (Twentieth Century–Fox, 1990), 85 minutes, R-rated; Co-P, D, SC.

Full Fathom Five (1990), 82 minutes, PG-rated; P.

The Haunting of Morella (1990), 87 minutes, R-rated; P.

Last Stand at Lang Mei, aka *Eye of the Eagle 3* (1990), 90 minutes, R-rated; P.

Overexposed (1990), 80 minutes, R-rated; P.

Play Murder for Me (1990), 80 minutes, R-rated; EP.

Streets (1990), 86 minutes, R-rated; EP.

The Terror Within II (1990), 90 minutes, R-rated; EP.

Watchers II (1990), 101 minutes, R-rated; P.

Immortal Sins (1991), 80 minutes, R-rated; P.

Bloodfist III: Forced to Fight (1991), 90 minutes, R-rated; P.

Field of Fire (1991), 96 minutes, R-rated; P.

Final Embrace (1991), 83 minutes, R-rated; P.

Future Kick (1991), 76 minutes, R-rated; EP.

Killer Instinct (1991), 92 minutes, R-rated; P.

The Silence of the Lambs (Orion, 1991), 118 minutes, R-rated; A.

Blackbelt (1992), 80 minutes, R-rated; EP.

Bloodfist IV: Die Trying (1992), 86 minutes, R-rated; EP.

Body Chemistry II: The Voice of a Stranger (1992), 84 minutes, R-rated; EP.

Body Waves (1992), 80 minutes, R-rated; EP.

Crisis in the Kremlin, aka *The Assassination Game* (1992), 85 minutes, R-rated; EP.

In the Heat of Passion (1992), 102 minutes, R-rated; EP.

Munchie (1992), 80 minutes, PG-rated; P.

Raiders of the Sun (1992), 80 minutes, R-rated; P.

Ultraviolet (1992), 80 minutes, R-rated; EP.

Ultra Warrior, aka *Welcome to Oblivion* (1992), 80 minutes, R-rated; EP, A.

Angelfist (1993), 80 minutes, R-rated; P.

Blackbelt II, aka *Fatal Force* (1993), 83 minutes, R-rated; EP.

Bloodfist V: Human Target (1993), 84 minutes, R-rated; EP.

Carnosaur (1993), 85 minutes, R-rated; EP.

Curse of the Crystal Eye (1993), 90 minutes, PG-13–rated; EP.

Dracula Rising (1993), 85 minutes, R-rated; P.

Dragon Fire (1993), 90 minutes, R-rated; EP.

Eight Hundred Leagues Down the Amazon (1993), 75 minutes, PG-13–rated; EP.

Kill Zone (1993), 81 minutes, R-rated; P.

The Liars' Club (1993), 95 minutes, R-rated; EP.

Little Miss Millions, aka *Home for Christmas* (1993), 90 minutes, PG-rated; EP.

Live by the Fist (1993), 77 minutes, R-rated; P.

Philadelphia (Columbia/TriStar, 1993), 119 minutes, PG-13–rated; A.

The Skateboard Kid (1993), 83 minutes, PG-rated; EP.

Angel of Destruction, aka *Furious Angel* (1994), 80 minutes, R-rated; EP.

Bloodfist VI: Ground Zero (1994), 86 minutes, R-rated; EP.

Cheyenne Warrior (1994), 90 minutes, PG-rated; EP.

Deadly Desire, aka *Saturday Night Special* (1994), 86 minutes, R-rated; EP.

Fantastic Four (1994)—produced but never released; EP.

The Flight of the Dove, aka *The Spy Within* (1994), 87 minutes, R-rated; EP.

In the Heat of Passion II: Unfaithful (1994), 88 minutes, R-rated; EP.

New Crime City (1994), 86 minutes, R-rated; EP.

No Dessert Dad, 'Til You Mow the Lawn (1994), 89 minutes, PG-rated; EP.

One Man Army (1994), 79 minutes, R-rated; P.

Body Chemistry III: Point of Seduction (1994), 90 minutes, R-rated; EP.

Reflections in the Dark, aka *Reflections on a Crime* (1994), 94 minutes, R-rated; EP.

Stranglehold (1994), 73 minutes, R-rated; EP.

Watchers III (1994), 80 minutes, R-rated; EP.

Apollo 13 (Universal, 1995), 139 minutes, PG-rated; A.

Baby Face Nelson (1995), 93 minutes, R-rated; EP.

Bloodfist VII: Manhunt (1995), 95 minutes, R-rated; EP.

Caged Heat 3000 (1995), 85 minutes, R-rated; EP.

Captain Nuke and the Bomber Boys, aka *Demolition Day* (1995), 90 minutes, PG-rated; EP.

Carnosaur 2 (1995), 83 minutes, R-rated; P.

The Crazysitter (1995), 92 minutes, PG-13–rated; EP.

Dillinger and Capone (1995), 94 minutes, R-rated; EP.

Droid Gunner, aka *Cyberzone* (1995), 90 minutes, R-rated; EP.

One Night Stand (1995), 88 minutes, R-rated; EP.

Twisted Love (1995), 85 minutes, R-rated; EP.

Where Evil Lies (1995), 83 minutes, R-rated; EP.

Bio-Tech Warrior (1996), 81 minutes, R-rated; EP.

Black Rose of Harlem, aka *Machine Gun Blues* (1996), 87 minutes, R-rated; EP.

Bloodfist VIII: Trained to Kill (1996), 85 minutes, R-rated; EP.

Carnosaur 3: Primal Species (1996), 81 minutes, R-rated; P.

Rumble in the Streets (1996), 74 minutes, R-rated; EP.

Born Bad (1997), 84 minutes, R-rated; EP.

Black Thunder (1997), 86 minutes, R-rated; P.

Criminal Affairs (1997), 90 minutes, R-rated; EP.

Macon County Jail, aka *Jailbreak* (1997), 88 minutes, R-rated; EP.

Detonator (1997), 86 minutes, R-rated; EP.

Don't Sleep Alone (1997), 80 minutes, R-rated; EP.

Eruption, aka *Volcano Run* (1997), 92 minutes, R-rated; EP.

The Sea Wolf (1997), 85 minutes, R-rated; EP.

Shadow Dancer, aka *Physical Attraction* (1997), 89 minutes, R-rated; EP.

Stripteaser II (1997), 77 minutes, R-rated; EP.

Termination Man (1997), 88 minutes, R-rated; Co-EP.

Urban Justice (1997), length unavailable, R-rated; EP.

Dangerous Curves, aka Stray Bullet II (1998), length unavailable, R; P.

Desert Thunder (1998), 88 minutes, R; EP.

Running Woman (1998), 87 minutes, R; P.

Star Portal (1998), 78 minutes, R; EP.

A Very Unlucky Leprechaun (1998), length unavailable, PG; P.

Watchers Reborn (1998), 83 minutes, R; EP.

*The Haunting of Hell House, aka The Ghostly Rental, aka Henry James' The
   Haunting of Hell House* (1999), 90 minutes, R; P.

Shepherd (1999), 86 minutes, R; EP.

Stray Bullet (1999), 86 minutes, R-rated; EP.

The Protector (1999), 85 minutes, R-rated; EP.

The White Pony (1999), 93 minutes, G; P.

The Doorway (2000), 91 minutes, R; P.

The Independent (2000), 95 minutes, R; A.

Nightfall, aka Isaac Asimov's Nightfall (2000), 82 minutes, R; P.

Scream 3 (2000), 116 minutes, R; A.

The Suicide Club, aka Robert Louis Stevenson's the Game of Death (2000),
   89 minutes, R; P.

The Arena, aka Gladiatrix (2001), 92 minutes, R; EP.

Raptor (2001), 81 minutes, R; P.

Escape From Afghanistan (2002), length unavailable, R; EP.

Shakedown (2002), 92 minutes, R; EP.

Slaughter Studios (2002), 90 minutes, R; EP.

Sting of the Black Scorpion (2002), 84 minutes, R; EP.

Wolfhound (2002), length unavailable, R; EP.

Barbarian (2003), length unavailable, R; EP.

Firefight (2003), length unavailable, R; EP.

Looney Tunes: Back in Action (2003), length unavailable, PG; A.

TELEVISION

The following were made specifically for airing on U.S. television. Beginning in 1995, Roger Corman launched a Showtime cable TV network series
known as *Roger Corman Presents:* many of the films listed here were origi-

nally part of that series. Some were entirely new projects; others were remakes of earlier Corman works. After their Showtime debut, they were released theatrically and on videodisc.

What's In It for Harry, aka *Target: Harry; How to Make It* (ABC-TV, 1969), theatrical version 81 minutes, R-rated; P, D, A (uncredited cameo).

Georgia Peaches, aka *Follow That Car* (CBS, 1980), length and rating unavailable; EP.

Body Bags (Showtime, 1993), 91 minutes, R-rated; A.

Runaway Daughters (Showtime, 1994), 83 minutes, PG-13-rated; A.

NOTE: From this point on, all Showtime cable-TV listings are part of the anthology series known as *Roger Corman Presents.*

Black Scorpion, (Showtime, 1995), 92 minutes, R-rated; EP.

Bucket of Blood, aka *Dark Secrets; The Death Artist* (Showtime, 1995), 83 minutes, R-rated; EP.

Bram Stoker's Burial of the Rats (Showtime, 1995), 78 minutes, R-rated; EP.

Hellfire, aka *Haunted Symphony* (Showtime, 1995), 85 minutes, PG-13-rated; P.

Last Chance, aka *Terminal Virus* (Showtime, 1995) 74 minutes, R-rated; EP.

Not Like Us (Showtime, 1995), 87 minutes, R-rated; EP.

Not of This Earth (Showtime, 1995), 92 minutes, R-rated; EP.

Piranha (Showtime, 1995), 89 minutes, R-rated; EP.

Sawbones, aka *Prescription for Murder* (Showtime, 1995), 85 minutes, R-rated; EP.

Suspect Device (Showtime, 1995), 90 minutes, R-rated; EP.

Unknown Origin, aka *The Alien Within* (Showtime, 1995), 75 minutes, R-rated; EP.

Virtual Seduction, aka *Addicted to Love* (Showtime, 1995), 84 minutes, R-rated; EP.

Wasp Woman, aka *Forbidden Beauty* (Showtime, 1995), 87 minutes, R-rated; EP.

Alien Avengers, aka *Welcome to Planet Earth* (Showtime, 1996), 81 minutes, R-rated; EP.

Black Scorpion II: Aftershock (Showtime, 1996), 85 minutes, R-rated; EP.

Death Game (Showtime, 1996), length unavailable, R-rated; EP.

Humanoids from the Deep (Showtime, 1996), 86 minutes, R-rated; EP.

Inhumanoid, aka *Circuit Breaker* (Showtime, 1996), 88 minutes, R-rated; EP.

Ladykiller (Showtime, 1996), 83 minutes, R-rated; P.

Last Exit to Earth (Showtime, 1996), length unavailable, R-rated; EP.

Marquis de Sade, aka *Dark Prince* (Showtime, 1996), length unavailable, R-rated; EP.

Spectre, aka *House of the Damned* (Showtime, 1996), 83 minutes, R-rated; EP.

Subliminal Seduction (Showtime, 1996), 81 minutes, R-rated; EP.

The Unspeakable, aka *Criminal Pursuit*, also *Shadow of a Scream* (Showtime, 1996), 88 minutes, R-rated; EP.

Vampirella (Showtime, 1996), 82 minutes, R-rated; EP.

Beverly Hills, 90210 (Fox TV, Season 6, Episode 17, "Fade In, Fade Out," January 10, 1996); A.

Alien Avengers II, aka *Welcome to Planet Earth II*, also *The Aliens Among Us* (Showtime, 1997), 89 minutes, R-rated; EP.

Club Vampire (Showtime, 1997), 76 minutes, R-rated; EP.

Falling Fire, aka *3 Minutes to Impact* (Showtime, 1997), 93 minutes, R-rated; EP.

Future Fear (Showtime, 1997), 82 minutes, R-rated; EP.

Haunted Sea, aka *Ghost Ship* (Showtime, 1997), 73 minutes, R-rated; EP.

Spacejacked (Showtime, 1997), 89 minutes, R-rated; EP.

Starquest II, aka *Mind Breakers* (Showtime, 1997), 92 minutes, R-rated; EP.

The Second Civil War (HBO, 1997), 97 minutes, R-rated; A.

The Practice (ABC, Season 3, Episode 13, "Judge and Jury," January 17, 1999); A.

The Phantom Eye (American Movie Classics, October 1999), 60 minutes, rating unavailable; EP, A.

Avalanche Alley (2001), 90 minutes, PG; EP.

Black Scorpion, aka *Roger Corman Presents Black Scorpion: The Series* (2001), 22 one-hour episodes; EP.

Appendix A

SOME DISTINGUISHED FRIENDS
AND ALUMNI OF THE ROGER CORMAN
SCHOOL OF FILM

GIVEN THE VAST number of people in the film community whose lives have been touched by Roger Corman, I have been faced with some hard choices in this appendix. I have decided to focus on major Hollywood names, and on those filmmakers whose careers have been indelibly stamped by their Corman days. Quotability was another determining factor: this is why I have chosen Samuel Z. Arkoff, rather than his late colleague, James Nicholson, as a representative of Roger's AIP period. Space considerations have prevented me from including many members of the Roger Corman Stock Company, among them Susan Cabot, Beverly Garland, Jonathan Haze, Barboura Morris, and Mel Welles from the early days. In the Concorde era, I have been forced to omit such familiar Corman actors as Rick Dean, Maria Ford, and Don "The Dragon" Wilson.

Arkoff, Samuel Z.

DATES: 1918–2001.

FIRST CORMAN CREDIT: Executive producer, *Apache Woman* (1955).

HONORS: Special guest at New York's Museum of Modern Art, AIP retrospective, 1979.

JOB DESCRIPTION: Producer, executive producer.

In 1954, attorney Sam Arkoff and exhibitor Jim Nicholson borrowed $3,000 to start American International Pictures, which distributed more than thirty of Corman's early works while also producing many of them. Though Corman ultimately went his own way, he and Arkoff shared a strong mutual respect. When Corman was honored at the Los Angeles County Museum of Art in 1997, *Variety* records that Arkoff described him to the audience as "a cautious man with a buck—which made him very good for us because we didn't have many bucks in those days." Arkoff added, "But sometimes he was too cheap, even for AIP."

AIP made its name on low-budget genre movies—horror, science fiction, beach party flicks, blaxploitation—tailored to the tastes of the burgeoning youth market. In 1972, after Arkoff's split from Jim Nicholson, he attempted bigger pictures, like *The Amityville Horror* (1979). Ultimately AIP merged with Filmways, which was swallowed up by Orion Pictures in 1982. Until late in his life, Arkoff remained active on behalf of his own small company, Arkoff International Pictures.

Arkoff's producer and executive producer credits include: *Reform School Girl* (1957); *Machine Gun Kelly* (1958); *House of Usher* (1960); *The Raven* (1963); *Beach Blanket Bingo* (1965); *Wild in the Streets* (1968);*Bloody Mama* (1970); *Dillinger* (1973); *The Island of Dr. Moreau* (1977); *The Amityville Horror* (1979); *Dressed to Kill* (1980); *Hellhole* (1985).

Arkush, Allan

BORN: 1948.

FIRST CORMAN CREDIT: Co-director and co-editor, *Hollywood Boulevard* (1976).

HONORS: Emmy (Best Director of a TV Miniseries or Movie), *The Temptations*, 1999.

JOB DESCRIPTION: Director, executive producer, editor.

Arkush came west in 1974 to join Joe Dante as a trailer-cutter at New World Pictures. Graduating into the position of second-unit director for Ron Howard's debut film, *Grand Theft Auto* (1977), he discovered the horrors of going on location Corman-style. On November 5, 1998 he described for me the catered lunch that was so foul that his crew ran it over with a prop automobile while the cameras rolled. Still, location shooting had its up-side: "You went out in the desert all day, you wrecked cars." Though Corman required a bargain-basement aesthetic, New World films were not without ingenuity. For a climactic chase scene in *Deathsport*, Corman pointed to photos taken at California's Nike Missile Base, insisting they could be made to resemble the sets from Sergei Eisenstein's epic, *Ivan the Terrible* (1945). When Arkush expressed surprise, Corman "showed me what he wanted, and he drew little things on the photos, and it made complete sense."

Arkush left New World after *Rock 'n' Roll High School* (1979), and has since made a steady living as a director, mostly for commercial television. He is also known for his music videos. Arkush told me, "Most of the people I work with today are young people. When they ask me what I've done, I say Roger Corman. It kind of draws a blank. If I say *Fame* [the television series], they go crazy."

Arkush's director credits include: *Hollywood Boulevard* (co-director, 1976); *Deathsport* (1978); *Rock 'n' Roll High School* (1979); *Fame* (TV series, 1982–87); *Moonlighting* (TV series, 1985–89); *Caddyshack II* (1988); *I'll Fly Away* (TV series, 1991–93); *Elvis Meets Nixon* (TV, 1997); *Ally McBeal* (TV series, 1997–2002); *The Temptations* (TV miniseries, 1998); *Crossing Jordan* (TV series, 2001–); *Prince Charming* (TV, 2001).

Bartel, Paul

DATES: 1938–2000.

FIRST CORMAN CREDIT: Second unit director, *Big Bad Mama* (1974).

HONORS: Special guest at the Locarno (Italy) Film Festival, 1999.

JOB DESCRIPTION: Director, actor, writer, producer.

Bartel's idiosyncratic career began when he directed *Private Parts* (1972), an erotic comedy thriller, for producer Gene Corman. The film failed dismally, as Bartel explained to me on December 1, 1998, because it was "much too hybrid and sophisticated for the audience for which it was actually destined, which was kids." Fortunately, Bartel got a second chance when Roger Corman hired him to direct *Death Race 2000* (1975). But their post-production wrangling instilled in Bartel a bitterness toward Corman that he couldn't always shake. Speaking to me of a recent Concorde employee who was accused of wrongdoing, Bartel sardonically put the blame on Roger's own paranoia: "Well, you know *everybody* steals from him. Everybody who works for him steals from him, and everybody who works for him betrays him. The directors betray him by ruining the films, and then he has to save them. And everybody else betrays him by stealing—sometimes it's paper clips, sometimes it's sheets of paper, sometimes it's illicit uses of the copying machine." Still, Bartel admitted to a soft spot for his old boss: "I have always thought of him as a kind of monster, but I do owe him the chance to make that second film and do all those other things that I did."

Those "other things" include several highly original features. In 1982, Bartel teamed with Andy Warhol alumna Mary Woronov (a featured player in *Death Race 2000*) to star as Paul and Mary Bland in Bartel's most memorable work, a biting satire about cannibalism entitled *Eating Raoul* (1982). The two friends ultimately acted together so often that on May 8, 1999 writer Chuck Griffith called them "The Lunts of Poverty Row." Bartel's biggest-budgeted film project was the ill-starred *Scenes from the Class Struggle in Beverly Hills* (1989), but within mainstream Hollywood he was best known as a comically pompous character actor. His sudden death at the age of sixty-one prompted hundreds of well-wishers to gather at the American Cinematheque to salute his memory.

Bartel's director credits include: *Private Parts* (1972); *Death Race 2000* (1975); *Cannonball* (1976); *Eating Raoul* (1982); *Scenes from the Class Struggle in Beverly Hills* (1989); *Shelf Life* (1993).

Bogdanovich, Peter

BORN: 1939.

FIRST CORMAN CREDIT: Actor and assistant director, *The Wild Angels* (1966).

HONORS: Oscar nominations (Best Director and Best Screenplay), *The Last Picture Show*, 1972.

JOB DESCRIPTION: Director, actor, producer, writer.

A stage director and film historian, Bogdanovich became Corman's all-purpose assistant on *The Wild Angels* (1966), then ended up directing the second unit. He told *American Film* that "I went from getting the laundry to directing the picture in three weeks. Altogether, I worked twenty-two weeks—pre-production, shooting, second unit, cutting, dubbing—I haven't learned as much since."

Corman rewarded Bogdanovich with the chance to make *Targets*

(1968), for which he intercut period horror footage from *The Terror* (1963) with a contemporary story about a sniper at a drive-in movie theatre. *Targets* led to *The Last Picture Show* (1971), which catapulted the young director into international prominence. His subsequent films, like *What's Up, Doc?* (1972) and *Paper Moon* (1973), display an affinity for the cinematic styles of past eras. After many career ups and downs, Bogdanovich found a new niche in popular culture by playing psychiatrist Elliott Kupferberg on the hit TV series, *The Sopranos* (1999–2000). In his 1998 book, *Who the Devil Made It?* he claimed to have returned full circle to "Roger Corman's guerrilla school of picture-making," with a strong sense of "how indolent, spoiled, and wasteful most feature productions have become."

Bogdanovich's director credits include: *Targets* (1968); *The Last Picture Show* (1971); *What's Up, Doc?* (1972); *Paper Moon* (1973); *At Long Last Love* (1975); *Saint Jack* (1979); *Mask* (1985); *Texasville* (1990); *Noises Off* (1992); *The Cat's Meow* (2001).

Cameron, James

BORN: 1954.

FIRST CORMAN CREDIT: Art director and miniature designer, *Battle Beyond the Stars* (1980).

HONORS: Oscars (Best Picture, Best Director, Best Editing), *Titanic*, 1998.

JOB DESCRIPTION: Director, writer, producer, editor, design and special effects consultant.

Jim Cameron's expertise in the realm of spectacle has transformed today's Hollywood. I've heard Corman praise a smart move by Cameron in *The Terminator* (1984): matching the truck in a crucial action sequence to an existing toy model, rather than trying to build a model to resemble the full-sized truck. Roger admires this decision because of its cost-consciousness. But on matters of budget, Cameron and Corman are generally poles apart. Randy Frakes, who did special effects work with Cameron on his debut film, *Battle Beyond the Stars* (1980), clarifies that Cameron is "not lavish for lavish[ness's] sake, but he won't spare any expense to get the effect he wants." He thinks on a grand scale, whereas Corman is a deliberate minimalist.

Frank Moreno, New World's head of sales in the 1970s, wishes Corman would join forces with his celebrity alumni to make quality movies. Still, he can't quite envision Corman and Cameron as a team. He suspects Roger would exclaim, "What do you mean, the budget is $220 million? In my whole life, I haven't spent $220 million!" To Moreno, one of Cameron's great achievements at New World was hooking up with the "incredibly talented and bright" Gale Anne Hurd who subsequently produced four of his most inventive features.

Cameron also met other key members of his creative circle at New World. Composer James Horner, whose score for *Battle Beyond the Stars* still turns up on the sound track of many Corman films, has gone on to win multiple honors, including two Academy Awards for *Titanic*. And visual effects specialists Robert and Dennis Skotak, who first worked with Cameron on *Battle Beyond*, have snagged Oscars for Cameron's *Aliens*, *The Abyss*, and *Terminator 2*.

Cameron's director credits include *Piranha II: The Spawning* (1981); *The Terminator* (1984); *Aliens* (1986); *The Abyss* (1989); *Terminator 2: Judgment Day* (1991); *True Lies* (1994); *Titanic* (1997); *Ghosts of the Abyss* (2003).

Carradine, David

BORN: 1936.

FIRST CORMAN CREDIT: Actor, *Boxcar Bertha* (1972).

HONORS: Golden Globe nomination (Best Actor in a Drama), *Bound for Glory*, 1977.

JOB DESCRIPTION: Actor, director, associate producer.

Carradine hails from an acting family: he is the son of the legendary character actor John Carradine (1906–1988), and half-brother to actors Keith (b. 1949) and Robert (b. 1954) Carradine. His own long string of Corman pictures started with *Boxcar Bertha* in 1972. The New World cult classic, *Death Race 2000* (1975), was shot just prior to the Oscar-nominated *Bound for Glory* (1976), in which Carradine starred as folksinger Woody Guthrie. Though his career includes studio productions, he insists he likes the challenge of making Corman action films, especially overseas. When we spoke in February 1999, he made clear that "all these movies are done too quickly, and there's not enough material—not enough film, the cameras are too old, the budget is extremely low for wardrobe and everything else—but somehow they're always exciting to do." Himself an iconoclast, Carradine respects Corman for thumbing his nose at industry bigwigs. He told me: "I don't think you could have the independent film industry that we have now, that's blooming out there, without Roger's example of how you can get away with things."

Many Corman alumni remember Carradine's on-set caprices: the potsmoking; the baby son (named "Free") who romped un-diapered through his trailer on the set of *Cannonball* (1976); the time in Argentina (for 1984's *The Warrior and the Sorceress*) when he smashed his hand into a concrete wall and then had to film his sword-fights while wearing a specially-decorated plaster cast. Carradine also once claimed to have misplaced his false teeth just before a key scene, necessitating a frantic search by the entire production team before the dentures were finally found tucked away in his costume. Remarkably, he was such a strong actor that, whatever his eccentric behavior on the set, his performance always made up for the aggravation he caused. But Gwyneth Gibby, who traveled to Hyderabad, India to direct him in the 2000 version of *Nightfall*, found Carradine to be thoroughly professional and a very good sport. Because none of the three Indian assistant directors attached to the film could manage to issue call sheets, Carradine would simply show up on the set every morning and ask if he was needed.

Carradine's actor credits include: *Boxcar Bertha* (1972); the two *Kung Fu* television series (1972–75 and 1992–1997); *Death Race 2000* (1975); *Bound for Glory* (1976); *Cannonball* (1976); *The Serpent's Egg* (1977); *Deathsport* (1978); *The Warrior and the Sorceress* (1984); *Wizards of the Lost Kingdom II* (1988); *Crime Zone* (1988); *Nowhere to* Run (1989); *Field of Fire* (in which he played "General Corman," 1991); *Kill Zone* (1993); The Rage (1997); *Macon County Jail* (1997); *Last Stand at Saber River* (*TV*, 1997); *The New Swiss Family Robinson* (1998); *Dangerous Curves* (1998); *Nightfall* (2000); *Kill Bill: Vol. 1* (2003); *Kill Bill: Vol. 2* (2004).

Coppola, Francis Ford

BORN: 1939.

FIRST CORMAN CREDIT: Producer/scenarist of U.S. version of *Nebo sovyot*, retitled *Battle Beyond the Sun* (1962).

HONORS: Oscars (Best picture, Best director, Best screenplay), *The Godfather Part II*, 1975.

JOB DESCRIPTION: Producer, director, writer.

Fresh out of UCLA, Coppola was asked by Corman in 1962 to improve upon a Russian-made science fiction film. He wangled a trip to Europe as a would-be soundman on *The Young Racers* (1963) before Corman staked him $22,000 to make his directorial debut with *Dementia 13* (1963). Less than ten years later, *The Godfather* (1972), an almost operatic treatment of the life of a Mafia family, made Coppola a cinematic legend. His tendency to think big has produced major achievements, including *Apocalypse Now* (1979), but has sometimes brought him to the brink of financial disaster.

In 1992, when *Bram Stoker's Dracula* was released, Coppola told Steven Rea of the *Chicago Tribune* that the impetus behind the film was "my love for those kind of movies that Roger [Corman] made, movies like *The Pit and the Pendulum* [1961]. . . . I learned from Roger the kind of low-budget approach to producing Gothic effects. *Dracula* is like a Roger Corman movie." He neglected to add that his *Dracula* was a Roger Corman movie on a $42 million budget. Inevitably, Corman was soon trying to capitalize on *Dracula*'s success by making his own low-budget Gothics, including *Dracula Rising* (1993), and *Bram Stoker's Burial of the Rats* (1995).

Coppola's director credits include: *The Terror* (1963—uncredited); *Dementia 13* (1963); *The Godfather* (1972); *The Godfather Part II* (1974); *The Conversation* (1974); *Apocalypse Now* (1979); *One from the Heart* (1982); *Tucker: The Man and His Dream* (1988); *The Godfather Part III* (1990); *Bram Stoker's Dracula* (1992); *John Grisham's The Rainmaker* (1997).

Corman, Gene

BORN: 1927.

FIRST CORMAN CREDIT: Co-producer, *I, Mobster* (1958).

HONORS: Emmy (Outstanding Drama Special), *A Woman Called Golda*, 1983.

JOB DESCRIPTION: Producer, executive, writer.

In an interview conducted by *Fangoria* in October, 1985, Gene Corman described his and his brother's long and sometimes stormy working relationship with Jim Nicholson and Sam Arkoff of American International Pictures. In Gene's words, "Like lovers, you have a spat, but you always find a need for each other." It's fair to see this phrase as capturing the essence of Gene's relationship with Roger as well. Director Jack Hill, for one, has vivid recollections of the Filmways era when the brothers worked together daily: "They'd slam doors and scream at each other and throw things and storm out of the office."

Gene has experienced the film industry from many vantage points. He has been a film and television executive as well as a hands-on producer, sometimes collaborating with Roger and sometimes keeping his distance. The *Fangoria* interview hints that he's proud of his sibling's accomplishments, but also a trifle envious. Says Gene, "Now that I look at it in retrospect, I probably should have directed, and I have had two or three different opportunities." He also seems nostalgic for the days when he would produce the films Roger directed, but, despite occasional announcements in the trade press, they have not worked on a set together since *Von Richtofen and Brown* in 1970.

Generally considered more easygoing than Roger, Gene loves tennis, well-tailored clothing, and fine art.

Gene Corman's producer and executive producer credits include: *Hot Car Girl* (1958); *Beast from Haunted Cave* (1959); *Attack of the Giant Leeches* (1960); *Tower of London* (1962); *The Intruder* (1962); *The Premature Burial* (1962); *Tobruk* (1967); *Von Richtofen and Brown* (1971); *The Slams* (1973); *F.I.S.T.* (1978); *The Big Red One* (1980); *A Woman Called Golda* (TV miniseries, 1982); *Blood Ties* (TV, 1991); *Vital Parts* (1999).

Dante, Joe

BORN: 1946.

FIRST CORMAN CREDIT: editor, *The Arena* (1973). Dante explains that this was a wholly bogus credit, courtesy of Jon Davison who was trying to lure his friend Joe to California to join him at New World Pictures.

HONORS: Leopard of Honor, Locarno (Italy) Film Festival, 1998.

JOB DESCRIPTION: Director, actor, producer, editor.

Arriving at New World Pictures in 1973, Dante was faced with cutting the "coming attractions" trailer for Jonathan Demme's debut film, *Caged Heat* (1974). Joe recalls cranking out "seven minutes of random, terrible junk," and then nearly missing the screening of his own trailer because his bus was late. As he remembers, "Roger's first words to me—because I had never met him—were, 'If I were you, I'd try to be on time for these things.'" Once the trailer was screened, Dante assumed he'd be fired on the spot, but Corman merely listed the changes he wanted made. "Apparently, nothing was too terrible for Roger to not figure he could fix it somehow."

After co-directing (with Allan Arkush) the quickie pastiche, *Hollywood Boulevard* (1976), Dante surprised himself by becoming a major studio director. Noted for his deft handling of action, fantasy, and popular culture in films like *Gremlins* (1984), he was recently honored at the Locarno Film Festival as "a poet whose heart is a toy shop filled with miniature spaceships." In 1999 this same festival devoted an entire sidebar session to "Joe Dante and the Second Corman Generation." Dante, Corman, Allan Arkush, Paul Bartel, Jon Davison, Monte Hellman, Dick Miller, Mary Woronov, and Dante's producing partner (and fellow New World alumnus) Mike Finnell were all invited to spend two weeks in Locarno as honored guests.

Though he may grouse about his Corman days, Joe insisted to me on November 5, 1998 that "if I had it to do over differently, I wouldn't have it any other way. I would never have wanted any other introduction to the movie business than the one I got." Dante hardly believes it was Corman's goal to make Hollywood a better place. Still, "this business, for good or ill, wouldn't be anywhere near full of as many interesting people if it wasn't for him. 'Cause they all started with him."

Dante's director credits include: *Hollywood Boulevard* (1976); *Piranha* (1978); *The Howling* (1980); *Gremlins* (1984); *Innerspace* (1987); *The 'Burbs* (1989); *Matinee* (1993); *Small Soldiers* (1998); *Looney Tunes: Back in Action* (2003).

Davison, Jon

BORN: 1949.

FIRST CORMAN CREDIT: Associate producer, *Big Bad Mama* (1974).

HONORS: Golden Satellite nomination (Best Motion Picture—Animated or Mixed Media), *Starship Troopers*, 1997.

JOB DESCRIPTION: Producer, executive producer.

A longtime Roger Corman fan, Davison wrote a ninety-page term paper on the filmmaker in high school. He studied film under Martin Scorsese at New York University (NYU), then became a low-rent Manhattan entrepreneur, operating a neighborhood repertory house and staging film retrospectives like "The All-Night Once-in-a-Lifetime Atomic Movie Orgy." Julie Corman described for *Vanity Fair* (1996) how Davison entered the New World organization. When he was visiting the set of *Night Call Nurses* (1972), she learned he had put himself through college by pirating and showing Corman flicks on campus. She conveyed this to Roger, who said "Send him around. I think we have a job for him in distribution."

Davison found his real niche in marketing, creating outrageous campaigns for such Corman classics as *Death Race 2000* (1975) and *Hollywood Boulevard* (1976), the film on which he earned his first producer credit. In a 1976 interview, he told the *Hollywood Reporter*, "For film students, Roger Corman is an oasis in the film desert." He has since moved on to a successful career as producer of *Airplane!* (1980) and other films marked by audacity and youth appeal.

Davison's producer credits include: *Hollywood Boulevard* (1976); *Grand Theft Auto* (1977); *Piranha* (1978); *Airplane!* (1980); *Robocop* (executive producer, 1987); *Starship Troopers* (1997); *The Sixth Day* (2000); *Starship Troopers 2* (2004).

Demme, Jonathan

BORN: 1944.

FIRST CORMAN CREDIT: Producer, co-writer, *Angels Hard as They Come* (1971).

HONORS: Oscar (Best Director), *The Silence of the Lambs*, 1992.

JOB DESCRIPTION: Director, producer, writer, actor.

A onetime film publicist, Demme first hooked up with Corman when he and a friend tried to craft a motorcycle movie in the style of Akira

Kurosawa's classic film, *Rashomon* (1950). After writing and producing several of Corman's Manila-made quickies, Demme made his directorial debut with the technically-crude but energetic *Caged Heat* (1974). He directed two more Corman movies before turning to studio projects, beginning with *Citizen's Band* in 1977. In a 1989 interview with David Thompson, Demme called Corman "one of my favorite people." He praised the latitude he was given as a fledgling director: "Having made sure that you accepted the rules of how to make a Corman movie, Corman then gave you an enormous amount of freedom to go ahead and do it."

Demme told Thompson he'd learned from Corman that "your villain has to be the most fascinating, if not likable, person in the piece." He would use this principle to good effect on his most acclaimed feature, *The Silence of the Lambs* (1991). Though Demme's career has been marked by a strong political consciousness, he recognizes the need to be entertaining. Thompson's comparison of his *Married to the Mob* (1988) to a Corman movie pleased him, "because that means our aggressive attempt to entertain is coming across."

Demme's director credits include: *Caged Heat* (1974); *Crazy Mama* (1975); *Fighting Mad* (1976); *Citizen's Band* (aka *Handle with Care*) (1977); *Melvin and Howard* (1980); *Something Wild* (1986); *Married to the Mob* (1988); *The Silence of the Lambs* (1991); *Philadelphia* (1993); *Beloved* (1998); *The Truth about Charlie* (2002).

Dern, Bruce

BORN: 1936.

FIRST CORMAN CREDIT: Actor, *The Wild Angels* (1966).

HONORS: Oscar Nomination (Best Supporting Actor), *Coming Home*, 1979.

JOB DESCRIPTION: Actor.

Spotted by Corman on the New York stage, Dern was cast in *The Wild Angels* (1966) after George Chakiris dropped out of the central role and Peter Fonda moved up from the second lead. In quick succession, Dern was then featured by Corman in *The St. Valentine's Day Massacre* and *The Trip* (both 1967). In a 1967 issue of the Canadian film journal *Take One*, Corman wrote, "Bruce Dern is extremely versatile; he is probably the best young actor I've ever worked with."

As Fonda's on-screen guide into the world of LSD, Dern was playing against type: he was a serious athlete, and Fonda recalled for documentary filmmaker Christian Blackwood that Dern had no use for alcohol, tobacco, or firearms. *Bloody Mama* (1970) was his last Corman movie before he won roles in major studio productions like the much-honored *Coming Home* (1978). Though grateful to Roger for picking him out of the crowd, Dern believes Corman should have ventured beyond low-budget film. He mused to Lois Armstrong of *People:* "I wonder why he never chose to go after the big ones. What happened to that director?"

Also appearing in *The Wild Angels* was Dern's then-wife, Diane Ladd. In 1993, the year that their daughter Laura starred in *Jurassic Park*, Ladd agreed to play the mad scientist role in Corman's low-rent dinosaur clone, *Carnosaur.*

Dern's actor credits include: *Marnie* (1964); *The Wild Angels* (1966); *The Trip* (1967); *They Shoot Horses, Don't They?* (1969); *Bloody Mama* (1970); *The Great Gatsby* (1974); *Smile* (1975); *Family Plot* (1976); *Coming Home* (1978); *That Championship Season* (1982); *After Dark, My Sweet* (1990); *Last Man Standing* (1996); *The Haunting* (1999); *All the Pretty Horses* (1999); *Masked and Anonymous* (2003).

Fonda, Peter

BORN: 1939.

FIRST CORMAN CREDIT: Actor, *The Wild Angels* (1966).

HONORS: Oscar nominations (Best Screenplay), *Easy Rider*, 1970; (Best Actor) *Ulee's Gold*, 1998.

JOB DESCRIPTION: Actor, director, producer, writer.

The son of screen legend Henry Fonda began his film career in the romantic comedy, *Tammy and the Doctor* (1963). But before *Easy Rider* (1969) made the tall, lanky Fonda a spokesman for the Counterculture, he had already become a 1960s icon as the chopper-riding Heavenly Blues in *The Wild Angels* (1966). Fonda was then an enthusiastic supporter of the drug scene. In Christian Blackwood's 1977 documentary, he chuckles over how, during *The Trip* (1967), he helped Corman shed his inhibitions by shoving a kilo of marijuana into Roger's mailbox as a Christmas gift. But Fonda could also be generous in more legal ways. Onetime Corman assistant Frances Doel recalled to me that when the film's hallucinogenic sequences were shot in Big Sur on the California coast, Fonda treated the hardworking cast and crew to a steak dinner.

Fonda has not made a Corman film since *Fighting Mad*, directed by Jonathan Demme in 1976. Once an aspiring director, he told Blackwood that he habitually phoned Roger several times a year for practical filmmaking advice. Though he has not directed since 1979, Fonda has developed into a respected actor who has moved beyond biker films to play sensitive character roles.

Fonda's actor credits include: *Tammy and the Doctor* (1963); *The Wild Angels* (1966); *The Trip* (1966); *Easy Rider* (1969); *Fighting Mad* (1976); *Futureworld* (1976); *Cannonball Run* (1981); *The Rose Garden* (1989); *Nadja* (1994); *Ulee's Gold* (1997); *The Limey* (1999); *The Laramie Project* (2002).

Franklin, Carl

BORN: 1949.

FIRST CORMAN CREDIT: Director, *Nowhere to Run* (1989).

HONORS: Independent Spirit Award (Best Director), *One False Move*, 1993.

JOB DESCRIPTION: Director, writer, actor.

Franklin's first feature as a director was the moody and intricate *Nowhere to Run* (1989) for Julie Corman. A former actor, he has also played roles in several Corman films. After leaving Concorde, Franklin made an indie thriller, *One False Move* (1991), distinguished by its sultry atmosphere and complex characterizations. His major studio releases include *Devil in a Blue Dress* (1995) starring Denzel Washington, and *One True Thing* (1998), which garnered an Oscar nomination for Meryl Streep.

Franklin will not speak for the record about his Corman films. But on September 18, 1998, he told Elvis Mitchell of radio station KCRW about his adventures when filming for Corman in Peru and the Philippines. In a Manila nightspot, he was drugged with an animal tranquilizer, probably by someone planning to rob him. Possibly, it was an attempt at something more sinister, like a kidnapping by a revolutionary group: "Which would have been hilarious, man. Can you imagine the rebels contacting Roger

Corman and asking for ransom? Can you imagine that? [imitating Corman's deep baritone] 'A million dollars! I can do six films for that!' "

Franklin's director credits include: *Nowhere to Run* (1989); *Eye of the Eagle 2* (1989); *Full Fathom Five* (1990); *One False Move* (1991); *Devil in a Blue Dress* (1995); *One True Thing* (1998); *High Crimes* (2002); *Out of Time* (2003).

Grier, Pam

BORN: 1949.

FIRST CORMAN CREDIT: Actress, *The Big Doll House* (1971).

HONORS: Golden Globe nomination (Best Actress in a Comedy/Musical), *Jackie Brown*, 1998.

JOB DESCRIPTION: Actress.

The voluptuous Grier started in Hollywood as an AIP switchboard operator. Back then, as she recently told Louis Hobson of the *Calgary Sun* (Alberta, Canada), "I was an angry thing. I really personified what was going on in the heads of women and particularly black women." In 1997, Corman recalled for the *Seattle Times*, "She was incredible-looking, but she was also hard as nails." When Roger suggested putting her in-your-face attitude on camera, she accepted $500 a week to play a tough prison inmate in *The Big Doll House*. This launched a series of films that made her the queen of blaxploitation in the 1970s. In later years, Grier's parts have become more challenging, culminating in the title role in *Jackie Brown* (1997), which Quentin Tarantino built around her talents and forceful screen presence.

Grier's actress credits include: *The Big Doll House* (1971); *The Big Bird Cage* (1972); *The Arena* (1973); *Coffy* (1973); *Foxy Brown* (1974); *Greased Lightning* (1977); *Fort Apache, the Bronx* (1981); *Escape from L.A.* (1996); *Jackie Brown* (1997); *Holy Smoke* (1999); *Love the Hard Way* (2001); *The Adventures of Pluto Nash* (2002); *The L Word* (TV series, 2004).

Hellman, Monte

BORN: 1932.

FIRST CORMAN CREDIT: Director, *Beast from Haunted Cave* (1959).

HONORS: Critics Prize, Venice Film Festival, 1988.

JOB DESCRIPTION: Director, editor, producer.

The distinctive austerity of such Hellman films as *Two-Lane Blacktop* (1971) is revered by fans of independent cinema. Hellman met Corman in the late 1950s; they sometimes socialized, and once enthusiastically discussed German philosopher Friedrich Nietzsche while driving up the California coast. When we spoke on December 4, 1998, Hellman described how Roger put money toward two 1966 westerns on which Hellman collaborated with Jack Nicholson. The deal was that any over-budget costs would come out of the filmmakers' pockets, and Hellman learned from the experience "how to make a movie whatever the budget was. I've never gone over budget." Back then, Hellman told me, it was a pleasure to work with Corman in the editing room. But "by the time we did *Cockfighter* [1974], he became a little bit more rigid and a little less patient. I think maybe he'd done just too many movies by that time."

Hellman, primarily a director, took on a new role in helping young Quentin Tarantino raise financing for his debut feature, *Reservoir Dogs* (1992). Though Tarantino, a B-movie aficionado, had dedicated the script of *Reservoir Dogs* to Corman and other cinematic heroes, the project never crossed Corman's desk. On July 25, 1996, *Variety*'s Richard Natale queried Corman: "If a Quentin Tarantino came to you with the script of *Reservoir Dogs*, and asked you for a million dollars to make it, what would you say?" Corman's reply: "I'd say I'll give you $750,000 and you'll do the film."

Hellman's director credits include: *Beast from Haunted Cave* (1959); *The Shooting* (1966); *Ride the Whirlwind* (1966); *Two-Lane Blacktop* (1971); *Cockfighter* (1974); *China 9, Liberty 37*, aka *Gunfire* (1978); *Avalanche Express* (finished directorial chores after death of original director, Mark Robson, 1979); *Silent Night, Deadly Night III* (1989).

Hopper, Dennis

BORN: 1936.

FIRST CORMAN CREDIT: actor, *Queen of Blood* (1966).

HONORS: Oscar nominations (Best Original Screenplay), *Easy Rider*, 1970; (Best Supporting Actor), *Hoosiers*, 1987.

JOB DESCRIPTION: actor, director, writer.

Early in his career, Hopper was featured in *Rebel without a Cause*

(1955) and *Giant* (1956). In 1966 he played the male lead in *Queen of Blood*, a stodgy Russian science-fiction film to which a Corman minion had added new vampire footage. Hopper was recommended for his drug-dealer role in *The Trip* (1967) by his friend Peter Fonda. In 1969 they joined forces to make *Easy Rider*.

When I spoke with Hopper on assignment for the *Hollywood Reporter* on March 14, 1997, he described the Roger Corman of the 1960s as "the only really close-to-independent filmmaker that existed at that time." Still, after *The Trip*, Hopper never worked for Corman again. But Concorde staffers remember an almost incoherent German film called *White Star* (1985), purchased by Corman because of the value of Hopper's name and the glitz promised by the film's music-industry setting. The task was to refashion *White Star* into something an American audience could watch. Staffer Anna Roth, who came from an experimental theatre background, remembers that the experience "was so avant-garde, it was almost post-modern. A totally different way of telling a story . . . a found object, this piece of celluloid that makes no sense, bringing sense to it. We would have to fill in the logic, and try to hire someone who looked like Dennis Hopper from an angle." Following a period of personal upheaval, Hopper has set-tled into a major career as one of Hollywood's favorite screen villains.

Hopper's actor credits include: *Rebel Without a Cause* (1955); *Queen of Blood* (1966); *The Trip* (1967); *Easy Rider* (1969); *Apocalypse Now* (1979); *White Star* (1985); *Hoosiers* (1986); *Blue Velvet* (1986); *River's Edge* (1987); *Speed* (1994); *Waterworld* (1995); *Meet the Deedles* (1998); *EDtv* (1999); *24* (TV series, 2002); *The Keeper* (2003); *The Crow: Wicked Prayer* (2004).

Howard, Ron

BORN: 1953
FIRST CORMAN CREDIT: Actor, *Eat My Dust!* (1976)
HONORS: Oscars (Best Picture, Best Director), *A Beautiful Mind*, 2002.
JOB DESCRIPTION: director, producer, actor, writer

In the opinion of some New World regulars, Ron Howard was too nice to be a movie director. Nonetheless, the former child star of *The Andy Griffith Show* (1960–68) is today one of Hollywood's most respected com-mercial filmmakers. Howard told me on January 29, 1999 that when he agreed to star in *Grand Theft Auto* (1977) in exchange for the chance to write and direct, "It wasn't my dream project, the film that I was trying to get off the ground, but it was the closest thing to a professional directing opportunity that I'd been able to generate." Howard recalled Corman saying, "I like to think I turn out directors for Hollywood the way the University of Southern California turns out running backs for the NFL." (Of course, those were the days when USC was a football powerhouse.) Corman had high praise for Howard's achievements, telling Mick Garris and Carl Macek of the *Los Angeles Herald Examiner,* "He was the coolest first-time director I'd ever seen in my life."

Howard's director credits include: *Grand Theft Auto* (1977); *Splash* (1984); *Cocoon* (1985); *Parenthood* (1989); *Backdraft* (1991); *Far and Away* (1992); *Apollo 13* (1995); *Ransom* (1996); *EDtv* (1999); *How the Grinch Stole Christmas* (2000); *A Beautiful Mind* (2001); *The Missing* (2003); *Cinderella Man* (2004).

Hurd, Gale Anne

BORN: 1955

FIRST CORMAN CREDIT: Co-producer, *Smokey Bites the Dust* (1981)

HONORS: Women in Film's Crystal Award, 1998. Independent Spirit Award (Best First Feature), *The Waterdance,* 1993

JOB DESCRIPTION: producer, executive producer

An economics major at Stanford University, Gale Anne Hurd planned a career in law or business. But during her year at Stanford's overseas campus in London, England, she developed a passion for film. Hurd ended up graduating Phi Beta Kappa with a double major in economics and communications. Soon Roger Corman came calling. Gale served as his assistant, then quickly was named New World's director of advertising. But when she decided to move into production, Corman decreed she must start at the bottom. In 1988, Hurd told journalist J. D. McCulley: "I went from director of advertising to production assistant. I learned a lot about making coffee and emptying chemical toilets in motor homes." Fortunately, Hurd was not disheartened, recognizing that "it's great to learn in the trenches. And with Roger you didn't stay in the trenches very long."

Hurd remained at New World for five years. By the time she and James

Cameron joined forces to make *The Terminator* (1984), she had absorbed every aspect of film production. As the producer of such blockbusters as *Aliens* (1986), *Terminator 2: Judgment Day* (1991), and *Armageddon* (1998), Gale has built her reputation on science fiction and action films that feature strong heroines. Corman credits her with bringing Jim Cameron's talents to his attention on the set of *Battle Beyond the Stars*. And he has high praise for Hurd's own abilities. As he told *Variety*'s Jerry Roberts in June 1998, "I've never met anyone like Gale. She's hard-working and creative, but above all she's intelligent, really a brilliant woman."

Hurd's producer and executive producer credits include: *The Terminator* (1984); *Aliens* (1986); *Alien Nation* (1988); *The Abyss* (1989); *Tremors* (1990); *Terminator 2: Judgment Day* (1991); *The Waterdance* (1992); *Raising Cain* (1992); *The Ghost and the Darkness* (1996); *The Relic* (1997); *Dante's Peak* (1997); *Armageddon* (1998); *Dead Man on Campus* (1998); *Virus* (1999); *Dick* (1999); *Clockstoppers* (2002); *Hulk* (2003); *Terminator 3: Rise of the Machines* (2003); *The Punisher* (2004).

Kaminski, Janusz

BORN: 1959
FIRST CORMAN CREDIT: gaffer, *Not of this Earth* (1988)
HONORS: Oscars (Best Cinematography), *Schindler's List*, 1994; (Best Cinematography), *Saving Private Ryan*, 1999
JOB DESCRIPTION: cinematographer, director

A true believer in the American dream, Kaminski came to the United States from Poland at age twenty-two to study filmmaking. Since then he has won two Oscars and married a movie star, Holly Hunter. While a student at the American Film Institute, Kaminski worked as a gaffer on Concorde films. Once he had convinced the Concorde production team to let him demonstrate his camera skills, he shot *The Terror Within II* (1990) and *The Rain Killer* (1991). From there it was only a short jump to *Schindler's List* (1993).

When we spoke on May 6, 1999, Kaminski told me that at Concorde "I learned how to work really fast, how to rely on my instincts." He also discovered how to cover up a lack of substance with flashy camera tricks. He had little direct contact with Corman on the Concorde lot, but remembers how dolly tracks would have to be hidden before the boss arrived on the set. (Roger felt that setting up tracks to guide the movement of the camera was overly time-consuming.) Looking back, Kaminski assured me he's "glad to be part of that tradition of young filmmakers coming in and working on twelve or sixteen-day movies, working twenty hours a day, getting fed nothing, being abused, being insulted by people who didn't know any better." Today he continues his creative collaboration with Steven Spielberg; he has also directed his own first feature, *Lost Souls* (1999).

Kaminski's cinematography credits include: *The Terror Within II* (1990); *The Rain Killer* (1991); *Schindler's List* (1993); *Jerry Maguire* (1966); *Amistad* (1997); *The Lost World* (1997); *Saving Private Ryan* (1998); *Artificial Intelligence: AI* (2001); *Minority Report* (2002); *Catch Me If You Can* (2002); *Terminal* (2004).

Kirkland, Sally

BORN: 1944

FIRST CORMAN CREDIT: actress, *The Young Nurses* (1973)

HONORS: Golden Globe, Independent Spirit Award, Los Angeles Film Critics Award (Best Actress), *Anna*, 1988.

JOB DESCRIPTION: stage and screen actress, producer, director, teacher

The flamboyant Kirkland met Corman, whom she considers a lifelong mentor, circa 1969. An Actors Studio graduate with a penchant for both physical and emotional nakedness, Kirkland was soon playing sexy roles in New World films, while also learning production. In that era, recalls Kirkland, Corman was training his wife Julie to be a producer. As Julie's head of casting on such films as *Candy Stripe Nurses* (1974), Kirkland too got a valuable education in working behind the camera. Sally affirmed when we spoke on May 20, 1999 that both Cormans treated her like family. She became a godmother to their eldest daughter, and they lent her their home for parties at which Hollywood's most interesting young aspirants could meet and mingle: "Because they're shy people in that sense—a social sense—I would act kind of like a social director." In return, said Kirkland, "they were always there for me—always."

Following Kirkland's Oscar nomination for *Anna* (1988), Corman made her a six-figure offer to star in *In the Heat of Passion* (1992), and urged her to try directing. He has gone out of his way to praise her in front of the media, and she's convinced that his encouragement helped lead to her directorial debut on Showtime's anthology series, *Women's Stories of Passion* (1997). Kirkland told me Roger has challenged her to come up with a project that is simultaneously provocative and arty. She quotes him as saying, "If you can find me a play combining *Pulp Fiction* [1994] and *Last Tango in Paris* [1973], I'll have it turned into a screenplay for you to direct."

Kirkland's actress credits include: *Coming Apart* (1969); *The Young Nurses* (1973); *The Sting* (1973); *Candy Stripe Nurses* (1974); *Big Bad Mama* (1974); *Crazy Mama* (1975); *Georgia Peaches* (TV, 1980); *Anna* (1987); *High Stakes* (1989); *Cold Feet* (1989); *Best of the Best* (1989); *Revenge* (1989); *JFK* (1991); *In the Heat of Passion* (1992); *EDtv* (1999); *Bruce Almighty* (2003).

Miller, Dick

BORN: 1928

FIRST CORMAN CREDIT: actor, *Apache Woman* (1955)

HONORS: appears in every feature shot by director Joe Dante.

JOB DESCRIPTION: actor

The short, pugnacious Miller was first hired by Corman for *Apache Woman* (1955), in which he played both a cowboy and an Indian. (As a member of the posse tracking the Indian, he almost killed himself off in the western's climax.) The Corman-Miller relationship was sometimes turbulent, and Dick still has mixed emotions about his old boss. When we spoke on September 11, 1998, he conceded that "I got the opportunity from him, multiple opportunities, some thirty films before I left, and every part was basically different. As an actor it was great; I was having a ball. But I never felt that Roger properly respected or rewarded the people who worked for him." Today, the two chat cordially at industry events held in Corman's honor. But Miller, who underwent major surgery in 1997, still feels hurt that Corman has never thought to inquire about his health.

Fortunately for Miller's career, "a lot of guys who started with Roger seemed to want to give me a shot some place along the line." He has played featured roles for Martin Scorsese, Jonathan Demme, Jim Cameron, Allan Arkush, and Jonathan Kaplan. Joe Dante, who considers him a good-luck charm, uses him regularly. In *Matinee* (1993), Dante's salute to B-movies set against the backdrop of the Cuban Missile Crisis, Miller and filmmaker John Sayles play a Mutt-and-Jeff pair of bad guys.

Miller's actor credits include: *Rock All Night* (1957); *Bucket of Blood* (1959); *The Little Shop of Horrors* (1960); *The Terror* (1963); *The Howling* (1980); *Heart Like a Wheel* (1983); *The Terminator* (1984); *Gremlins* (1984); *Fame* (TV series,1985–87); *After Hours* (1985); *Matinee* (1993); *Small Soldiers* (1998); *Looney Tunes: Back in Action* (2003).

Nicholson, Jack

BORN: 1937

FIRST CORMAN CREDIT: actor, *The Cry Baby Killer* (1958)

HONORS: Oscars (Best Actor), One Flew Over the Cuckoo's Nest, 1976; (Best Supporting Actor), *Terms of Endearment*, 1984; (Best Actor), *As Good as It Gets*, 1998

JOB DESCRIPTION: actor, writer, producer, director

In accepting the Cecil B. DeMille Award at the 1999 Golden Globe ceremony, Nicholson thanked Corman ahead of a long list of industry folk. When he made his big-screen debut as the lead in Corman's *The Cry Baby Killer* (1958), Nicholson's success as an actor was by no means assured. Longtime Corman assistant director Paul Rapp, to whom I spoke on October 22, 1998, thought Nicholson had a poor speaking voice and advised the young man to go into real estate. But Nicholson impressed Corman's story editor Frances Doel as being hip and knowledgeable about films. She also found him surprisingly relaxed: "He didn't seem scared of Roger at all, unlike me."

Before he met Corman, Nicholson had been mired in daytime television, playing roles on *Matinee Theatre* and *Divorce Court*. He is quoted in Earl Blackwell's *Celebrity Register* (1990) as saying, "I always sort of stunk of TV. At the time Roger [Corman] was the only guy who would employ me as a professional." Today, Nicholson looks back on his nearly twenty Corman films with amused affection. In Corman's 1990 autobiography, Nicholson recalls budgets so low that cast members would all share the same script. The book also reveals Nicholson's special fondness for the zany shenanigans involved with *The Terror* (1963): "I had a great time. Paid the rent. They don't make movies like *The Terror* any more."

Nicholson's actor credits include: *The Cry Baby Killer* (1958); *The Little Shop of Horrors* (1960); *The Raven* (1963); *The Terror* (1963); *Easy Rider* (1969); *Five Easy Pieces* (1970); *The Last Detail* (1973); *Chinatown* (1974); *One Flew Over the Cuckoo's Nest* (1975); *The Shining* (1980); *Reds* (1981); *Terms of Endearment* (1983); *Prizzi's Honor* (1985); *The Witches of Eastwick* (1987); *Ironweed* (1987); *A Few Good Men* (1992); *Hoffa* (1992); *As Good as It Gets* (1997); *Blood and Wine* (1997); *The Pledge* (2001); *About Schmidt* (2002); *Anger Management* (2003); *Something's Gotta Give* (2003).

Price, Vincent

DATES: 1911–1993

FIRST CORMAN CREDIT: actor, *House of Usher* (1960)

HONORS: Career Achievement Award, Los Angeles Film Critics Association, 1991

JOB DESCRIPTION: actor, author

Educated at Yale University and the University of London, Price was an established Broadway star when he came to Hollywood in 1938 to play costume roles, usually as treacherous or effete villains. He was starring in horror films long before Corman cast him as Roderick Usher in 1960. Though Price was known for his sophisticated tastes—he was an art collector and gourmet chef—he did not seem to mind appearing in drive-in fare. Earl Blackwell's *Celebrity Register* (1990) quotes him as saying, "I sometimes feel that I'm impersonating the dark unconscious of the whole human race. I know this sounds sick but I love it."

In eulogizing the star of nine of his best-known features, Corman praised Price's professionalism and flexibility. Roger pointed especially to *The Raven* (1963), in which Price successfully adjusted to three different acting styles, that of Jack Nicholson (trained in the Method), Boris Karloff (classically schooled in the English manner), and Peter Lorre, who "did anything that came into his mind at any given moment."

Price's actor credits include: *The Private Lives of Elizabeth and Essex* (1939); *The Invisible Man Returns* (1940); *Laura* (1944); *The Three Musketeers* (1948); *The Baron of Arizona* (1950); *House of Wax* (1953); *The Fly* (1958); *House of Usher* (1960); *The Raven* (1963); *The Tomb of Ligeia* (1965);

The Abominable Dr. Phibes (1971); *Theatre of Blood* (1973); *The Whales of August* (1987); *Edward Scissorhands* (1990).

Sayles, John

BORN: 1950

FIRST CORMAN CREDIT: writer and actor, *Piranha* (1978)

HONORS: Oscar nominations (Best Screenplay), *Passion Fish*, 1993; (Best Screenplay), *Lone Star*, 1997

JOB DESCRIPTION: director, writer, actor, editor

Sayles, who wears many hats in his own independent productions, learned screenwriting on such Corman movies as *Battle Beyond the Stars* (1980). On February 10, 1999, he described for me the challenge of crafting a low-budget action script: "It would be great if you were James Cameron and you knew you could have the hero surf into a iron foundry on the side of a oil truck that had just tipped over and was shooting up sparks. You can write that all you want, but if you don't have the budget to do it, it doesn't solve the problem of how to end the movie." Unlike Cameron and other Corman alumni, Sayles has never gone the studio route. More interested in human drama than in spectacle, he likes working on a smaller scale, free of outside interference.

Sayles confirmed for me that he turned down Corman's offer to invest in his own first film, *Return of the Secaucus 7* (1980), because "I actually didn't need a producer to come in at that point." Prepared to make the picture on his own terms, he did not want the obligation connected with using someone else's money. Still, said Sayles, "It was very generous of him. He really hadn't even read the script, as far as I know." To this day, Sayles continues to chart his own course, on such films as the Spanish-language *Hombres armados* (*Men With Guns*, 1997).

Sayles' director credits include: *Return of the Secaucus 7* (1980); *The Brother from Another Planet* (1984); *Matewan* (1987); *Eight Men Out* (1988); *City of Hope* (1991); *Passion Fish* (1992); *The Secret of Roan Inish* (1994); *Lone Star* (1996); *Men with Guns* (1997); *Limbo* (1999); *Sunshine State* (2002); *Casa de los Babys* (2003).

Scorsese, Martin

BORN: 1942

FIRST CORMAN CREDIT: director, *Boxcar Bertha* (1972)

HONORS: American Film Institute's Life Achievement Award, 1997. Oscar nominations (Best Director), *Raging Bull*, 1981; (Best Director), *The Last Temptation of Christ*, 1989; (Best Director and Best Screenplay), *GoodFellas*, 1991; (Best Screenplay), *The Age of Innocence*, 1994; (Best Director), *Gangs of New York*, 2003.

JOB DESCRIPTION: director, writer, producer, actor

Scorsese and his fellow NYU film students were mesmerized by Corman's 1960 horror classic, *House of Usher*. He says in *Scorsese on Scorsese* (1989), "We loved this blend of English Gothic and French *grand guignol* mixed together in an American film." When Corman hired Scorsese to direct *Boxcar Bertha* (1972), the young filmmaker was surprised to find his new boss "very sweet and very suave." Still, Roger knew how to get results. Scorsese recalled in his book that when Corman visited the *Boxcar Bertha* set in Arkansas, "he walked around scowling and the crew shaped up immediately." Scorsese quickly learned about Corman's pet theories: "Remember, Marty, that you must have some nudity at least every fifteen pages. Not complete nudity. Maybe a little off the shoulder, or some leg, just to keep the audience interest up."

Warned by another mentor, John Cassavetes (1929–1989), to avoid getting sucked into the world of exploitation films, Scorsese turned down further Corman assignments to make his own feature, *Mean Streets* (1973). He looked to Corman for financing, but Gene Corman's success with an urban ghetto drama, *Cool Breeze* (1972), caused Roger to demand one key change. In Scorsese's words, "Roger said to me, 'If you want to make *Mean Streets*, and if you're willing to swing a little'—I'll never forget that phrase—'and make them all black, I'll give you $150,000 and you can shoot it all with a non-Union crew in New York.'" Scorsese ultimately raised money elsewhere, and made the film he wanted to make, using his *Boxcar Bertha* crew and shooting most of the New York exteriors in Southern California. He has since become a pre-eminent American director, respected for work as diverse as the domestic comedy, *Alice Doesn't Live Here Anymore* (1974), and the philosophical epic, *Kundun* (1997). He is chiefly linked, however, with explorations of male violence in such unsparing films as *Taxi Driver* (1976) and *Raging Bull* (1980).

Scorsese's director credits include: *Who's that Knocking at My Door* (1968); *Boxcar Bertha* (1972); *Mean Streets* (1973); *Alice Doesn't Live Here Anymore* (1974); *Taxi Driver* (1976); *Raging Bull* (1980); *After Hours* (1985); *The Last Temptation of Christ* (1988); *Goodfellas* (1990); *The Age of Innocence* (1993); *Casino* (1995); *Kundun* (1997), *Bringing Out the Dead* (1999); *Gangs of New York* (2002).

Shire, Talia

BORN: 1946

FIRST CORMAN CREDIT: actress, *Gas-s-s-s!* (1970)

HONORS: Oscar nominations (Best Supporting Actress), *The Godfather Part II*, 1975; (Best Actress), *Rocky*, 1977

JOB DESCRIPTION: actress, producer, director

Shire, who first met Corman through her brother, Francis Ford Coppola, appeared on screen in *Gas-s-s-s!* (1970), worked behind the scenes on other films, and dated Corman briefly. Her biggest successes came as Connie Corleone Rizzi in *The Godfather* trilogy and as Adrian, opposite Sylvester Stallone, in five *Rocky* films. In 1995, Corman agreed to back *One Night Stand*, a thriller starring Ally Sheedy that marked Shire's directing debut. Alida Camp, the film's producer, noted on December 17, 1998 that Corman had always thought highly of Shire. For that reason, said Camp, "he was willing to let her have a lot of freedom. And he put more money into her movie also. Well, it ended up being more money than he wanted to put in." The upshot was that Roger abruptly slashed several hundred thousand dollars from the budget, but Shire refused to believe he was serious. She ended up owing him money, and the once-cordial relationship soured.

Shire's acting credits include: *Gas-s-s-s!* (1970); *The Godfather* (1972); *The Godfather Part II* (1974); *Rocky* (1976), and four more *Rocky* films; *The Godfather Part III* (1990).

Stallone, Sylvester

BORN: 1946

FIRST CORMAN CREDIT: actor, *Death Race 2000* (1975)

HONORS: Oscar nominations (Best Actor and Best Screenplay), *Rocky*, 1977
JOB DESCRIPTION: actor, writer, director

While an aspiring actor, Stallone supported himself as a zookeeper, a pizza chef, and a bit player in a porno film. Robert Rehme, once Corman's head of sales at New World, recalls how he used to see Stallone "hanging around in the halls, working for pennies." It was director Paul Bartel who first brought the young actor to Roger's attention. He was cast as the comic heavy, Machine-Gun Joe Viterbo, in *Death Race 2000* (1975), and that same year played buttoned-down mafioso Frank Nitti in New World's *Capone*. *Rocky* (1976) made him a star, and he continues to be a major box office draw in action films. In 1980, Stallone told *People* magazine, "Roger is one of the few men who will give a new artist an honest break."

Stallone's actor credits include: *The Lords of Flatbush* (1974); *Death Race 2000* (1975); *Capone* (1975); *Rocky* (1976, followed by four sequels); *Paradise Alley* (1978); *F.I.S.T.* (1978); *First Blood* (1982); *Rhinestone* (1984); *Rambo* (1985); *Cobra* (1986); *Cliffhanger* (1993); *Judge Dredd* (1995); *Cop Land* (1997); *D-Tox* (2002); *Spy Kids 3-D: Game Over* (2003).

ART FILMS

THIS LIST IS composed chiefly of foreign-language films associated with Roger Corman. Although he had no part in their production, they were distributed by his companies in North American markets, and his involvement greatly contributed to their critical and financial success. I've chosen to list these films in chronological order, by their original release dates, using their English-language titles. All films are in color, unless otherwise noted.

Cries and Whispers (1972, Swedish), 106 minutes.
Director: Ingmar Bergman.
With Harriet Andersson, Liv Ullmann, Ingrid Thulin.

The Harder They Come (1973, Jamaican), 98 minutes.
Director: Perry Henzell.
With Jimmy Cliff, Janet Barkley, Carl Bradshaw.

The Last Days of Man on Earth (1973, British), 78 minutes.
Director: Robert Fuest.
With Jon Finch, Jenny Runacre, Sterling Hayden.

Fantastic Planet (1973, French), 72 minutes.
Director: René Laloux.
Animated. (Corman's English-language version features the voice of Barry
   Bostwick.)

Amarcord (1974, Italian), 127 minutes.
Director: Federico Fellini.
With Magali Noel, Bruno Zanin, Pupella Maggio.

The Romantic Englishwoman (1975, British), 115 minutes.
Director: Joseph Losey.
With Michael Caine, Glenda Jackson, Helmut Berger.

The Story of Adele H (1975, French), 97 minutes.
Director: François Truffaut.
With Isabelle Adjani, Bruce Robinson, Sylvia Marriott.

The Lost Honor of Katharina Blum (1975, German), 106 minutes.
Directors: Volker Schlöndorff, Margarethe von Trotta.
With Angela Winkler, Mario Adorf, Dieter Laser.

Dersu Uzala (1975, Japanese-Russian), 140 minutes.
Director: Akira Kurosawa.
With Maxim Munzuk, Yuri Solomine.

Small Change (1976, French), 104 minutes.
Director: François Truffaut.
With Geory Desmouceaux, Philippe Goldman.

Lumiere (1976, French), 95 minutes.
Director: Jeanne Moreau.
With Jeanne Moreau, Francine Racette, Lucia Bose.

Andy Warhol's Bad (1977, American), 100 minutes.
Director: Jed Johnson.
With Carroll Baker, Perry King, Susan Tyrell.

A Hero Ain't Nothin' but a Sandwich (1978, American), 105 minutes.
Director: Ralph Nelson.
With Cicely Tyson, Paul Winfield, Larry B. Scott.

Autumn Sonata (1978, Swedish), 97 minutes.
Director: Ingmar Bergman.
With Ingrid Bergman, Liv Ullmann, Lena Nyman.

A Little Night Music (1978, American), 124 minutes.
Director: Harold Prince.
With Elizabeth Taylor, Diana Rigg, Len Cariou.

Breaker Morant (1979, Australian), 107 minutes.
Director: Bruce Beresford.
With Edward Woodward, Jack Thompson, John Waters.

The Kids Are Alright (1979, American), b&w and color, 108 minutes.
Director: Jeff Stein.
Documentary featuring rock band The Who.

The Tin Drum (1979, German), 142 minutes.
Director: Volker Schlöndorff.
With David Bennent, Mario Adorf, Angela Winkler.

Mon Oncle d'Amerique (1980, French), 123 minutes.
Director: Alain Resnais.
With Gérard Depardieu, Nicole Garcia, Roger Pierre.

Richard's Things (1980, British), 104 minutes.
Director: Anthony Harvey.
With Liv Ullmann, Amanda Redman, Tim Pigott-Smith.

Christiane F. (1981, German), 124 minutes.
Director: Ulrich Edel.
With Nadja Brunkhorst, Thomas Haustein, Jens Kuphal.

Fitzcarraldo (1982, German), 157 minutes.
Director: Werner Herzog.
With Klaus Kinski, Claudia Cardinale, Jose Lewgoy.

Cabeza de Vaca (1991, Mexican), 112 minutes.
Director: Nicolás Echevarría.
With Juan Diego, Daniel Giménez Cacho, Roberto Sosa.

SOURCE NOTES

SOURCES OF OPENING QUOTES FOR CHAPTERS

1. Roger Corman, in Alford, Henry, "The Fast Tycoon," *Vanity Fair* (April 1996), 148.
2. Roger Corman, in Oppenheimer, Jean, "The Mentor," *Village View* (October 9–15, 1992), 9.
3. Roger Corman, in Berges, Marshall, "Home Q&A: Julie and Roger Corman," *Los Angeles Times Home Magazine* (October 22, 1978), 43.
4. Roger Corman, in *Directors on Directing*, directed for Telepiu (Italy) by Adam Simon (1997).
5. Howard Thompson, review of *The Pit and the Pendulum*, *New York Times* (August 24, 1961), C-25.
6. Corman, Roger, with Jim Jerome, *How I Made a Hundred Movies in Hollywood and Never Lost a Dime* (New York: Random House, 1990), 145.
7. Roger Corman, in Thomas, Kevin, "Roger Corman—Director Who Changed the Face of Hollywood," *Los Angeles Times* (January 9, 1972).
8. Roger Corman, in Honeycutt, Kirk, " 'Corman School' Days Are Out," *Hollywood Reporter* (May 14, 1998), 65.

9. John Sayles, in "Filmmaker," *The New Yorker* (March 23, 1981).

10. Roger Corman, in Armstrong, Lois, "Roger Corman's Films May 'B' Shlock, but No One in Hollywood Has Nurtured More 'A' Talent," *People* (November 12, 1980), 90.

11. Roger Corman, quoted by casting executive Steve Rabiner in Duke, Paul Francis, "Movie Maverick." *Stanford* (July–August 1997), 63.

12. Carl Franklin, in Duke, *Ibid.*, 62.

13. Roger Corman, in Citron, Alan, "Corman Nears Sale of B Movie Library," *Los Angeles Times* (February 11, 1994).

14. Roger Corman, in Jolson-Colburn, Jeffrey, "Corman May Sell to Kastner," *Hollywood Reporter* (December 9, 1996).

NOTE: Sources for each chapter/section are listed in alphabetical order.

INTRODUCTION

Brock, Deborah, taped conversation, October 14, 1998.

Broderick, John, taped conversation, October 26, 1998.

Carradine, David, taped conversation, February 3, 1999.

Cohen, Howard R., taped conversation, September 4, 1998.

Dante, Joe, taped conversation, November 5, 1998.

Dickerson, Beach, taped conversation, October 2, 1998.

Flender, Rodman, taped conversation, September 23, 1998.

Frakes, Randy, taped conversation, November 19, 1998.

Grier, Pam, in "Roger Corman: Shoot to Thrill," *California Stories*, directed for KCET-TV by Joseph Kwong (November 1988).

Griffith, Charles B., e-mail message, November 15, 1998.

Haney, Daryl, taped conversation, December 12, 1998.

Honeycutt, Kirk, " 'Corman School' Days Are Out," *Hollywood Reporter* (May 14, 1998).

King, Robert, taped conversation, December 22, 1998.

Krevoy, Brad, taped conversation, September 25, 1998.

Mark, Ellen, conversation, September 15, 1998.

Martinez-Holler, Ana (Hollywood Chamber of Commerce), conversation, July 20, 1999.

Rehme, Robert, taped conversation, December 3, 1998.

Vlastas, Pamm, taped conversation, October 7, 1998.

CHAPTER 1: A BOY'S LIFE

Armstrong, Lois, "Roger Corman's Films May 'B' Shlock, but No One in Hollywood Has Nurtured More 'A' Talent," *People* (November 12, 1980), 90.

Beverly Hills Citizen (July 31, 1942 through June 18, 1943).

[Beverly Hills High School] *Watchtower* (Summer 1943).

Beverly Hills Historical Society.

Bloch, Flo, e-mail messages, January 13 and February 10, 1999, regarding Post Intermediate.

Corman, Roger, with Jim Jerome, *How I Made a Hundred Movies in Hollywood and Never Lost a Dime* (New York: Random House, 1990), 5.

Ibid., 177.

Davidson, Bill, "King of Schlock," *New York Times Magazine* (December 28, 1975), 30.

Doel, Frances, informal conversations dating back to 1973.

Florence, Mal, conversation, January 12, 1999.

Haller, Kinta, taped conversation, January 5, 1999.

Louie, Barbara, archivist, Burton Historical Collection at Detroit Public Library, e-mail message, February 25, 1999.

Monicker magazine, 1974.

Mount, Thom, taped conversation, November 13, 1998.

"Off the Cuff," *Hollywood Reporter* (March 18, 1987).

Stanford University Register (1943–44).

CHAPTER 2: A GENTLEMAN AND A SCHOLAR

Brock, Deborah, taped conversation, October 14, 1998.

Corman, Roger, "Sideline Slants" column, *Stanford Daily* (November 15, 1943).

Ibid., (April 21, 1944).

Corman, Roger, with Jim Jerome, *How I Made a Hundred Movies in Hollywood and Never Lost a Dime* (New York: Random House, 1990), 8–10.

Digby Diehl, "Roger Corman: The Simenon of Cinema," *Show* (May 1970), 28.

Griffith, Charles B., e-mail message, November 20, 1998.

Haller, Kinta, taped conversation, January 5, 1999.

Krevoy, Brad, taped conversation, September 25, 1998.

McGee, Mark Thomas, *Faster and Furiouser: The Revised and Fattened Fable of American International Pictures* (Jefferson, NC: McFarland, 1996), 20.

Rapp, Paul, taped conversation, October 21, 1998.

Stanford Daily (September 1943–June 1947).

Stanford Directory (1946–47).

[Stanford University] *Quad* (1947).

CHAPTER 3: ONE FOR THE MONEY

Almond, Paul, taped conversation, November 25, 1998.

Bartel, Paul, taped conversation, December 1, 1998.

Campbell, R. Wright, e-mail message, September 29, 1998.

Ibid., October 1, 1998.

Cohen, Howard R., taped conversation, September 4, 1998.

Corman, Roger, with Jim Jerome, *How I Made a Hundred Movies in Hollywood and Never Lost a Dime* (New York: Random House, 1990), 10.

Ibid., 14.

Ibid., 19.

Ibid., 33.

Ibid., 225.

"Corman Sets Up Oxford Scholarship," *Variety* (July 31, 1969).

Dante, Joe, taped conversation, November 5, 1998.

Davison, Jon, taped conversation, November 5, 1998.

Dickerson, Beach, taped conversation, October 2, 1998.

Dietz, Lawrence, "The Quickie Master," *New York World Journal Tribune* (January 8, 1967).

Doel, Frances, informal conversations dating back to 1973.

Garland, Beverly, taped conversation, October 27, 1998.

Griffith, Charles B., e-mail message, November 17, 1998.

Ibid., November 20, 1998.

Haller, Kinta, taped conversation, January 5, 1999.

Hollywood Reporter [review of *It Conquered the World*], quoted in Frank, Alan, *The Films of Roger Corman: "Shooting My Way Out of Trouble"* (London: BT Batsford Ltd, 1998), 37.

McGee, Mark Thomas, *Roger Corman: The Best of the Cheap Acts* (Jefferson, NC: McFarland, 1988), 39.

Miller, Dick, taped conversation, September 11, 1998.

Moreno, Frank, taped conversation, November 27, 1998.

Morris, Gary, *Roger Corman* (Boston: Twayne Publishers, 1985), 4.

Ibid., 143.

Naha, Ed, *The Films of Roger Corman: Brilliance on a Budget* (New York: Arco, 1982), 96.

Ibid., 98.

Rabkin, Bill, taped conversation, September 13, 1998.

Roth, Anna, taped conversation, October 6, 1998.

"Roger Corman Honors," *Hollywood Reporter* (August 17, 1966).

Variety [review of *The Monster from the Ocean Floor*], quoted in Frank, *The Films of Roger Corman*, 15.

Variety [review of *Swamp Women*], quoted in Frank, Alan, 31.

Weaver, Tom, and John Brunas, "The Other Corman," *Fangoria*, no. 48 (October 1985).

Welles, Mel, taped conversation, February 1, 1999.

Williams, Whitney, " 'Exploitation Pictures' Pay Off Big for Majors, Also Indies," *Weekly Variety* (January 9, 1946).

Wynorski, Jim, taped conversation, September 15, 1998.

CHAPTER 4: MAKER OF MONSTERS

Almond, Paul, taped conversation, November 25, 1998.

Arkoff, Sam, in Brosnan, John, *The Horror People* (New York: St. Martin's Press, 1976), 135.

Arkush, Allan, taped conversation, November 5, 1998.

Barnett, Steve, taped conversation, October 29, 1998.

Cohen, Howard R., taped conversation, September 4, 1998.

"Corman Custom-Tailors His Pix to 'Monstrous' Tastes of Prep Scholars," *Variety* (November 19, 1957).

Dante, Joe, taped conversation, November 5, 1998.

Dickerson, Beach, taped conversation, October 2, 1998.

Doel, Frances, informal conversations dating back to 1973.

Frakes, Randy, taped conversation, November 19, 1998.

Griffith, Charles B., e-mail message, November 14, 1998.

Ibid., November 17, 1998.

Ibid., December 5, 1998.

Ibid., June 3, 1999.

Ibid., June 23, 1999.

Griffiths, Mark, taped conversation, December 2, 1998.

Haller, Kinta, taped conversation, January 5, 1999.

Hellman, Monte, *Take One*, quoted in Brosnan, *The Horror People*, 135.

Hellman, Monte, taped conversation, December 4, 1998.

Krevoy, Brad, taped conversation, September 25, 1998.

McCarty, John, and Mark Thomas McGee, *The Little Shop of Horrors Book* (New York: St. Martin's Press, 1988), 125ff.

Miller, Dick, taped conversation, October 11, 1998.

Naha, Ed, *The Films of Roger Corman: Brilliance on a Budget* (New York: Arco, 1982), 152.

Rapp, Paul, taped conversation, October 21, 1998.

Roger Corman segment, *Directors on Directing*, directed for Telepiu (Italy) by Adam Simon (1997).

Roger Corman segment of *PM Magazine* (syndicated TV, May 1987).

"Roger Corman Unit Readying Three Pix for Three Companies," *Hollywood Reporter* (April 19, 1966).

Spear, Ivan, *Boxoffice* (December 15, 1956).

Tube., review of *The Little Shop of Horrors*, *Variety* (May 10, 1961).

Weaver, Tom, and John Brunas, "The Other Corman," *Fangoria*, no. 48 (October 1985).

Welles, Mel, taped conversation, February 1, 1999.

CHAPTER 5: THE RISE OF THE HOUSE OF CORMAN

Archer, Eugene, review of *The Masque of the Red Death*, New York Times (September 17, 1964).

Armstrong, Lois, "Roger Corman's Films May 'B' Shlock, but No One in Hollywood Has Nurtured More 'A' Talent," *People* (November 12, 1980), 91.

Bailey, Fred, taped conversation, November 12, 1998.

Barnett, Steve, taped conversation, October 29, 1998.

Brand, Larry, taped conversation, October 29, 1998.

Brock, Deborah, taped conversation, October 14, 1998.

Corman, Roger, in *Directors on Directing*, directed for Telepiu (Italy) by Adam Simon (1997).

————, letter to Professor Susan Madigan (September 23, 1993).

————, "Vincent Price as I Remember Him," unpublished press release, 1993.

Corman, Roger, with Jim Jerome, *How I Made a Hundred Movies in Hollywood and Never Lost a Dime* (New York: Random House, 1990), 101.

Ibid., 103.

Ibid., 124.

Crowther, Bosley, review of *The Intruder*, New York Times (May 15, 1962).

Diehl, Digby, "Roger Corman: The Simenon of Cinema," *Show* (May 1970), 27.

Ibid., 86.

Doel, Frances, informal conversations dating back to 1973.

Griffith, Charles B., e-mail message, November 17, 1998.

Haller, Kinta, taped conversation, January 5, 1999.

Hellman, Monte, taped conversation, December 4, 1998.

Hirsch, Tina, taped conversation, November 6, 1998.

Hurd, Gale Anne, taped conversation, January 14, 1999.

"'Intruder' Movie Sparks New Censorship Controversy," *Hollywood Citizen-News* (February 6, 1962).

Kauffmann, Stanley, review of *The Intruder*, New Republic (May 28, 1962).

Krevoy, Brad, taped conversation, September 25, 1998.

McGee, Mark Thomas, *Faster and Furiouser: The Revised and Fattened Fable of American International Pictures* (Jefferson, NC: McFarland, 1996), 196–97.

————, *Roger Corman: The Best of the Cheap Acts* (Jefferson, NC: McFarland, 1988), 40.

Ibid., 49.

Miller, Dick, taped conversation, October 11, 1998.

Nicholson, Jack, in Davidson, Bill, "King of Schlock," *New York Times Magazine* (December 28, 1975), 31.

Rehme, Robert, taped conversation, December 3, 1998.

Roger Corman: Hollywood's Wild Angel, produced and directed by Christian Blackwood (New World Pictures, 1977).

Sayles, John, taped conversation, February 10, 1999.

Shatner, William, e-mail message, February 3, 1999.

Thompson, Howard, review of *The Secret Invasion*, *New York Times* (September 17, 1964).

————, review of *X—The Man with the X-Ray Eyes* and *Dementia 13*, *New York Times* (October 24, 1963).

Tube., review of *House of Usher*, *Variety* (June 17, 1960).

————, review of *The Intruder*, *Variety* (May 15, 1962).

"Up From Monsters," *Show* (May 1962).

Variety, June 16, 1961 [regarding casting for *The Intruder*].

Weekly Variety, January 4, 1961 [rentals for *House of Usher*].

CHAPTER 6: ANGELS AND ACID

Arkoff, Sam, with Richard Trubo, *Flying Through Hollywood by the Seat of My Pants* (New York: Carol Publishing Group, 1992), 177.

Ibid., 197.

Bailey, Fred, taped conversation, November 12, 1998.

Bartel, Paul, taped conversation, December 1, 1998.

Bloody Mama, screenplay by Robert Thom (1970).

Bradford, Jack, column, *Hollywood Reporter* (May 12, 1967).

Canby, Vincent, "Roger Corman: A Good Man Gone to 'Pot,'" *New York Times* (September 18, 1966).

Compton, Sharon, e-mail message, October 11, 1998.

Corman, Roger, *Films and Filming*, quoted in Brosnan, John, *The Horror People* (New York: St. Martin's Press, 1976), 134.

————, *Take One*, vol. 2, no. 12, quoted in Brosnan, 130.

Corman, Roger, with Jim Jerome, *How I Made a Hundred Movies in Hollywood and Never Lost a Dime* (New York: Random House, 1990), 143.

Ibid., 146.

Ibid., 152–53.

Ibid., 236–37.

"Corman: 'Took LSD, then Shot Pic'; Takes 'Trips' from AIP to Other Cos," *Weekly Variety* (July 19, 1967).

Crowther, Bosley, review of *The Wild Angels*, *New York Times* (December 22, 1966).

Dante, Joe, taped conversation, November 5, 1998.

Diehl, Digby, "Roger Corman: The Simenon of Cinema," *Show* (May 1970), 27.

Ibid., 28.

Ibid., 87.

Doel, Frances, informal conversations dating back to 1973.

Fonda, Peter, in *Take One*, vol. 2, no. 3 (1969).

Goldman, Charles, "An Interview with Roger Corman," *Film Comment*, vol. 7, no. 3 (fall 1971), 54.

Hellman, Monte, taped conversation, December 4, 1998.

McGee, Mark Thomas, *Faster and Furiouser: The Revised and Fattened Fable of American International Pictures* (Jefferson, NC: McFarland, 1996), 250.

————, *Roger Corman: The Best of the Cheap Acts* (Jefferson, NC: McFarland., 1988), 57.

Moreno, Frank, taped conversation, November 27, 1998.

Rapp, Paul, taped conversation, October 21, 1998.

Ibid., October 22, 1998.

Roger Corman segment of *Directors on Directing*, directed for Telepiu (Italy) by Adam Simon (1997).

Roger Corman: Hollywood's Wild Angel, documentary film produced and directed by Christian Blackwood (New World Pictures, 1977).

Simon, Adam, taped conversation, October 8, 1998.

Weekly Variety, January 4, 1967 [rentals for *The Wild Angels*].

Weekly Variety, January 3, 1968 [rentals for *The Trip*].

Welles, Mel, taped conversation, February 1, 1999.

The Wild Angels, screenplay by Charles B. Griffith (1966)

CHAPTER 7: SUNSET BOULEVARD

Almond, Paul, taped conversation, November 25, 1998.

The Arena press materials (1973–74).

Arkush, Allan, taped conversation, November 5, 1998.

Candy Stripe Nurses press materials (1974).

Carradine, David, taped conversation, February 3, 1999.

Clarkson, Wensley, *Quentin Tarantino: Shooting from the Hip* (Woodstock, NY: The Overlook Press, 1995), 273.

Cohen, Howard R., taped conversation, September 4, 1998.

Corman, Roger, remarks to author for *Hollywood Reporter*'s Cannes Film Festival article, April 13, 1998.

Corman, Roger, with Jim Jerome, *How I Made a Hundred Movies in Hollywood and Never Lost a Dime* (New York: Random House, 1990), 181.

Dante, Joe, taped conversation, November 5, 1998.

Davidson, Bill, "King of Schlock," *New York Times Magazine* (December 28, 1975), 13.

Davison, Jon, taped conversation, November 5, 1998.

Demme, Jonathan on *The Charlie Rose Show*, Transcript #2277, PBS-TV (October 26, 1998).

Flender, Rodman, taped conversation, September 23, 1998.

Grant, Hank, "Rambling Reporter," *Hollywood Reporter* (July 9, 1974).

Hayden, Laurette, taped conversation, October 30, 1998.

Henderson, Clark, taped conversation, October 15, 1998.

Hurd, Gale Anne, taped conversation, January 14, 1999.

Kirkland, Sally, taped conversation, May 20, 1999.

Kit, Zorianna, "Cruise Driven to 'Death Race,'" *Hollywood Reporter*, July 12, 1999.

Kit, Zorianna, and Anita M. Busch, "Anderson Slate to Make Impact," *Hollywood Reporter*, July 13–19, 1999.

Miller, Dick, taped conversation, September 11, 1998.

Moldo, Julie, conversation, September 11, 1998.

Moreno, Frank, taped conversation, November 27, 1998.

Mount, Thom, taped conversation, November 13, 1998.

Raskin, Judy, "Corman Formula: Exploitation and Current Themes and Trailers," *Independent Film Journal* (May 25, 1972).

Roger Corman: Hollywood's Wild Angel, documentary film produced and directed by Christian Blackwood (New World Pictures, 1977).

Roth, Anna, taped conversation, October 6, 1998.

Shayne, Linda, taped conversation, October 1, 1998.

Thomas, Kevin, "Upping the Genre of Prison Flicks" [review of *Caged Heat*], *Los Angeles Times*, 1974.

TNT Jackson press kit (1974).

Tusher, Will, "The Economics of Runaway: Corman in the Philippines," *Hollywood Reporter* (January 18, 1972).

Valenti, Jack, "The Voluntary Movie Rating System," in Jason E. Squire, ed., *The Movie Business Book*, second edition (New York: Simon and Schuster, 1992), 397–406.

Vlastas, Pamm, taped conversation, October 7, 1998.

Warga, Wayne, "*Cries and Whispers* a Departure for the King of the Bs," *Los Angeles Times* (March 25, 1975).

Weekly Variety, January 7, 1976 [rentals for *Death Race 2000*].

CHAPTER 8: ARTISTIC LICENSE

Arkush, Allan, taped conversation, November 5, 1998.

Bailey, Fred, taped conversation, November 12, 1998.

Bartel, Paul, "Another Evening with David Carradine," *Take One*, vol. 6, no. 8, July 1978.

———, taped conversation, December 1, 1998.

Berges, Marshall, "Home Q&A: Julie and Roger Corman," *Los Angeles Times Home Magazine* (October 22, 1978), 43.

Brand, Larry, taped conversation, September 17, 1998.

Camp, Alida, taped conversation, December 17, 1998.

Carradine, David, taped conversation, February 3, 1999.

Corman, Roger, with Jim Jerome, *How I Made a Hundred Movies in Hollywood and Never Lost a Dime* (New York: Random House, 1990), 237.

Dante, Joe, taped conversation, November 5, 1998.

"Daughter for the Cormans," *Boxoffice* (May 12, 1975).

Davidson, Bill, "King of Schlock," *New York Times Magazine* (December 28, 1975), 13.

Dickerson, Beach, taped conversation, October 2, 1998.

Grant, Hank, "Rambling Reporter," *Hollywood Reporter* (July 23, 1974).

Haney, Daryl, taped conversation, November 12, 1998.

Hayden, Laurette, taped conversation, October 30, 1998.

Hellman, Monte, taped conversation, December 4, 1998.

Henderson, Clark, taped conversation, October 15, 1998.

Howard, Alan R., review of *Big Bad Mama*, *Hollywood Reporter* (July 2, 1974).

Hurd, Gale Anne, taped conversation, January 14, 1999.

Jones, Gwen, "My Style," *Los Angeles Herald Examiner* (May 9, 1983).

Krevoy, Brad, taped conversation, September 25, 1998.

Los Angeles Herald Examiner (September 29, 1977). [regarding birth of second Corman son].

McBride, Joseph, "After 6 Years of Steady Profits, Corman Swings for Fences," *Weekly Variety* (May 1989).

Moreno, Frank, taped conversation, November 27, 1998.

Nugent, Ginny, taped conversation, October 6, 1998.

————, telephone conversation, March 31, 1999.

Rehme, Robert, taped conversation, December 3, 1998.

Roth, Anna, taped conversation, October 6, 1998.

Variety (April 24, 1978). [birth announcement for Brian Corman].

Warga, Wayne, "*Cries and Whispers* a Departure for the King of the Bs," *Los Angeles Times* (March 25, 1975).

Winfrey, Jonathan, taped conversation, November 18, 1998.

CHAPTER 9: PIRANHAS AND OTHER FISH STORIES

Alpert, Sasha (American Cinematheque), conversation, May 10, 1999.

Almond, Paul, taped conversation, November 25, 1998.

Arkush, Allan, taped conversation, November 5, 1998.

Boxoffice ad for *I Never Promised You a Rose Garden* (November 14, 1997).

Canby, Vincent, review of *Jackson County Jail, New York Times* (July 12, 1976).

Cohen, Howard R., taped conversation, September 4, 1998.

Corman, Roger, letter to the editor, *Los Angeles Times Sunday Calendar* (May 25, 1980).

Dante, Joe, taped conversation, November 5, 1998.

Davidson, Bill, "King of Schlock," *New York Times Magazine* (December 28, 1975), 29.

Davison, Jon, taped conversation, November 5, 1998.

Golab, Jan, "King of the Killer Bs," *KCET Magazine* (November 1988), 43.

Governor, Mark, taped conversation, November 3, 1998.

Hayden, Laurette, taped conversation, October 30, 1998.

Hollywood Boulevard, screenplay by Patrick Hobby [pseudonym for Danny Opatashu] (1976).

Honeycutt, Kirk, " 'Corman School' Days Are Out," *Hollywood Reporter* (May 14, 1998), 10.

Howard, Ron, taped conversation, January 29, 1999.

Hurd, Gale Anne, taped conversation, January 14, 1999.

Kawin, Bruce, "Please Sir, They're Eating the Guests," *Take One*, vol. 7, November 1978, 10.

King, Robert, taped conversation, December 22, 1998.

McBride, Joseph, "Corman: 'He Wins Most Who Guards against Burst Budget,' " *Weekly Variety* (June 9, 1976).

Moreno, Frank, taped conversation, November 27, 1998.

Piranha press materials, published in *Take One*, vol. 7 (November 1978).

Roger Corman: Hollywood's Wild Angel, documentary film produced and directed by Christian Blackwood (New World Pictures, 1977).

Roth, Anna, taped conversation, October 6, 1998.

Sayles, John, taped conversation, February 10, 1999.

Schreger, Charles, "Ron Howard's Baptism Under Showmanship Creed of Corman," *Weekly Variety* (April 15, 1977).

Silverman, Jeff, ed., "And Sinking 'Deeper' All the Time," *Los Angeles Herald Examiner* (April 21, 1980).

Simon, Adam, taped conversation, October 8, 1998.

Weekly Variety, January 4, 1978 [rentals for *Grand Theft Auto*].

Wynorski, Jim, taped conversation, September 15, 1998.

CHAPTER 10: TO THE STARS

Almond, Paul, taped conversation, November 25, 1998.

Brand, Larry, taped conversation, September 17, 1998.

Brock, Deborah, taped conversation, October 14, 1998.

Corman, Roger, with Jim Jerome, *How I Made a Hundred Movies in Hollywood and Never Lost a Dime* (New York: Random House, 1990), 214.

Ibid., 219.

Frakes, Randy, taped conversation, November 19, 1998.

Franklin, BJ, "Corman Reaches New Frontiers," *Screen International* (June 18, 1983).

Haller, Kinta, taped conversation, January 5, 1999.

Hayden, Laurette, taped conversation, October 30, 1998.

Henderson, Clark, taped conversation, October 15, 1998.

Hirsch, Tina, taped conversation, November 6, 1998.

Holzman, Allan, taped conversation, September 28, 1998.

Hurd, Gale Anne, taped conversation, January 14, 1999.

Klein, Richard, "Roger Corman: Emotional Ties are with Production," *Variety* (June 13, 1983).

Krevoy, Brad, taped conversation, September 25, 1998.

Maloney, Lane, "Roger Corman Plans to Restructure His New World," *Variety*, (September 9, 1980).

"Power Fifty," Gale Anne Hurd profile, *Hollywood Reporter*, Women in Entertainment Special Issue (December 1–7, 1998).

Rehme, Robert, taped conversation, November 3, 1998.

Shea, Katt, taped conversation, December 23, 1998.

Weekly Variety, January 13, 1982 [rentals for *Galaxy of Terror*].

Winfrey, Jonathan, taped conversation, November 15, 1998.

CHAPTER 11: SEX, SURPRISE, AND VIDEOTAPE

Barnett, Steve, taped conversation, October 29, 1998.

Briggs, Joe Bob, "Cleavage and Cleavers," *We Are the Weird*, vol. 7, no. 38 (September 23, 1991), 3.

Corliss, Richard, "There's Gold in That There Shlock, *Time* (August 26, 1996), 55.

"Corman II," *L.A. Weekly* (July 22, 1988).

Crosby, Joan, "Roger and Julie Corman Form Concorde Pictures," *Drama-Logue*, vol. 16, no. 16 (April 18–24, 1985).

Dante, Joe, taped conversation, November 5, 1998.

Dickerson, Beach, taped conversation, October 2, 1998.

Eastman Kodak ad, *Variety* (May 12, 1976).

Griffiths, Mark, taped conversation, December 2, 1998.

Krevoy, Brad, taped conversation, September 25, 1998.

McBride, Joseph, "Concorde Keeps On Ticking," *Variety* (May 30, 1990).

Moreno, Frank, taped conversation, November 27, 1998.

Mount, Thom, taped conversation, November 13, 1998.

Nugent, Ginny, taped conversation, October 6, 1998.

Rabkin, Bill, conversation, September 13, 1998.

Roger Corman segment of *PM Magazine* (syndicated TV, May 1987).

Roth, Anna, taped conversation, October 6, 1998.

Schneider, Wolf, "Corman to Up Prod'n Under Solidified Concorde Banner," *Hollywood Reporter* (March 26, 1987).

Shea, Katt, taped conversation, December 23, 1998.

Wynorski, Jim, taped conversation, September 15, 1998.

CHAPTER 12: GOING PLACES

Bailey, Fred, taped conversation, November 12, 1998.

Brand, Larry, taped conversation, September 17, 1998.

Canby, Vincent, review of *Roger Corman's Frankenstein Unbound, New York Times* (November 2, 1990).

Carradine, David, taped conversation, February 3, 1999.

Cohen, Howard R., taped conversation, September 4, 1998.

Combs, Richard, "Roger Corman's Frankenstein Unbound," *Sight and Sound* (1990).

Corman, Roger, with Jim Jerome, *How I Made a Hundred Movies in Hollywood and Never Lost a Dime* (New York: Random House, 1990), 226–28.

Franklin, Carl, taped conversation, April 16, 1996.

Giddins, Gary, "The Walking Dead," *Village Voice* (November 13, 1990).

Governor, Mark, taped conversation, November 3, 1998.

Griffiths, Mark, taped conversation, December 2, 1998.

Haney, Daryl, taped conversation, November 12, 1998.

Henderson, Clark, taped conversation, October 15, 1998.

Howard, Ron, taped conversation, January 29, 1999.

Jolson-Colburn, Jeffrey, "Corman Trip to 'Paradise' with Early Bullock," *Hollywood Reporter* (August 16, 1996).

Jones, Gwen, "My Style," *Los Angeles Herald Examiner* (May 9, 1983).

Karridene, Kathleen, taped conversation, October 30, 1998.

King, Robert, taped conversation, December 22, 1998.

Krevoy, Brad, taped conversation, September 27, 1998.

Lifson Pompan, Byrdie, taped conversation, October 28, 1998.

Mattison, Sally, taped conversation, November 3, 1998.

McBride, Joseph, "Concorde Keeps On Ticking," *Variety* (May 30, 1990).

Mount, Thom, taped conversation, October 6, 1998.

MovieBuff database [www.moviebuff.net].

Murphy, Art, *Art Murphy's 1990 Boxoffice Register* (Hollywood, California: 1991).

Nugent, Ginny, taped conversation, October 6, 1998.

Simon, Adam, taped conversation, October 8, 1998.

Wilson, Don "The Dragon," taped conversation, October 30, 1998.

CHAPTER 13: FAST-FORWARD

Amato, Michael, taped conversation, October 2, 1998.

Arkush, Allan, telephone conversation, October 18, 1998.

Breitrose, Dr. Henry S., through Margaret Kimball, archivist, Green Library, Stanford University, March 5, 1999.

Corman, Roger, with Jim Jerome, *How I Made a Hundred Movies in Hollywood and Never Lost a Dime* (New York: Random House, 1990), 232.

Dante, Joe, taped conversation, November 5, 1998.

Flender, Rodman, taped conversation, September 23, 1998.

Greenberg, Matt, taped conversation, November 9, 1998.

Haller, Kinta, taped conversation, January 5, 1999.

King, Andrea, "Corman Leaps into 'Quake!' Feature," *Hollywood Reporter* (October 26, 1989).

———, "'Roger Corman Film School' Reunites to Honor Teacher," *Hollywood Reporter* (June 13, 1991).

Krevoy, Brad, taped conversation, September 25, 1998.

Long, Marion, "Balletomaniac," *GQ* (May 1990).

"Loot Shoot," *People* (June 1, 1992).

Moreno, Frank, taped conversation, November 27, 1998.

Murphy, Art, *Art Murphy's 1989 Boxoffice Register* (Hollywood, California: 1990).

O'Steen, Kathleen, "Corman Kinder, Gentler," *Variety* (December 2, 1993).

"Rambling Reporter," *Hollywood Reporter* (April 12, 1994).

Roth, Anna, taped conversation, October 6, 1998.

Schiff, Laura, taped conversation, October 20, 1998.

Shayne, Linda, taped conversation, October 1, 1998.

Simon, Adam, taped conversation, October 8, 1998.

Stevens, Andrew, taped conversation, December 21, 1998.

Weaver, Tom, and John Brunas, "The Other Corman," *Fangoria*, no. 48 (October 1985).

Zimmerman, Paul, "How the Blair Witch Project Evolved into Two Entertainments, One on the Web and One on the Screen," *iF Magazine*, issue 5.1 (July 9, 1999). [www.ifmagazine.com]

CHAPTER 14: FUTURE TENSE

Amato, Michael, taped conversation, November 25; 1998.

Bailey, Fred, taped conversation, November 12, 1998.

Bates, James, "B-Movie King to Sell Company," *Los Angeles Times* (February 10, 1997).

Beck, Marilyn, and Stacy Janel Smith, "Celebrities," *Los Angeles Daily News* (September 10, 1999).

Carradine, David, taped conversation, February 3, 1999.

Carver, Benedict, "Corman Sells Up to Kastner," *Screen International* (December 13, 1996).

Citron, Alan, "Corman Nears Sale of B-movie Library," *Los Angeles Times* (February 11, 1994).

Clark, John, " 'Some Nudity' Provided a Catharsis," *Los Angeles Times* (January 24, 1998).

Corman, Roger, brief conversation, August 7, 1998.

Corman, Roger, with Jim Jerome, *How I Made a Hundred Movies in Hollywood and Never Lost a Dime* (New York: Random House, 1990), 234.

"Corman's Concorde is Selling Most Assets to Producer Kastner," *Wall Street Journal* (February 10, 1997).

Dante, Joe, taped conversation, November 5, 1998.

Dean, Rick, taped conversation, November 6, 1998.

Devlin, Martina, "A Taxing Issue for Concorde," *Hollywood Reporter International* (September 5–7, 1997), 13–14.

Doel, Frances, informal conversations dating back to 1973.

Fabrikant, Geraldine, "A Lion of B Movies to Sell Company to an Independent," *New York Times* (February 10, 1997).

Feeley, Gregory, e-mail message, June 12, 1999.

"Film Shorts," *Hollywood Reporter* (May 11, 1993) [Golden Crab Award].

Glaser, Jan, taped conversation, February 5, 1999.

Haney, Daryl, taped conversation, November 12, 1998.

Harrington, Richard, review of *Nightfall*, *Washington Post* (May 30, 1988).

Harris, Dana, "Corman Sells Shop in Venice," *Hollywood Reporter* (January 19, 2000), 1, 35.

Hettrick, Scott, "Corman Puts Finishing Touch on CNH Product," *Hollywood Reporter* (September 3, 1997).

Hindes, Andrew, "Corman Embarks on New Eire," *Variety* (November 1, 1995).

Hollywood Reporter (January 31, 1967) [Corman honored by Cinémathèque Française].

Jolson-Colburn, Jeffrey, "Corman May Sell to Kastner," *Hollywood Reporter* (December 9, 1996).

Kenny, Glenn, "It's Showtime for Corman," *TV Guide* (June 10, 1995).

Klady, Leonard, "L.A. Pix Crix Honor Corman," *Variety* (September 23, 1996).

"L.A. Raw," *Los Angeles* (March 1997).

Looseleaf, Victoria, "A Horror Movie, Dismembered," Los Angeles Times (October 25, 1999). [on The Pantom Eye

Lovell, Glenn, review of Some Nudity Required, Variety (January 29, 1998).

McCarthy, Todd, "Kazan's Career Atill Under a PC Shadow," Variety (January 10, 1997).

Mobley-Anderson, Marta, phone conversations, October 4 and October 1999.

Moreno, Frank, taped conversation, November 27, 1998.

Patterson, John, review of *Some Nudity Required, L.A. Weekly* (October 1998).

Some Nudity Required, produced and directed by Odette Springer Child Productions, 1998).

Stalter, Katharine, "Golden Eddie for Corman," *Variety* (February 4,

Stevens, Andrew, taped conversation, December 21, 1998.

Vlastas, Pamm, taped conversation, October 7, 1998.

Welkos, Robert W., "A Few New Tricks to the Hollywood Trade *Los Angeles Times* (August 8, 1999).

Welles, Mel, taped conversation, February 1, 1999.

Wilson, Don "The Dragon," taped conversation, October 30, 1998.

Winfrey, Jonathan, taped conversation, November 18, 1998.

Wolynetz, Vlad, phone conversation, October 7, 1999.

EPILOGUE

Roger Corman, in Mallory, Michael, "AFM Honors—Lifetime Achievement," *Variety* (February 21, 2001).

Additional sources for the epilogue are:

Boyle, Barbara, taped conversation, February 9, 2001.

Coppola, Francis, e-mail message, January 25, 2001.

Dante, Joe, taped conversation, January 23, 2001.

Dargis, Manohla, "Riding Low," *Los Angeles Times* (June 6, 2003).

Doel, Frances, taped conversation, June 17, 2003.

"Film Shorts," *Hollywood Reporter* (May 15, 2000).

Gibby, Gwyneth, conversation, August 4, 2003.

Goldstein, Patrick, "In Dad's Footsteps," *Los Angeles Times* (June 10, 2003).

"Just for Variety," *Daily Variety* (August 8, 2002).

"Just for Variety," *Daily Variety* (January 11, 2001).

Graham, Chad, "Corman Studio Goes Out Blazing," *Hollywood Reporter* (April 5, 2001).

Harris, Dana, "Corman Sells Shop in Venice," *Hollywood Reporter* (January 19, 2000).

Hill, Jack, taped conversation, November 2, 2000.

Juliano, Lenny, taped conversation, July 28, 2003.

Kit, Zorianna, "Attack of the $20 Mil Budget," *Hollywood Reporter* (May 17, 1999).

Kit, Zorianna, "Film Shorts," *Hollywood Reporter* (June 11, 2001).

Long, Marion, "Balletomaniac," *G.Q.* (May 1990).

Mohr, Ian, "Corman Hatches 'DinoCroc' Pic," *Hollywood Reporter* (February 21–23, 2003).

Moreno, Frank, conversation, September 16, 2000.

Moreno, Susan, conversation, September 16, 2000.

Nevius, Craig, taped conversation, June 23, 2003.

New York University press release, June 20, 2000.

Nichols, Peter M., "Roger Corman's Grateful Alumni," *New York Times* (April 6, 2001).

Nicholson, Jack, fax message, January 25, 2001.

Purdy, Jon, conversation, April 25, 2000; e-mail message August 8, 2003.

Ryon, Ruth, "Hot Property," *Los Angeles Times* (November 30, 2000).

T.L., "Roger Corman," *Hollywood Reporter 70th Anniversary Special Issue* (November 20, 2000).

APPENDIX A: SOME DISTINGUISHED FRIENDS AND ALUMNI OF THE ROGER CORMAN SCHOOL OF FILM

Alford, Henry, "The Fast Tycoon," *Vanity Fair* (April 1996), 147–48.

Arkush, Allan, taped conversation, November 5, 1998.

Armstrong, Lois, "Roger Corman's Films May 'B' Shlock, But No One in Hollywood Has Nurtured More 'A' Talent," *People* (November 1980), 91.

Bartel, Paul, taped conversation, December 1, 1998.

Blackwell, Earl, *Celebrity Register* (Detroit: Gale Research Inc., 1990), *Ibid.*, 345.

Bogdanovich, Peter, "Dialogue on Film," *American Film* (1978), quoted in Biskind, Peter, *Easy Riders, Raging Bulls* (New York: Simon and Schuster, 1998), 115.

———, *Who the Devil Made it?* (New York: Ballantine Books, 1998), 30.

Camp, Alida, taped conversation, December 17, 1998.

Carradine, David, taped conversation, February 2, 1999.

Corman, Roger, "A Letter from Roger Corman," *Take One*, vol. 12 (1967), 14.

———, "Vincent Price as I Remember Him," unpublished press release, 1993.

Corman, Roger, with Jim Jerome, *How I Made a Hundred Movies in Hollywood and Never Lost a Dime* (New York: Random House, 1990), 67.

Ibid., 94.

Dante, Joe, taped conversation, November 5, 1998.

"Demme on Demme" (1989) in *Projections: A Forum for Film Makers*, eds. John Boorman and Walter Donohue, issue no. 1 (London: Faber and Faber, 1992), 167–68.

Ibid., 187.

Doel, Frances, informal conversations dating back to 1973.

Frakes, Randy, conversation, February 2, 1998.

Garris, Mick, and Carl Macek, "Bergman to Bombast: Corman Calls Them Films," *Los Angeles Herald Examiner* (December 13, 1977).

Gibby, Gwyneth, conversation, August 4, 2003.

Griffith, Charles B., e-mail message, May 8, 1999.

Hellman, Monte, taped conversation, December 4, 1998.

Hill, Jack, taped conversation, November 2, 2000.

Hobson, Louis B., "Hollywood Shifts into Grier," *Calgary* (Alberta, Canada) *Sun* (August 22, 1996).

Hoelscher, Jean, "New Faces" [on Jon Davison], *Hollywood Reporter* (October 15, 1976).

Hopper, Dennis, brief conversation, March 14, 1997.

Howard, Ron, taped conversation, January 29, 1999.

Kaminski, Janusz, taped conversation, May 6, 1999.

Kirkland, Sally, taped conversation, May 20, 1999.

Krohn, Bill, Locarno (Italy) Film Festival program notes honoring Joe Dante, 1998.

Lawson, Terry, "Pam Grier Has Eye on Life after 'Jackie Brown' Role," *Seattle* (Washington) *Times*, (December 30, 1997).

McCulley, J.D., "Termination of Endearment," *BAM* (July 1, 1988) [Interview with Gale Anne Hurd].

Miller, Dick, taped conversation, September 11, 1998.

Moreno, Frank, taped conversation, November 27, 1998.

Natale, Richard, "Corman Pop Quiz," *Variety* (July 25, 1996).

Petrikin, Chris, "Corman Toasted, Roasted at L.A. Film Crix' Tribute," *Variety* (February 26, 1997).

Rapp, Paul, taped conversation, October 22, 1998.

Rea, Steven, "Coppola First Did Horror Films for Roger Corman," *Chicago Tribune*, (November 1992).

Rehme, Robert, taped conversation, December 3, 1998.

Roberts, Jerry, "Colleagues, Crew Praise Sense, Sensibility" [showbiz expo tribute to Gale Anne Hurd], *Variety* (June 25, 1999).

Roger Corman: Hollywood's Wild Angel, documentary film produced and directed by Christian Blackwood (New World Pictures, 1977).

Roth, Anna, taped conversation, October 6, 1998.

Sayles, John, taped conversation, February 10, 1998.

Thompson, David, and Ian Christie, eds., *Scorsese on Scorsese* (London: Faber and Faber, 1989), 20.

Ibid., 34.

Ibid., 36.

Ibid., 39.

The Treatment, with Elvis Mitchell [interview with Carl Franklin], radio station KCRW (September 18, 1998).

BIBLIOGRAPHY

PERSONAL INTERVIEWS CONDUCTED BY THE AUTHOR

Ackerman, Forrest J. (June 21, 2003).

Almond, Paul (November 25, 1998, and July 21, 1999).

Amato, Michael (October 2, 1998).

Arkush, Allan (November 5, 1998).

Bailey, Fred (November 12, 1998).

Barnett, Steve (October 29, 1998).

Bartel, Paul (December 1, 1998).

Bean, Karen (March 25, 2003).

Bloch, Flo (e-mail messages, January 13, 1999, and February 10, 1999).

Borack, Carl (June 29, 1998).

Boyle, Barbara (February 9, 2001).

Brand, Larry (September 17, 1998).

Brock, Deborah (October 14, 1998).

Broderick, John (October 26, 1998).

Camp, Alida (December 17, 1998).

Campbell, Robert Wright (e-mail conversations, September 23–October 2, 1998).

Carradine, David (February 3, 1999).

Clement, Shirley (February 2, 2003).

Cohen, Howard R. (September 4, 1998).

Compton, Sharon (e-mail message, October 11, 1998).

Coppola, Francis (e-mail message, January 25, 2001).

Dante, Joe (November 5, 1998, and January 23, 2001).

Davison, Jon (November 5, 1998).

Dean, Rick (November 6, 1998).

Dickerson, Beach (October 2, 1998).

Doel, Frances (series of informal conversations beginning in 1973 and continuing through 2003).

Flender, Rodman (September 23, 1998).

Florence, Mal (January 12, 1999).

Frakes, Randy (February 2, 1998, and November 19, 1998).

Franklin, Carl (April 16, 1996).

Garland, Beverly (October 27, 1998).

Gibby, Gwyneth (August 4, 2003).

Glaser, Jan (February 5, 1999).

Governor, Mark (November 3, 1998).

Greenberg, Matt (November 9, 1998).

Griffith, Charles B. (e-mail conversations, November 7, 1988–July 23, 1999).

Griffiths, Mark (December 2, 1998).

Guarino, Al (October 4, 1998).

Haller, Kinta (January 5, 1999).

Haney, Daryl (November 12, 1998).

Hayden, Laurette (October 30, 1998).

Haze, Jonathan (October 21, 2000).

Hellman, Monte (December 4, 1998).

Henderson, Clark (October 15, 1998).

Henderson, Isabel (October 15, 1998).

Hill, Jack (November 2, 2000).

Hickenlooper, George (December 5, 2001).

Hirsch, Tina (November 6, 1998).

Holzman, Allan (September 28, 1998).

Howard, Ron (January 29, 1999).

Hurd, Gale Anne (January 14, 1999).

Johnson, George Clayton (October 22, 2000).

Juliano, Lenny (July 28, 2003).

Kaminski, Janusz (May 6, 1999).

Kanefsky, Rolfe (September 26, 1998).

Karridene, Kathleen (October 30, 1998).

King, Robert (December 22, 1998, and September 24, 2003).

Kirkland, Sally (January 17, 1999, and May 20, 1999).

Krevoy, Brad (September 25, 1998).

Levy, Scott (May 24, 1999).

Lifson Pompan, Byrdie (October 28, 1998).

Mark, Ellen (September 15, 1998).

Mattison, Sally (November 3, 1998).

Miller, Dick (September 11, 1998).

Mittelman, Gina (October 3, 1998).

Moldo, Julie (September 11, 1998).

Moreno, Frank (November 27, 1998, and September 16, 2003).

Moreno, Susan (September 16, 2000).

Mount, Thom (November 13, 1998).

Nevius, Craig (June 23, 2003).

Nicholson, Jack (fax message, January 25, 2001)

Nugent, Ginny (October 6, 1998).

Purdy, Jon (April 25, 2000; e-mail message August 8, 2003).

Rabkin, Bill (September 13, 1998).

Rapp, Paul (October 21, 1998, and October 22, 1998).

Ratajczak, Paul (February 11, 1998).

Rehme, Robert (December 3, 1998).

Reilly, Ed (December 11, 1998).

Rosen, Robert (February 25, 1999).

Roth, Anna (October 6, 1998).

Sayles, John (February 10, 1999).

Schiff, Laura (October 20, 1998).

Shatner, William (e-mail message, February 3, 1999).

Shayne, Linda (October 1, 1998).

Shea, Katt (December 23, 1998).

Simon, Adam (October 8, 1998).

Springer, Odette (March 3, 2000).

Stevens, Andrew (December 21, 1998).

Vlastas, Pamm (October 7, 1998).

Welles, Mel (February 1, 1999).

Wilson, Don "The Dragon" (October 30, 1998).

Winfrey, Jonathan (November 18, 1998).

Wynorski, Jim (September 15, 1998).

Zwang, Ron (September 18, 1998).

BOOKS

Arkoff, Sam, with Richard Trubo. *Flying Through Hollywood by the Seat of My Pants*. New York: Carol Publishing Group, 1992.

Biskind, Peter. *Easy Riders, Raging Bulls: How the Sex-Drugs-and-Rock 'n' Roll Generation Saved Hollywood*. New York: Simon and Schuster Touchstone Books, 1998.

Blackwell, Earl. *Celebrity Register*. Detroit: Gale Research Inc., 1990.

Bliss, Michael, and Christina Banks. *What Goes Around Comes Around: The Films of Jonathan Demme*. Carbondale: Southern Illinois University Press, 1996.

Bogdanovich, Peter. *Who the Devil Made It? Conversations with Legendary Film Directors*. New York: Ballantine Books, 1998.

Bogle, Donald. *Blacks in American Films and Television: An Encyclopedia*. New York: Garland Publishing, 1988.

Bourgoin, Stéphane. *Roger Corman*. Paris: Edilig, 1983.

Brosnan, John. *The Horror People*. New York: St. Martin's Press, 1976.

Clarkson, Wensley. *Quentin Tarantino: Shooting from the Hip*. Woodstock, New York: The Overlook Press, 1995.

Connors, Martin, and Jim Craddock. *VideoHound's Golden Movie Retriever 2000.* Detroit: Visible Ink Press, 1999.

Corman, Roger, with Jim Jerome. *How I Made a Hundred Movies in Hollywood and Never Lost a Dime.* New York: Random House, 1990.

Dawson, Jeff. *Quentin Tarantino: The Cinema of Cool.* New York: Applause Books, 1995.

Di Franco, J. Philip. *The Movie World of Roger Corman.* New York: Chelsea House, 1979.

Frank, Alan. *The Films of Roger Corman: "Shooting My Way Out of Trouble."* London: BT Batsford Ltd., 1998.

Katz, Ephraim. *The Film Encyclopedia,* 3rd edition. New York: HarperCollins, 1998.

Maltin, Leonard, ed. *Leonard Maltin's Movie and Video Guide,* 1999 edition. Bergenfield, NJ: Viking Penguin, 1998.

McCarthy, Todd, and Charles Flynn, eds. *Kings of the Bs: Working Within the Hollywood System.* New York: E. P. Dutton, 1975.

McCarthy, John, and Mark Thomas McGee. *The Little Shop of Horrors Book.* New York: St. Martin's Press, 1988.

McGee, Mark Thomas. *Faster and Furiouser: The Revised and Fattened Fable of American International Pictures.* Jefferson, NC: McFarland, 1996.

——. *Roger Corman: The Best of the Cheap Acts.* Jefferson, NC: McFarland, 1988.

Morris, Gary. *Roger Corman.* Boston: Twayne Publishers, 1965.

Murphy, Art. *Art Murphy's 1989 Boxoffice Register.* Hollywood, California: 1990.

——. *Art Murphy's 1990 Boxoffice Register.* Hollywood, California: 1991.

Naha, Ed. *The Films of Roger Corman: Brilliance on a Budget.* New York: Arco, 1982.

Parish, James Robert, and George H. Hill. *Black Action Films.* Jefferson, NC: McFarland, 1989.

Squire, Jason E., ed. *The Movie Business Book.* second edition. New York: Simon and Schuster, 1992.

Stanford University Register, 1943–44.

Thompson, David, and Ian Christie, eds. *Scorsese on Scorsese*. London: Faber and Faber, 1989.

Thomson, David. *A Biographical Dictionary of Film*. New York: Alfred A. Knopf, 1994.

Turroni, Giuseppe. *Roger Corman*. Il Castoro Cinema. Firenze: La nuova Italia, 1976.

Video Sourcebook, 29th edition. Detroit: Gale, 2002.

Whitehead, Mark. *Roger Corman*. Harpenden, Herts., UK: Pocket Essentials, 2003.

Will, David, and Paul Willemen, eds. *Roger Corman: The Millennic Vision*. Edinburgh, Scotland: Edinburgh Film Festival, 1970.

ARTICLES

Alford, Henry. "The Fast Tycoon." *Vanity Fair*, April 1996, pp. 136, 138, 147–50.

Archer, Eugene. Review of *The Masque of the Red Death*. *New York Times*, September 17, 1964.

Armstrong, Lois. "Roger Corman's Flicks May 'B' Schlock, But No One in Hollywood Has Nurtured More 'A' Talent." *People*, November 12, 1980, pp. 89–91.

Bartel, Paul. "Another Evening with David Carradine." *Take One*, vol. 6, no. 8, July 1978, pp. 15–19.

Bates, James. "B-Movie King to Sell Company." *Los Angeles Times*, February 10, 1997.

Beck, Marilyn, and Stacy Janel Smith. "Celebrities" [on AMC *Monster-Fest*]. *Los Angeles Daily News*, September 10, 1999.

Berges, Marshall. "Home Q&A: Julie and Roger Corman." *Los Angeles Times Home Magazine*, October 22, 1978, pp. 40–45.

Beverly Hills Citizen, July 21, 1942–June 18, 1943.

Boxoffice, November 14, 1977 [ad for *I Never Promised You a Rose Garden*].

Bradford, Jack. Column, *Hollywood Reporter*, May 12, 1967.

Briggs, Joe Bob. "Cleavage and Cleavers." *We Are the Weird*, vol. 7, no. 38, September 23, 1991, pp. 1–3.

Brooks, Richard. "Corman's Mother Earth Film Deemed Distasteful." *The* [London] *Observer*, June 30, 1996.

Canby, Vincent. Review of *Jackson County Jail. New York Times*, July 12, 1976.

———. Review of *Roger Corman's Frankenstein Unbound. New York Times*, November 2, 1990.

———. "Roger Corman: A Good Man Gone to 'Pot.' " *New York Times*, September 18, 1966.

Carver, Benedict. "Corman Sells Up to Kastner." *Screen International*, December 13, 1996.

Caulfield, Deborah. "Another Corman Heard From." *Los Angeles Times*, May 15, 1986.

———. "Corman Names His Baby." *Los Angeles Times*, June 13, 1983.

Citron, Alan. "Corman Nears Sale of B Movie Library." *Los Angeles Times*, February 11, 1994.

Clark, John. " 'Some Nudity' Provided a Catharsis." *Los Angeles Times*, January 24, 1998.

Combs, Richard. "Roger Corman's Frankenstein Unbound." *Sight and Sound*, 1990.

Corliss, Richard. "There's Gold in That There Schlock." *Time*, August 26, 1996, pp. 55–56.

"Corman II" [interview with Julie Corman]. *L.A. Weekly*, July 22, 1988.

"Corman Custom-Tailors His Pix to 'Monstrous' Tastes of Prep Scholars." *Variety*, November 19, 1957.

Corman, Roger. "A Letter from Roger Corman." *Take One*, vol. 1, no. 12, 1967, pp. 13–14.

———. Letter to Professor Susan Madigan. September 23, 1993.

———. Letter to the editor. *Los Angeles Times Sunday Calendar*, May 25, 1980.

———. "Sideline Slants" column. *Stanford Daily*, April 21, 1943.

———. "Sideline Slants" column. *Stanford Daily*, November 15, 1943.

———. "Vincent Price as I Remember Him." Unpublished press release, 1993.

"Corman Sets Up Oxford Scholarship." *Variety*, July 31, 1969.

"Corman: 'Took LSD, then Shot Pic'; Takes 'Trips' from AIP to Other Cos." *Weekly Variety*, July 19, 1967.

"Corman's Concorde is Selling Most Assets to Producer Kastner." *Wall Street Journal*, February 10, 1997.

Crosby, Joan. "Roger and Julie Corman Form Concorde Pictures." *Drama-Logue*, vol. 16, no. 16, April 18–24, 1985.

Crowther, Bosley. Review of *The Intruder*. *New York Times*, May 15, 1962.

———. Review of *The Wild Angels*. *New York Times*, December 22, 1966.

Dargis, Manohla. "Riding Low." *Los Angeles Times*, June 6, 2003.

"Daughter for the Cormans." *Boxoffice*, May 12, 1975.

Davidson, Bill. "King of Schlock." *New York Times Magazine*, December 28, 1975, pp. 13, 29–31.

Dawes, Amy. "Corman Tells Tyros to Get Pic Jobs 'Any Way You Can.'" *Variety*, March 30, 1989.

"Demme on Demme," compiled from two 1989 interviews with David Thompson. In *Projections: A Forum for Film Makers*, eds. John Boorman and Walter Donohue, issue no. 1. London: Faber and Faber, 1992, pp. 158–97.

Devlin, Martina. "A Taxing Issue for Concorde." *Hollywood Reporter International*, September 5–7, 1997, pp. 13–14.

Duke, Paul Francis. "Movie Maverick." *Stanford*, July–August 1997, pp. 60–63.

Diehl, Digby. "Roger Corman: The Simenon of Cinema." *Show: The Magazine of Films and the Arts*, vol. 1, no. 5, May 1970, pp. 27–30, 86–87.

Dietz, Lawrence. "The Quickie Master." *New York World Journal Tribune*, January 8, 1967.

Ewing, Iain. "Interview with Peter Fonda." *Take One*, vol. 2, no. 3, 1969, p. 8.

"Expo Honoree" [tribute to Gale Anne Hurd]. *Variety*, June 25, 1999.

Fabrikant, Geraldine. "A Lion of B Movies to Sell Company to an Independent." *New York Times*, February 10, 1997.

"Film Shorts." *Hollywood Reporter*, May 11, 1993.

"Film Shorts." *Hollywood Reporter*, May 15, 2000.

"Filmmaker." [interview with John Sayles]. *The New Yorker*, March 23, 1981.

Franklin, BJ. "Corman Reaches New Frontiers." *Screen International*, June 18, 1983.

Garris, Mick, and Carl Macek. "Bergman to Bombast: Corman Calls Them Films." *Los Angeles Herald Examiner*, December 13, 1977.

Gaydos, Steven. "Monte Hellman and *Two-Lane Blacktop*." *Movie Talk from the Front Lines*. eds. Jerry Roberts and Steven Gaydos. Jefferson, NC: McFarland, 1995, pp. 7–22.

Gaydos, Steven. "On Roger Corman." In *Writers on Directors*, conceived and photographed by Susan Gray. New York: Watson-Guptill Publications, 1999.

Giddins, Gary. "The Walking Dead." *Village Voice*, November 13, 1990.

Golab, Jan. "King of the Killer Bs." *KCET Magazine*, November 1988, pp. 43–45.

Goldman, Charles. "An Interview with Roger Corman." *Film Comment*, vol. 7, no. 3, Fall 1971, pp. 49–54.

Goldstein, Patrick. "You Know His Face, But Can You Give His Name?" [on Dick Miller]. *Los Angeles Times*, July 31, 1984.

Goldstein, Patrick. "In Dad's Footsteps." *Los Angeles Times*, June 10, 2003.

Graham, Chad. "Corman Studio Goes Out Blazing." *Hollywood Reporter*, April 5, 2001.

Grant, Hank. "Rambling Reporter." *Hollywood Reporter*, July 9, 1974.

———. "Rambling Reporter." *Hollywood Reporter*, July 23, 1974.

Gray, Beverly. "Show Neuf" [regarding producer honorees at Cannes Film Festival]. *Hollywood Reporter*, Cannes Special Issue, May 1998, p. 14.

Harrington, Richard. Review of *Nightfall*. *Washington Post*, May 30, 1988.

Harris, Dana. "Corman Sells Shop in Venice." *Hollywood Reporter*, January 19, 2000, pp. 1, 35.

Harwood, Jim. "Corman and NWP Trade Suits Over Pic Company Sale." *Variety*, March 5, 1985.

Hettrick, Scott. "Corman Puts Finishing Touch on CNH Product." *Hollywood Reporter*, September 3, 1997.

Hindes, Andrew. "Corman Embarks on New Eire." *Variety*, November 1, 1995, pp. 3, 15.

Hobson, Louis B. "Hollywood Shifts into Grier." *Calgary* (Alberta, Canada) *Sun*, August 22, 1996.

Hoelscher, Jean. "New Faces" [on Jon Davison]. *Hollywood Reporter*, October 15, 1976.

Hollywood Reporter, January 31, 1967. [Corman honored by Cinémathèque Française.]

Honeycutt, Kirk. "Concorde Vets Have Capital Idea." *Hollywood Reporter*, November 7, 1995, pp. 3, 134.

———. "'Corman School' Days Are Out." *Hollywood Reporter*, May 14, 1998, pp. 10, 65.

Howard, Alan R. Review of *Big Bad Mama*. *Hollywood Reporter*, July 2, 1974.

"'Intruder' Movie Sparks New Censorship Controversy." *Hollywood Citizen-News*, February 6, 1962.

Jolson-Colburn, Jeffrey. "Corman May Sell to Kastner." *Hollywood Reporter*, December 9, 1996.

———. "Corman Trip to 'Paradise' with Early Bullock." *Hollywood Reporter*, August 16, 1996.

Jones, Gwen. "My Style" [conversation with Julie Corman]. *Los Angeles Herald Examiner*, May 9, 1983.

"Just for Variety," *Daily Variety* (August 8, 2002

———, *Daily Variety* (January 11, 2001).

Kauffmann, Stanley. Review of *The Intruder*. *New Republic*, May 28, 1962.

Kawin, Bruce. "Please Sir, They're Eating the Guests." *Take One*, Vol. 6, November 1978, pp. 9–11.

Kendrick, Walter. Review of Corman's memoir, *Village Voice Literary Supplement*, July 8, 1990.

Kenny, Glenn. "It's Showtime for Corman." *TV Guide*, June 10, 1995.

King, Andrea. "Corman Leaps into 'Quake!' Feature." *Hollywood Reporter*, October 26, 1989.

———. "'Roger Corman Film School' Reunites to Honor Teacher." *Hollywood Reporter*, June 13, 1991.

King, Susan. "Master of His Cult." *TV Times*, July 9–15, 1995.

Kit, Zorianna. "Attack of the $20 Million Budget." *Hollywood Reporter*, May 17, 1999.

Kit, Zorianna. "Cruise Driven to 'Death Race.'" *Hollywood Reporter*, July 12, 1999.

———. "Film Shorts." *Hollywood Reporter*, June 11, 2001.

———. "Pryce, Corman Plan 'Suicide.'" *Hollywood Reporter*, March 31, 1999.

Kit, Zorianna, and Anita M. Busch. "Anderson Slate to Make Impact." *Hollywood Reporter*, July 13–19, 1999.

Klady, Leonard. "L.A. Pix Crix Honor Corman." *Variety*, September 23, 1996.

Klein, Richard. "Roger Corman: Emotional Ties Are with Production." *Variety*, June 13, 1983.

Krohn, Bill. Locarno (Italy) Film Festival program notes honoring Joe Dante, 1998.

"L.A. Raw." *Los Angeles* magazine, March 1997.

Lawson, Terry. "Pam Grier Has Eye on Life after 'Jackie Brown' Role." *Seattle* (Washington) *Times*, December 30, 1997.

London, Michael. "Corman, New World Sue in a Battle for Control." *Los Angeles Times*, March 6, 1985.

Long, Marion. "Balletomaniac." *GQ*, May 1990.

"Loot Shoot." *People*, June 1, 1992.

Los Angeles Herald Examiner, September 29, 1977. [on birth of second son].

Looseleaf, Victoria. "A Horror Movie, Dismembered." [On *The Phantom Eye*.] *Los Angeles Times*, October 25, 1999.

Lovell, Glenn. Review of *Some Nudity Required*. *Variety*, January 29, 1998.

Maloney, Lane. "Roger Corman Plans to Restructure His New World." *Variety*, September 9, 1980.

McBride, Joseph. "After 6 Years of Steady Profits, Corman Swings for Fences." *Weekly Variety*, May 1989.

———. "Concorde Keeps on Ticking." *Variety*, May 30, 1990.

———. "Corman: 'He Wins Most Who Guards Against Burst Budget.'" *Weekly Variety*, June 9, 1976.

———. "Roger Corman's Concorde Keeps Title as Busiest Indie in Hollywood." *Weekly Variety*, February 21, 1990.

McCarthy, Todd. "Kazan's Career Still Under a PC Shadow." *Variety*, January 10, 1997.

———. "A Swarm of B's from Roger Corman." *Los Angeles Times Calendar*, February 5, 1978, pp. 31–32.

Mohr, Ian. "Corman Hatches 'DinoCroc' Pic." *Hollywood Reporter*, February 21–23, 2003.

Natale, Richard. "Corman Pop Quiz." *Variety*, July 25, 1996.

Nichols, Peter M. "Roger Corman's Grateful Alumni." *New York Times*, April 6, 2001.

"Off the Cuff." *Hollywood Reporter*, March 18, 1987.

Oppenheimer, Jean. "The Mentor." *Village View*, October 9–15, 1992, pp. 9, 17.

O'Steen, Kathleen. "Corman Kinder, Gentler." *Variety*, December 2, 1993, pp. 1, 17.

Patterson, John. Review of *Some Nudity Required*. *L.A. Weekly*, October 16, 1998.

Petrikin, Chris. "Corman Toasted, Roasted at L.A. Film Crix' Tribute." *Variety*, February 26, 1997, p. 10.

"Power Fifty" [Gale Anne Hurd profile]. *Hollywood Reporter*, Women in Entertainment Special Issue, December 1–7, 1998.

"The Rambling Reporter" [Regarding *Vesco*]. *Hollywood Reporter*, April 12, 1994.

Raskin, Judy. "Corman Formula: Exploitation and Current Themes and Trailers." *Independent Film Journal*, May 25, 1972.

Rea, Steven. "Coppola First Did Horror Films for Roger Corman." *Chicago Tribune*, November 1992.

Rice, Lynette. "Corman Sets Up 'Scorpion' Camp." *Hollywood Reporter*, Thursday, August 13, 1998, pp. 3, 25.

"Roger Corman." *Monicker*, 1974.

"Roger Corman" ad for Eastman Kodak. *Variety*, May 12, 1976.

"Roger Corman Honors." *Hollywood Reporter*, August 17, 1966.

"Roger Corman Unit Readying Three Pix for Three Companies." *Hollywood Reporter*, April 19, 1966.

Russi, John. "Roger Corman." *Filmfox*, October–January 2000.

Ryon, Ruth. "Hot Property." *Los Angeles Times*, November 30, 2000.

Salvato, Larry. "Discovering Monte Hellman." *Millimeter*, vol. 3, no. 7–8 (no date).

Schneider, Wolf. "Corman to Up Prod'n Under Solidified Concorde Banner." *Hollywood Reporter*, March 26, 1987.

Schreger, Charles. "Ron Howard's Baptism Under Showmanship Creed of Corman." *Weekly Variety*, April 15, 1977.

Seidenberg, Robert. "Frankenstein Unbound." *American Film*, March 1990, pp. 50–51.

Silverman, Jeff, ed. "And Sinking 'Deeper' All the Time." *Los Angeles Herald Examiner*, April 21, 1980.

Singer, Mark. "Whose Movie is This?" *The New Yorker*, June 22 and 29, 1998, pp. 110–16.

Spear, Ivan. *Boxoffice*, December 15, 1956.

Stalter, Katharine. "Golden Eddie for Corman." *Variety*, February 4, 1997.

Stanford [University] *Daily*, 1943–47.

Thomas, Kevin. "Roger Corman—Director Who Changed the Face of Hollywood." *Los Angeles Times*, January 9, 1972.

———. "Upping the Genre of Prison Flicks" [review of *Caged Heat*]. *Los Angeles Times*, 1974.

Thonen, John. "The Roger Report: Roger Corman on the B-Video Biz." *VideoScope*, Fall 1999, pp. 46–47.

Thompson, Howard. *Review of House of Usher*. *New York Times*, September 15, 1960.

———. Review of *The Pit and the Pendulum*. *New York Times*, August 24, 1961.

———. Review of *The Secret Invasion*. *New York Times*, September 17, 1964.

———. Review of *X—The Man with the X-ray Eyes* and *Dementia 13*. *New York Times*, October 24, 1963.

T.L. "Roger Corman." *Hollywood Reporter 70th Anniversary Special Issue*, November 20, 2000.

Tube. Review of *House of Usher*. *Variety*, June 17, 1960.

———. Review of *Little Shop of Horrors*. *Variety*, May 10, 1961.

————. Review of *The Intruder*. *Variety*, May 15, 1962.

Tuchman, Mitch. "A New Dimension for the Girl Gang Genre." *Los Angeles Times*, July 28, 1974.

Tusher, Will. "The Economics of Runaway: Corman in the Philippines." *Hollywood Reporter*, January 18, 1972.

"Up From Monsters." *Show*, May 1962.

Variety, April 24, 1978 [birth announcement for Brian Corman].

————. June 16, 1961 [casting for *The Intruder*].

Warga, Wayne. "*Cries and Whispers* a Departure for the King of the Bs." *Los Angeles Times*, March 25, 1975.

Weaver, Tom. "Michael Forest: An Interview." *Classic Images*, no. 282, December 1998.

Weaver, Tom, and John Brunas. "The Other Corman." *Fangoria*, no. 48, October 1985 [on Gene Corman].

Weekly Variety, January 4, 1961 [rentals for *House of Usher*].

————. January 4, 1967 [rentals for *The Wild Angels*].

————. January 3, 1968 [rentals for *The Trip*].

————. January 7, 1976 [rentals for *Death Race 2000*].

————. January 4, 1978 [rentals for *Grand Theft Auto*].

————. January 13, 1982 [rentals for *Galaxy of Terror*].

Weiner, Rex. "Thrifty Corman Healthy in 4th Decade." *Variety*, July 10–16, 1995.

Welkos, Robert W. "A Few New Tricks to the Hollywood Trade." *Los Angeles Times*, August 8, 1999.

Williams, Whitney. "'Exploitation Pictures' Pay Off Big for Majors, Also Indies." *Weekly Variety* (January 9, 1946).

Zimmerman, Paul. "How *The Blair Witch Project* Evolved into Two Entertainments, One on the Web and One on the Screen." *iF Magazine*, issue 5.1 (July 9, 1999). [www.ifmagazine.com].

DATABASES AND WEB SITES

The Astounding B Monster
www.bmonster.com

Bright Lights Film Journal
www.brightlightsfilm.com

Concorde—New Horizons Official Web Site
www.concorde-newhorizons.com

Images Journal
www.imagesjournal.com/issue09/features/rogercorman/

Internet Movie Database
www.imdb.com

New Concorde Site
www.newconcorde.com

The Onion
www.theavclub.com/avclub3512/avfeature3512.html

The Other Cinema (spring 2002)
www.othercinema.com/ozframe.html

FILM AND TELEVISION DOCUMENTARIES

The Directors: Roger Corman, Encore, 2003.
It Conquered Hollywood! The Story of American International Pictures, 2001.
Roger Corman segment of *Directors on Directing*, directed for Telepiu (Italy) by Adam Simon (1997).
Roger Corman segment of *PM Magazine* (syndicated TV, May 1987).
Roger Corman: Hollywood's Wild Angel, documentary film produced and directed by Christian Blackwood (New World Pictures, 1977).
"Roger Corman: Shoot to Thrill," *California Stories*, directed for KCET-TV by Joseph Kwong (November, 1988).
Some Nudity Required, produced and directed by Odette Springer (Only Child Productions, 1998).

TRANSCRIPTIONS OF BROADCAST INTERVIEWS

The Charlie Rose Show [interview with Jonathan Demme]. Transcript #2277, PBS-TV, October 26, 1998.

The Treatment, with Elvis Mitchell [interview with Carl Franklin]. Radio station KCRW, September 18, 1998.

INDEX

ABOUT THE AUTHOR

BEVERLY GRAY holds a Ph.D. in Twentieth-Century American Literature from UCLA. Upon completing her doctorate, she spent sixteen months at New World Pictures as Roger Corman's assistant. She then returned to academia, accepting a position in the department of English at USC that allowed her to teach "fiction into film" courses. She also explored the performing-arts scene for the *Los Angeles Times*, the *New York Times*, and a number of magazines. Ultimately she resumed her Corman connection, devoting eight years to the post of "story editor" at Concorde-New Horizons Pictures. Since 1994, she has covered the film industry for the *Hollywood Reporter* and taught screenwriting through UCLA Extension's Writers Program. Gray's first book, *Roger Corman: An Unauthorized Biography of the Godfather of Indie Filmmaking*, appeared in May 2000, and quickly reached the #4 spot on the *Los Angeles Times* hardcover non-fiction bestseller list. In March 2003, she published her second critically-acclaimed biography, *Ron Howard: From Mayberry to the Moon . . . and Beyond.*

Gray lives in Santa Monica, California with her husband. She misses her daughter in Albuquerque, her son in Eagle Rock, and Muffin the cockatiel in New York City.